Personal Economic Planning

6.95

Personal Economic Planning

Glen A. Mumey
The University of Alberta

HOLT, RINEHART AND WINSTON, INC.
New York Chicago San Francisco Atlanta
Dallas Montreal Toronto London Sydney

To Brendan Marshall Mumey
and Sol Timothy Mumey

ISBN: 0-03-082868-6
Library of Congress Catalog Card Number: 76–148379
Printed in the United States of America
5 4 3 2 090 1 2 3 4 5 6 7 8 9

Preface

This book is an attempt to involve its readers in an analysis of some everyday, but complex, personal economic issues. The theme of *Personal Economic Planning* is the development of an integrated plan for personal choices in which alternative courses of action are judged by their contribution to the attainment of the decision maker's particular set of economic objectives.

Although this book covers the same topics as conventional "personal finance" or "consumer economics" books, its approach differs in three basic ways. A theoretical thread, the *overall personal economic plan*, runs through the book and unites such diverse topics as inflation, insurance, and the purchase of household assets in a mutually reinforcing way. The book also is decision oriented and attempts not only to expose its readers to alternative ways of doing things, but to lead the reader toward a personal rational solution. Finally, the book provides less descriptive materials than standard texts; this limits its effectiveness as a reference work, but allows more attention toward the development of *methods of decision making.*

The book shares some common ground with investment books. It contains similar analytic equipment, such as present value and internal rate of return analysis, an introduction to the concept of risk, and a basic treatment of financial accounting. The nature of common stocks, bonds, and related investment alternatives is set forth. It contains less detail on security analysis than the usual investments text, but it suggests that such detail may not be of use to all investors.[1] However, it goes beyond the conventional texts in tying investment decisions into the investor's overall structure of personal planning.

[1] This treatment has been influenced considerably by recent literature relating to the "random walk" hypotheses.

Because of the difference in approach between this text and others now available, *Personal Economic Planning* will also be useful in a variety of college classes. It should appeal to instructors in personal finance and consumer economics who wish for a more decision-oriented text. Its questions and problems are keyed to the stimulation of student involvement in the economic choices process. Its lack of dogma and deference to the personal values of each individual or family should also contribute to "reaching" its audience.

The text will also be useful to an investments class. Many standard investments texts are not well-attuned to contemporary thinking about investments, providing only limited treatment of such vital concepts as risk and portfolio theory. The investments teacher is then left with the choice of an approach: one built around classical investment and security analysis, or the introduction of more avant garde material, such as Sharpe's *Portfolio Theory and Capital Markets*, which may be too difficult for the beginning student. This text would appear to be well suited for introducing the topic of investments in a broad, personally-related context and thus serve as a stepping stone to more detailed development of modern investments material.

Personal Economic Planning is intentionally nonmathematical. Although a slight amount of algebra is included, the student is provided with conventional financial tables and can rely on these for necessary problem solving. A word of caution may still be in order, though; the student will find it essential to cover the material in Chapter 3 carefully and learn to translate practical problems into a form to which these tables can be applied. Although the actual "doing" of mathematics will be avoided, the planning process which is developed will rely heavily on the student's ability to work with actual numbers; talking in generalities will not be enough.

I wish to acknowledge a number of valuable contributions to the development of this book. First, my wife, Lois, has participated at every step—planning, critical reviews of earlier drafts, even some typing. Without her help, both direct and indirect, the work would probably never have been completed or, for that matter, begun.

Conversations with past colleagues, particularly Professors Charles Bown, now at Eastern Washington State College, Lloyd Barber and John Cooke of the University of Saskatchewan, and Alex Whitmore, now at McGill University, have provided me with an inventory of observations and stimuli. Professor Eva Tihanyi of the University of Saskatchewan not only shared in that general process of inventory building, but also provided very helpful criticisms of my material on human capital.

A grant from the Canada Council gave impetus for this project during its formative stage. Purdue University not only provided me with a delightful year as a Visiting Professor (during which most of this text was written) but with extensive secretarial services. Gloria Schimmel rendered much of this secretarial help in an especially pleasant and intelligent manner.

Of course, I bear full responsibility for any errors the text may contain.

Edmonton, Canada G. A. M.
July 1971

Contents

chapter one

Basic concepts for personal economic decisions

Each individual has his own tastes and preferences. Individuals in a family may prefer owning a Ford to owning a Chevrolet or they may have a strong desire to educate their children or to travel. Individuals must also make choices; no one can indulge all of his or her preferences. This book is an attempt to provide an individual with a systematic way of approaching economic choices.

Economic choices are those choices that relate to money and material goods. If one chose a spouse because of her good looks, we might say she is chosen for noneconomic reasons, but if her earning power or the value of her work as a housewife is allowed to enter the selection process, the choice has become at least partly an economic decision.

Before describing further what the book tries to do, it may be useful to point out the approaches the book tries to avoid. First, it does not attempt to pass moral judgments on what is right or wrong in individual desires and preferences. Nowhere is the reader told that saving is a virtuous act or that absence of saving has merit, or that he will waste money if he buys a new car but will gain a great deal of satisfaction from his money if he improves the diets of his children. These matters must depend basically on individual concepts of right and wrong, of like and dislike.

Second, this book is not an attempt to provide any sure, practical techniques that will immediately lead the reader to a higher level of personal wealth and well-being. No insights are advanced for spotting a suit of clothes that will fall apart at the seams in a month or for finding real estate speculations that will result in sure profits. The author does not pretend to be an expert on each of the thousands of transactions and problems that the reader is likely to encounter.

Instead the book stresses the fact that in many cases economic choices have far-reaching implications. The purchase of a car, for example, may mean that a couple cannot provide as well as they would like for satisfying some other preference, such as a comfortable retirement. For this reason we will work toward the development of a personal economic plan that aids the reader in sorting out the implications of his choices. If the couple is concerned about assuring a luxurious retirement income, guidelines will be suggested to enable them to develop a plan to attain this goal.

The development of the plan could also cause the couple to reconsider their original goal because the plan might point out undesirable sacrifices that will be required to bring about the goal. Goals are frequently revised after the cost of their attainments is more fully understood.

To develop a logical plan for personal finances, it is necessary to do some foundation laying. Terms need to be defined carefully and procedures for record keeping and calculating need to be discussed. Therefore the first three chapters are concerned with the development of methods of analysis. After that we turn to problems of everyday affairs.

The planning unit

Although much personal planning is centered around the family, with the husband and wife planning jointly for themselves and for the needs of their children, planning is also appropriate for single persons. Except where necessary we do not make any distinction between the single individual and the family. Sometimes the term family or household may be used and sometimes the words person or individual.

The principle of simplification

Suppose that you were required to teach someone to operate an automobile. For his first attempt at driving you would probably take him to a quiet street. If he protested that he wanted to learn on a crowded, high-speed highway, you would explain to him that he first needed to grasp the basic ideas of starting, steering, and stopping a car and that after he learned this he could go on to more complicated situations.

This process of taking one basic theme at a time, and developing it with care, is an essential technique for understanding a complicated environment. Until a person understands the basic main idea, he must temporarily ignore many complications. This is called *simplification* (or *abstraction*) and we employ it frequently. For example, a consumer makes one financial decision repeatedly—to spend money on one item, or on another. In developing *methods* of making this decision, however, we would not focus on a method which is applicable solely to a choice between, say, buying a car and a pleasure boat. Such a technique, although practical, would be too limited in its application. It is far more useful to develop a method of making choices from among all consumable objects. If so, then we must first *abstract* or *simplify* when appropriate. This means that we exclude information pertaining to nonessential complications. More is said about this process later.

The choice process

Decisions require making selections among alternative courses of action. These choices are required because there are limits on the degree to which various courses of action can be pursued. For example, if an individual decides how many hours a day he is to work, his decision is made subject to the fact that a day contains only 24 hours. Therefore, when he decides to increase his income by "moonlighting," he has less time for nonwork activities such as sleeping and recreation. Thus the choice to "moonlight" presents only one side of the total decision, which is a choice between moonlighting and alternative uses of time. Similarly if a family decides to spend $1000 on a car, it has really selected the car from the almost limitless number of possible uses for the $1000.

The concept of choice leads us to a term that we use repeatedly—*opportunity cost.* Every time someone understakes one course of action he gives up the opportunity of following other courses of action. Thus the cost of following the course of action he selects is the loss of the opportunity to do something else. Normally a dollar value can be placed on this lost opportunity. For example, when the family buys the car referred to previously, we can readily say that it passed up the opportunity to buy $1000 worth of other goods. If an individual works an extra hour per day and therefore gives up an extra hour's leisure, he must place a dollar value on the amount of leisure he has foregone to identify the opportunity cost of working.

Consider another example of opportunity cost. Suppose that a family wins a refrigerator in a contest. Can it regard the use of the refrigerator as costless? Not if it employs the concept of opportunity cost, for it could sell the refrigerator to someone else for, let us say, $200. If the family uses the refrigerator, it passes up the opportunity of getting the $200 to use for other things; so it may regard the refrigerator as free only in describing the history of how the refrigerator was obtained.

The marginal approach

Suppose that a family considers selling its house to build a larger one. Its present house can be sold for $15,000 and the house it wants to buy costs $25,000. It can break down its decision to buy the larger house into two parts: extra costs and extra benefits. The extra cost associated with changing houses is the difference between $25,000 and $15,000, or $10,000. The family can now try to identify the extra benefit that it will get from changing houses, such as another bedroom or a location in a nicer neighborhood. The decision can then be reduced to whether the extra benefits identified are worth the extra $10,000 in cost.

The term *marginal* is usually employed to denote these extra benefits and costs. We would speak of the marginal cost of the better house as being $10,000 and the marginal benefits of the house as being the dollar value placed on the difference in the qualities of the new house over the qualities of the old one. We could also restructure the question into an opportunity cost approach and ask whether the marginal benefits from housing are more desirable than those obtainable from $10,000 used in another way.

Consider another example. A person must go to a city 300 miles away to attend to some family business. If he drives, the operating costs on his car plus one night's stay in a motel will cost $25. It will take two days to make the round trip and complete his business. On the other hand he can fly for a cost of $45 including taxi fare and return home the same day. In comparing flying with driving, he can identify a marginal cost of $20. The marginal benefit is the saving of one day's time. If he earns $30 a day, he can value the marginal benefit of flying at $30. Hence his decision to fly has a marginal cost of $20 and marginal benefits of $30; so he will presumably make the decision to fly. The gain that he expects to make from the decision (marginal net benefit) is the difference between marginal costs and marginal benefits, or $10.

In almost every decision a marginal concept can be employed. We are interested in knowing what will change as a result of the decision. We may refine this concept a little further by applying marginal analysis to successive stages in a decision process. For instance, in buying a new car we might decide that the lowest priced new car we would consider costs $2800. We might then apply marginal analysis to various possible "extras." Should we spend $350 on an air conditioner or can we obtain more benefit from the extra $350 by spending it on other types of assets or as consumption goods? Should we spend the $200 necessary to buy a more deluxe model? Do the marginal benefits from this $200 exceed the marginal cost? Only if our answers are Yes on these marginal decisions should we increase our spending on the car above the minimum $2800.

Earning power and income

It is common to talk about an individual rationing his income among its alternative uses. To examine the whole financial choice process we need to begin at a somewhat more basic level. This is true because there is an element of choice in the amount of income that the individual obtains. The name *earning power* may be used to denote the largest possible amount of current income that a person could earn by concentrating his efforts solely on making money. This earning power is determined for the individual by his cultural, educational, and ethnic makeup. Not only do mental prowess and physical endurance limit the amount that an individual can earn, but background and education may also be limiting factors. In addition, most individuals' standards of right and wrong do not permit them to accept certain types of employment, such as bank robbery.

One might ask, will not the individual always try to obtain as much income as possible? The answer is almost always No. Obtaining income has a major opportunity cost, the surrender of leisure time. If freedom from work has an advantage for the individual, he can apply step-by-step marginal analysis to decide whether increases in the length of his work week produce marginal benefits (in the form of additional earnings) that are greater than marginal costs (opportunity costs of giving up greater and greater amounts of leisure time). Most persons do not work as long or as hard each week as they are capable of working, and therefore probably do not earn as high an income as they are capable of earning. They have, perhaps without even thinking about it, made a decision to use some of their earning power to provide themselves with leisure.

The prevalence of a 40-hour or shorter work week in this country indicates that most people have individually, or through their unions, been willing to limit their incomes. They did not do this because they dislike additional income, but because the additional income was not worth the opportunity cost of earning it. The presence of moonlighting and the long work weeks commonly adopted by small businessmen provide examples of exceptions to the general pattern. Here are people whose tastes have led them to earnings that are closer to their total earning power.

There is a second reason for giving up income. If income is thought of as money income, the family may prefer to receive benefits in a nonmoney form. For example, a home that yields benefit in the form of housing may be purchased, even though the purchase price might have been used to make investments that would have yielded money income. As another example of nonmoney benefits, families often desire the services of the wife and mother at home, and thus much of her earning power is used in providing care for children and other duties.

Another reason why an individual may elect to give up income is that he may chose to use some of his earning power for self-improvement. Attending college is a familiar example. An individual who goes to college gives up the opportunity to earn income so that he may have time to study, perhaps for the purpose of providing himself with increased income in the future.

Earning power can be used in four different ways. This relationship is summarized in the following equation:

$$\text{Earning power} = \text{money income} + \text{nonmoney services} + \text{self-improvement} + \text{leisure}$$

There are no neat boundaries between these classifications. If someone goes to college "for the fun of it," do we call this leisure or do we call it self-improvement? There is no need, in this analysis, to draw a fine distinction. In general the term self-improvement will be used to denote the giving up of earning power with the *motive* of self-improvement rather than immediate pleasure.

To summarize, the financial planning process must begin with the decision about how to use earning power. If only the use of income is considered, the whole financial choice process is not being brought into view.

Consumption and savings

In the preceding section we noted the division of the earning power into income, nonmoney services, self-improvement, and leisure. Two commonly used terms can be emphasized to make another classification of earning power: *consumption* or *savings*. The word consumption is used here in the ordinary sense, that is, the act of using up or consuming. To take a simple example, if a man knows that he can earn $500 during a month, that sum is his earning power. Actually he works at a part-time job that pays $300 per month because it affords extra leisure. During a particular month he spends $100 on food, $100 on rent, and $100 on entertainment. At the end of the month nothing remains of the potential $500. If there is nothing to show for the $500 in earning power at the end of the month (fond memories do not count), we may conclude that something, the earning power, has been used up; that is, all of the $500 was consumed. Even the leisure was gone at the end of the month; it has produced all the satisfaction that it is ever going to produce.

In contrast, suppose that the same individual takes a $400-a-month job, puts his extra $100 in the bank, and spends his spare time studying. Instead of spending $100 on current entertainment, he uses this money to enlarge his collection of stereo records. Now the individual has something left over at the end of the month, and we may conclude that he has not used up all his earning power. In this case, he ends the month with $100 worth of records and $100 on deposit at a bank. He also ends the month as an "improved" person, an end toward which he devoted time with an opportunity cost of $100. This total amount of $300, which was not consumed, may be called savings. Saving is the opposite of consuming; it means abstaining from using up.

The relationship between these concepts can be shown in the form of some equations. We may rephrase the discussion of the last paragraph by saying that earning may or may not be used up. We may also write this as

$$\text{Earning power} = \text{savings} + \text{consumption}$$

From the preceding section, recall that

$$\text{Earning power} = \text{money income} + \text{nonmoney services} + \text{self-improvement} + \text{leisure}$$

We have already recognized that leisure is a form of consumption and that self-improvement is a form of saving. Since nonmoney services are also used up as they are received, they can be classed as consumption. We also know that money income can be either consumed or saved. To identify this latter relationship we can use the equation

$$\text{Money income} = \text{saved money income} + \text{consumed money income}$$

To identify the total amount of savings by an individual for a part-time period, we can use the expression

$$\text{Savings} = \text{saved money income} + \text{self-improvement}$$

Similarly, for consumption we may write

$$\text{Consumption} = \text{consumed money income} + \text{nonmoney services} + \text{leisure}$$

A word of caution is in order at this point. Sometimes we find the words consumption and savings used in a slightly different sense. For example, in the keeping of official national income accounts, saving is defined somewhat more narrowly, partly to facilitate measurement. However, all of the definitions in general use share the same approximate intention: the distinction between using up something of value during a current period and retaining it.

The concept of stocks and flows

The word stocks is often used to refer to the shares of corporations; we will reserve the term common stocks for this purpose. Here the word stock is employed in the sense that a businessman uses it when he says that he has a stock of merchandise on hand. *Stock* is a quantity of something that can be measured at a particular time. For example, if we measure the quantity of water in a tank at 3 o'clock in the afternoon and find 60 gallons, we could say that at a certain time a stock of 60 gallons of water existed.

Flow is a quantity that is not measured at one particular time but during a time period. For example, one might observe that between 3 o'clock and 5 o'clock, 10 gallons flowed out of the reservoir. He could then say that water was flowing at the rate of 10 gallons per 2-hour period or at an average rate of 5 gallons an hour.

The concepts of stocks and flows are very closely related. Stocks build up or decrease because of flows. For example, our reservoir held 60 gallons at 3 o'clock and if outflows continue for two hours at the rate of 5 gallons per hour we could calculate that the stock of water at 5 o'clock would be 50 gallons, provided that no water had flowed into the reservoir during this same period. Similarly, if we knew that the stock was 40 gallons at 6 o'clock and 70 gallons at 8 o'clock, we could state that, during the two hours, inflows into the reservoir must have been exceeding outflows by a rate of 15 gallons per hour.

Our concepts of earning power, consumption, and savings are all in the form of flows. To say that a family has an earning power of $1000 means nothing; we must say that it has an earning power of $1000 per month or per year or per some other unit of time. Similarly, when we talk about a level of consumption or saving we are talking about rates per time period.

Suppose that an individual has an earning power of $1000 per month and consumes at the rate of $700 per month. His income is equal to his earning power and he deposits all of this income in a bank account as he receives it. He then spends from this bank account to maintain his desired rate of consumption. The balance in the bank account would be comparable to the level of water in a reservoir. As the individual earns money there is an inflow to the bank account and as he spends it, an outflow. The difference between the rate of inflow and outflow causes the gradual accumulation of a money balance in the account at a rate of $300 per month. The rate of accumulation is equal to the individual's savings rate.

We now introduce another term. Let us refer to all items owned by a family as that family's *assets*. To the extent that a family has earning power in excess of its consumption, it accumulates a stock of assets. This stock is not limited to money, although that is included. The collection of stereo records referred to earlier would be among the collection of assets; so would a home, or for that matter, a college education. All result because an individual did not consume all his earning power during a current period but instead maintained a flow of saving during the time period.

Savings and assets

When one talks about the act of saving and the accumulation of assets, there is a suggestion that this is a process of hoarding, and that saver and miser might be closely related words. This notion needs to be contradicted. As we are using the term saving, it is a process that is undertaken by many people who might be commonly called extravagant. As we just noted, stereo records are assets which can be accumulated by saving. Or an individual may buy an automobile on a time payment plan. As long as he makes payments at a rate great enough so that the car is paid for before it wears out, the individual is working toward the ownership of a fully paid-for asset and therefore performing acts of saving. This is true even if the car is a very high-priced, "impractical" model.

No one knows for sure why people perform all acts of saving. Some people may save without any idea of the future in mind. They simply get pleasure from the accumulation of assets. For many others, however, saving is merely an act of waiting, a shifting of consumption from the present to the future. These persons have decided to spend money on something that will provide consumption over many time periods, rather than on something like restaurant meals that will yield only immediate pleasure.

Types of Assets

The assets that accumulate from the act of saving may take many forms. For the family or individual we can classify these forms into three groups. The family may directly buy "real" goods such as appliances, motorboats, or garages which result in the holding of a form of wealth that we may call *physical capital.* The individual may also accumulate assets in the form of self-improvement. If a boy out of high school turns down a $125-a-week job that he thinks has "no future" so that he can take a $100 job that involves learning a trade, he has saved $25 a week of his earning power and used it in developing his own skills. This form of asset, which results when earning power has been used to make some improvement in an individual is normally called *human capital.*

In addition to physical and human capital, assets of the individual may take another form. They may be held in the form of money, insurance policies, shares of corporation common stock, or even lottery tickets. All of these forms represent some type of power to accumulate "real" goods. Money can be easily exchanged for almost anything. A life insurance policy represents a right for the family of the insured to receive money under a certain condition. The share of common stock represents the right to obtain a share of the profits of a company, and a lottery ticket represents the right to receive a prize if a "lucky number" is drawn. Let us call all of these forms of assets simply *claims*. To summarize, the act of saving may result in the accumulation of assets. (Another use for savings is discussed later in the chapter.) The assets may be in the form of physical capital, human capital, or claims.

Opportunity cost of saving

At first glance it might appear that the cost of saving is lost consumption since consumption in a particular time period must be given up if saving is to take place. However, this concept is too shortsighted. A stock of assets may result from the saving; a distinction needs to be made between something called assets and an accumulation of valueless junk. Assets have the power to provide future consumption. A house has value and is an asset when it can still be lived in. Technically, we would describe it as being still capable of producing a flow of housing services. A stock of money has value because it can be exchanged for good which can be consumed. A college education will enable its possessor to earn more money in the future or to lead a more satisfying life; thus it is an asset since it has the power to provide future consumption to its owner.

As noted earlier saving does not mean the giving up of consumption for all time, since saving results in assets which contain the power to provide future consumption. The opportunity cost of saving is not doing without consumption goods but simply waiting for them. If one does not mind waiting, saving appears to be a cost-free act.

Of course, all of us do mind waiting, at least to some extent. A person certainly would not be willing to restrict his consumption to the point where he attempted to postpone eating for a year. Therefore some waiting probably has an immeasurably high opportunity cost since waiting on all consumption would mean the foregoing of life.

Although a person may be unwilling to wait for some items of consumption, others may not matter so much. Once "bare necessities" are provided, waiting is a less critical matter. Thus, although all saving requires waiting, all saving does not have the same opportunity cost since waiting for part of one's consumption is much less unpleasant than waiting for all of it. Although we will not try to develop the concept in any precise way, it is apparent that a marginal viewpoint is appropriate here. Suppose a family starts with a total earning power of $10,000 a year and considers saving various parts of it in $500 steps. The first $500 would decrease consumption to $9500; perhaps the family would not mind waiting at all on this $500 component. As subsequent steps encroach further on consumption, the family would surely want to assign increasing amounts of marginal opportunity cost to represent the increasing unpleasantry of the marginal waiting required.

The reward for waiting: interest

Some marginal waiting may be very undesirable, whereas other marginal waiting for consumption may not matter very much. Some individuals might even prefer to wait for some consumption. Irrespective of their degree of like or dislike for marginal waiting, all individuals are normally afforded the opportunity of a reward in the form of an interest rate on some types of assets.

An *interest rate* is a fee that is paid to those who allow someone else to make use of some of their assets. The existence of an interest rate allows someone who gives up consumption now and accumulates assets to enjoy consumption in the future in an amount greater than that originally given up. Thus the individual, in making a savings decision, needs to consider the interest rate. If he prefers some marginal waiting or if marginal waiting does not matter to him, certainly the existence of an interest rate ought to encourage him to do some marginal saving. His savings decision can consist of increasing his savings as long as the interest rate available is sufficient to compensate him for marginal waiting.

The existence of an interest rate also enables the development of another useful opportunity cost concept, the opportunity cost of assets. Saving has an opportunity cost that we have not identified precisely, that is, waiting. If the saving takes place, assets are formed that can be in the form of a claim, such as a government savings bond on which interest is paid. Therefore, if someone saves and accumulates assets in the form of physical capital or human capital, he does so subject to cost, the opportunity cost on assets. Assets can be used to earn interest, and when they are used for other purposes that interest is foregone.

To summarize, there is no easy guideline for deciding how much to save since this decision depends on one's attitude toward marginal waiting. Once saving has taken place, however, an opportunity cost for the use of the savings can be identified. That opportunity cost is the interest rate that could be earned on claims. Many different interest rates are in existence at any one time, but we will not yet try to take one of these as being *the* opportunity cost of wealth. However, we now have a general idea about the nature of this cost. If, for example, one plans to form some human capital by going to college instead of working, he must ask himself whether this capital is as productive as the assets he would accumulate if he worked at a job and used his savings to buy claims. If the benefits that he identifies from college do not exceed this opportunity cost, going to college is a wasteful use of savings. (In measuring benefits we, of course, want to consider not just extra earnings but any other benefits such as the pleasure derived from having more knowledge and the personal value attached to the social contacts obtained in college.)

Dissaving

So far we have been talking about flows of savings that build up stocks of assets. Just as flows can reduce the level in a reservoir as well as increase it, so the stock of assets can also be decreased by flows. If an individual owns a stock of wealth, he has the power to consume in excess of his current earning power. For instance, an individual may have an earning power of $10,000 in a given year, but he may consume at a level of $15,000 a year by drawing down $5000 in bank deposits that were accumulated in a previous period. When consumption exceeds earning power, then an outflow from assets may take place. This outflow can be called *dissaving.* Dissaving is a very common occurrence. For example, if any of us "live off savings" during a period of unemployment, illness, or retirement, we are probably performing an act of dissaving. One of the purposes for which individuals accumulate assets is for the privilege of being able to dissave later.

Borrowing

We have just observed that the direction of flow in the savings process can be reversed to get outflows from assets in the form of dissaving. Another aspect of assets is also capable of reversal. A family can hold assets in the form of claims which entitle it to receive money or substitutes for money under specified conditions. In addition to owning claims for the receipt of money, families may also *issue* negatives claims for the payment of money. When a family borrows money, it gives someone else a claim against its wealth or earnings. It promises to pay out money (or a substitute for money) in the future. These negative claims are usually called *liabilities.*

Borrowing, or the issuing of liabilities, may be used to secure money for either of two major purposes. The money may be used to purchase other types of assets (or simply be held as money, although that would be rather unusual behavior). Thus assets can be accumulated by borrowing as well as by saving.

For example, very few people initially save the full amount of money necessary to buy a home. Instead they buy the house and borrow to pay for it. Then they save in subsequent periods to repay their borrowed money. Thus saving can be used not only to accumulate assets but also to reduce the amount of liabilities. In this case, the flow is being used to decrease the stock of negative claims which have been issued by the individual.

A family may also use money obtained from borrowing to pay for its current consumption. Thus a family could consume more than its earning power either by reducing its stock of previously accumulated assets or by borrowing. So borrowing also offers another way in which dissaving can take place.

When a family identifies its stock of assets, it is also useful to identify the negative claims, or liabilities, that the family has issued. Assets are capable of providing future flows of consumption. Liabilities, on the other hand, require the surrender of future potential flows of consumption. To evaluate the *net* prospects for future consumption that are implied by the family's assets and liabilities, it is useful to calculate *net worth*. This is done by subtracting liabilities from assets. We have much more to say about this concept in Chapter 2.

Transfers

In addition to saving out of current earnings, a family may occasionally receive assets without earning them. The unearned receipts, such as inheritances or gifts, are called *transfer payments*. In an individual's overall financial plan, transfer payments have to be considered. Note that once the family acquires assets via a transfer the assets cannot be regarded as cost-free. Regardless of how acquired, assets are always subject to an opportunity cost as long as an interest rate exists.

In addition to receiving transfer payments from other individuals, families may receive transfers from a government. In one sense they will probably have already "earned" this wealth by having paid taxes. However, because such a payment is unrelated to the taxes (those who have not paid taxes also get it) we will classify this as a transfer.

Similarly, a family may make transfer payments in a negative direction. Taxes constitute the foremost example of this type of payment. However, it is not necessary to think about these outgoing transfer payments as a separate category. Taxes are almost always paid in connection with some particular activity so that they can be taken into consideration at that time. For example, earning power may be viewed in an after-tax sense: the difference left over after potential income taxes are deducted from potential earnings. Similarly, if there are taxes levied on the purchase of particular goods, such as cigarettes, these taxes may be lumped with the price of the goods as part of consumption.

Similarly, when an individual makes gifts to others or when, at the end of his lifetime, he bequeaths an inheritance to others, these outgoing transfers are also basically consumption expenditures. We will assume, with a liberal helping of the principle of simplification, that individuals make gifts or bequests for their own satisfaction and that they obtain the satisfaction from the transfers at (or before) the time the transfer is made. (This places them safely within our definition of consumption.)

To summarize, a family will want to specifically take incoming transfer payments into consideration when it makes its financial plans. Outgoing transfer payments, however, will be considered as by-products of the family's estimates of future earning power and consumption.

Future prospects

We have already considered many important elements for financial planning. The principal purpose of personal economic planning is to search for a pattern of present behavior that enables the family to come nearest to the attainment of its desires for consumption, both now and in the future.

We have observed that earning power can provide either current consumption or savings. Savings can be used to form assets, which in turn will provide the family with increased nonmoney services (such as housing) or increased money income (such as interest) in future periods. Thus the family, in deciding how much it should currently consume, is also deciding how much earning power it will save and make available for consumption in the future.

Similarly, when a family decides to borrow, this imposes a drain on the family's future consumption. Hence, together, the family's accumulation of assets and issuance of liabilities play a large part in determining the balance that the family strikes between the present and the future.

Consideration of the family's assets and liabilities is not the only ingredient in economic planning. The family must try to decide what its future consumption needs and desires are and what its total earning power will be in various future time periods. It will then be able to examine the use of assets and liabilities to influence the timing of its consumption.

For example, a family that has children in school and a prospect for good salary increases in the future might want to borrow and surrender some future consumption to provide for present needs. Or a young couple who are both working might want to set aside rather large savings to provide for future periods when consumption needs will be higher, both because the wife's earning power may have to be used to provide nonmoney services (like caring for children) and because other costs of an enlarged family must be met.

In Chapters 2 and 3 we look at two important planning tools, accounting methods and calculations, which are used to compare present and future money values. We then examine the problem of taxes in Chapter 4, since these will have a large influence on financial plans. From there we continue to a more detailed examination of asset types that are available to families (Chapters 5 to 8). The remainder of the book takes up other issues, such as insurance and borrowing, that bear on a family economic plan.

Summary

A personal economic plan must be individually developed, since both personal goals and the means for meeting these goals differ from individual to individual.

Planning must involve the use of simplification. If an attempt is made to consider all complexities of a problem at once, confusion inevitably results.

The concept of opportunity cost is vital to planning. This concept says that the taking of any action needs to be weighed against the losses caused by giving up an alternative course of action.

Marginal analysis is also essential to planning. Decisions can be analyzed step by step. Marginal costs and benefits are the costs and benefits associated with going one step further, or one step back.

An individual's earning power is equal to the amount of income he could potentially make. The actual money income he receives is usually less than his earning power. This difference arises because individuals do not use all their time to earn money but instead use their time also for leisure, for self-improvement, and for providing nonmoney services.

When an individual's earning power during a particular time period is used up during the current time period, we say that this earning power has been consumed. If earning power is not used up currently, but is instead employed in building up the potential for future consumption, saving has taken place. All earning power is either consumed or saved.

A stock is a quantity of something at a particular time; a flow is a change in quantity expressed as a rate per time period. The savings process is a flow, which may, for example, be described in dollars per year. Savings may be used to accumulate assets; an asset is a stock of value that has been accumulated. Assets may be measured in dollars at a particular time.

When an individual saves, he gives up the opportunity of present consumption. Saving, however, can result in the accumulation of assets, which in turn may be used to provide future consumption. Assets may be held in the form of claims, physical capital, or human capital. When assets are consumed, dissaving takes place.

Individuals may augment the consumption they receive from their earning power by borrowing and by receiving unearned transfer payments. Borrowing can be thought of as an "asset in reverse," since future consumption must be given up in exchange for present consumption.

QUESTIONS

1. How will the economic planning of a single individual differ from one who is married? Will the planning of the single individual be affected by the fact that he intends to marry sometime in the future?
2. Describe some of the "good things" you would like for yourself or your family in future years (such as travel plans, type of house, and type of retirement living).
3. What do you think each of the "good things" described in Question 2 will cost?
4. Define opportunity cost. Give at least three examples of opportunity costs that could affect your decisions.
5. You can buy a Chevrolet with an $800 down payment and monthly payments of $100 per month, or a Volkswagen for $500 down and $60 per month. What are the marginal down payment and marginal monthly payments that must be made if you buy the Chevrolet instead of the Volkswagen?
6. What do you think your earning power is?
7. How is your earning power divided up among money income, nonmoney services, self-improvement, and leisure?
8. Define savings and consumption.
9. How much do you save each month? consume?
10. Do your answers on Question 9 total to your answer on Question 6?
11. Define interest. How can an interest rate be used as an opportunity cost?
12. How can borrowing be useful? Why may it sometimes lead to harmful results?
13. Are taxes consumption or savings?
14. What claims do you own? What physical assets? What human capital have you accumulated?

PROBLEMS

1. You are working at a part-time job for ten hours per week, with pay of $3 per hour. You are offered another job in which you would work 12 hours per week at $3.25 per hour. What is the marginal benefit of the second job? What are marginal earnings *per hour*?
2. Charlie works 40 hours per week, but he feels that he is physically able to work 60 hours. He is paid $4 per hour. What is Charlie's earning power? his money income?

   Charlie usually spends about three hours per week doing work on his house, and another two hours per week working on a correspondence course. How is Charlie's earning power divided?

Money income	$__________
Leisure	$__________
Nonmoney services	$__________
Self-improvement	$__________
Total Earning Power	$__________

Charlie puts $10 per week into a savings account. He is also making payments on a house and he understands that every month he owns about $50 more of his house than he did the month before.

From the information given, what do you think Charlie's savings are per week? his consumption?

3. The Thomas family owns its own home. It has a chance to sell this house for $20,000. The Thomases know that they can buy assets that yield 6½% interest. What is their opportunity cost of home ownership each year? Can you think of any other costs of home ownership?

chapter two

Accounting as a planning tool

As one develops a financial plan, he will find himself dealing with financial information. He will want to estimate his economic resources and needs far into the future and he will want to look back into the past to evaluate the decisions he has previously made. Because the amount of information may be too large to be effectively handled "in his head," he may need a systematic way of recording economic information and recasting it into a form in which it can be used efficiently. For this reason, and also because we live in a world where much useful information is available in the form of accounting statements, we now consider some elementary principles of accounting, or record keeping.

As just noted an accounting system should be of use both in evaluating past performance and in developing plans for the future. These separate goals should be kept in mind as various accounting methods are examined. One may want to record information in one manner when measuring performance and then switch to a different method when planning for future decisions.

"Traditional" accounting

One type of accounting system is now in use in the great majority of businesses. This "traditional" system is subject to much criticism by economists and by many professional accountants, but it has one property that probably provides the principal explanation for its existence. The traditional accounting system relies heavily on measurable money values; that is, it uses money amounts that are directly drawn from actual events or conditions. (With this system of objective measurement, it is possible for accountants to check each other's work.) Although this may at first seem like a very good idea, there are some serious problems.

One immediate difficulty with applying the measurability requirement to a personal financial situation is that some forms of personal assets do not have readily measurable money values. Physical capital is normally acquired through purchase, so a receipt or some other record of payment or promise to pay will normally exist as objective evidence of the asset's purchase price. Similarly, claims may be actually held in the form of money or else they have usually been acquired through purchase. Human capital, however, is different; although there may be some money costs, such as tuition, involved in its accumulation, its major costs are usually the giving up of leisure or other employment. These costs are very real, but they are never set forth in a money transaction. Therefore traditional accounting does not normally include the recognition of human capital and confines its concept of assets to physical capital and claims.

The "traditional" accounting system displays weaknesses both in its role as a device for evaluating past performance and in its use as a tool for planning. However, it is important to understand the methods of traditional accounting, since income tax legislation is built around this system. Also, when one considers the purchase of corporate stocks or bonds, he may wish to base his decision on accounting information, and this information is usually prepared in the traditional form.

The balance sheet

The balance sheet of an individual describes his stock of assets and the claims against those assets at a particular time. In summary form it consists of the following equation:

$$\text{Net worth} = \text{assets} - \text{liabilities}$$

Net worth, the net wealth position of the business or individual for whom the balance sheet is constructed, is equal to assets—all of the things owned by the business or individual—minus the liabilities.

This equation can be rearranged into another equation:

$$\text{Assets} = \text{liabilities} + \text{net worth}$$

In this form the equation says that all things owned, assets, are subject to property rights. Creditors, to whom something is owed, have rights in the form of liabilities. The business or individual who owns the assets has rights to everything left over after liabilities are subtracted.

A typical balance sheet might look like this.

Constance O'Flaherty
Balance Sheet
June 30, 1971

Assets:	Bank account	$ 1,000	Liabilities:	Bank loan	$ 500
	Car	3,000		Mortgage on house	10,000
	House	20,000	Net Worth		13,500
		$24,000			$24,000

Assets

Two aspects of each balance sheet category need to be examined: what items are included in the category and how their values are determined. Since the traditional balance sheet excludes human capital, assets included are in the form of either claims or physical capital.

Cash, or bank accounts, is the claim that is usually listed first. Receivables are amounts of money owed to you. As such they are assets on your balance sheet but liabilities on the balance sheet of the debtor. Other items in the claims category are investments that have been made in corporation bonds and common stock (to be explained later) or in other businesses.

Among items of physical capital inventories are usually listed first. Inventories include the "stock in trade" of a business and miscellaneous goods. These goods are of a type that are sold quickly or consumed by the business or individual rather than goods which are held and used for an extended period of time. The longer-lived physical assets are shown under separate headings and include items such as land and real estate holdings, machinery, automobiles, appliances and equipment, houses, and factories.

In keeping with its measurability requirements, traditional accounting relies on what is called the *historical cost* principle in placing an initial value on assets. When an asset is acquired by a business or individual, it is valued at the *actual* amount paid for it. Sometimes this payment may have been direct, as, for instance, when an individual writes a check for an automobile. Other times it may be indirect, as, for instance, when a business acquires "accounts receivable." These receivables are assets that arise when a business extends credit to its customers. For example, if a store allows a customer 30 days to pay for a $10 purchase, the amount owed by the customer is recorded as a $10 asset because there is an identifiable money price involved even though the $10 has not yet been paid.

This historical cost method of evaluation rejects the recognition of human capital accumulation; it also does not allow the recognition of increases in the value of assets after they are acquired. If a suburban lot is purchased for $1000 and subsequently is enveloped by a growing city so that it becomes worth $100,000, its value remains, under the traditional accounting method, at $1000. A recognition of the current value would be an estimate, which would violate the principles of historical cost and direct measurability. Thus, especially if a traditional balance sheet lists many assets that are several years old, there is a good chance that its published values may be out of date.

Liabilities and Net Worth

Under the caption of liabilities are included all the contractual promises that have been made for payment to others. These promises do not have to be in writing or highly formal in nature as long as money (or a service measurable in money) is owed. A person who bought goods on a charge account would record the amount as a liability on his records. (It would probably be included in a heading called accounts payable.) The historical method of valuation also reigns in the area of liabilities. The amount shown in the liability account is the amount of the original debt less any repayments prior to the time that the balance sheet was prepared.

Net worth, or net wealth, is determined by subtracting liabilities from assets. Therefore any problems in the evaluation of assets or liabilities will also be reflected in the net worth account. For example, if an individual were to depart from traditional accounting and include human capital among his assets, his net worth account would show a corresponding increase.

The traditional balance sheet constitutes an attempt to measure the stock of assets and net worth of an individual or a business. It is prepared for one particular date just as the stock of water in a reservoir is measured at one point in time. In spite of criticisms of the traditional method, its general approach to the balance sheet is a sound one. For financial planning it is useful to know where one stands, what his current wealth position is. Before going further, let us look at the other facet of traditional accounting, its recording of flows, such as income and savings.

The business income statement

Although we are principally concerned with records that apply to the individual or family, it is useful to first examine the most commonly used presentation of flow accounting, the traditional business income statement. This is an accounting for the flows which increase and decrease the net worth of the business enterprise. After a discussion of this statement, we examine its adaptability to the accounting for personal financial affairs.

The business income statement for a specific period of time is based on another equation:

$$\text{Income} = \text{revenues} - \text{expenses}$$

Revenues are defined as those flows during the period that tend to increase the firm's net worth and *expenses* are the flows during the period that tend to decrease it. Included in revenues would be items such as the money coming in from the sales of goods, interest collected by the business, and rents received on property owned by the business. Expenses would include items such as purchases of goods that are going to be resold to the business' customers, wages of the business' employees, and payments of interest on the liabilities of the business.

Because the income statement deals with flows, it is prepared for a time period, such as June 1971 or the year ending December 31, 1971. The following is an example of a business income statement.

Jones Company
Income Statement
January 1, 1971 to March 31, 1971

Revenues		
Sales		$10,000
Interest income		500
Total revenues		$10,500
Expenses		
Purchases	$5,000	
Salaries	2,000	
Interest expense	700	
Miscellaneous expense	300	
Total expenses		8,000
Net Income		$ 2,500

Since revenues increase net worth and expenses decrease it, the $2500 difference between these amounts, net income, will be equal to the change in the Jones Company's net worth between the dates of January 1 and March 31.

Degree of Simplification

Additional explanation is needed about this statement. The Jones Company expenses section contains $300 in miscellaneous expenses; this is an example of the principle of simplification. Many small expenses have probably been added together to reach the amount shown. The other expense amounts may also represent simplifications. For example, the Jones Company may have hired two different types of employees, executives and salesmen, but the amounts paid to both of these groups were added together into salaries expense. A more detailed presentation might have shown those amounts separately.

Simplification is sometimes more desirable than at other times. If a large business prepares a report to be circulated to the people who own shares in it, it may want to keep the statement very simple. Some of the people who own shares in this company may also own shares in many other companies and they cannot take the time to study very detailed statements. On the other hand, the same firm may wish to prepare statements in much greater detail for use by managers within the business. Here the readers of the statement will have the time, the knowledge, and the desire to examine much smaller details. Thus we observe that we will probably find no single, correct form for preparing a financial statement. Instead the form of the statement will be dependent on the readers for whom it is intended. It will be important to remember this point as we consider personal accounting systems.

The personal savings statement

A business accounts for flows in the form of an income statement. This form of statement can be readily adapted to the use of the individual who wishes to account for the flows that change his wealth position. The individual receives inflows to his net worth position in the form of earnings, much as the business receives revenues. These earnings may be the individual's salary, interest that he has collected, income from business property he owns, transfer payments, or other inflows. The individual's wealth position is depleted by consumption; therefore, in place of the expenses on the business statement, the personal statement would include consumption. The difference between earnings and consumption during a particular period is the individual's savings for the period. A simple example of a personal savings statement is shown on p. 24.

Thus far we have followed the traditional method in preparing this personal savings statement. Therefore we included only earnings and consumption that can be measured. Not included were concepts such as earning power or leisure; since we included only earnings, we were not

Keith Johnson
Personal Savings
June 1971

Income		
Wages	$450	
Rental income	75	
Total Income		$525
Consumption		
Food	$125	
Clothing	35	
Interest expense	50	
Entertainment	25	
Total Consumption		235
Savings		$290

able to take into account the time spent by the individual in the development of human capital.

Note that we do not necessarily reach positive final figures in all income or savings statements. It is possible for a business, during a particular time period, to have expenses that are greater than revenues. In that period its financial statement will show a loss, that is, a net flow that reduces the business' net worth. Similarly, consumption for the individual may exceed earnings with the result that dissaving must be shown; again this represents a flow that reduces personal net worth.

Accounting for transactions: the double entry system

The traditional accounting system is built on data recorded from transactions such as purchases and sales. Now consider a simple transaction: An individual buys a meal in a restaurant and pays for it with cash. We may describe the transaction by saying that one of his assets, cash, was depleted by being exchanged for consumption. Thus two financial statements are affected. The balance sheet must be changed to show that an asset has been reduced in quantity. The savings statement for the period must be changed to show that expense, or outflow of assets, took place.

In a formal accounting system it is customary to write down a description of each transaction; businesses often use computers for the purpose. We will simply note the changes that must take place in the two financial statements. If a meal cost $3, the person at the time the transaction took place would write down the description

Cash	—$3
Food expense	+$3

He could then make use of this description and those of other transactions in preparing his two statements.

Occasionally transactions will not result in inflows to or outflows from the person's total assets but simply a switch from one asset to another. For example, suppose that he makes a loan to a friend for the amount of $200. He gives the friend cash and in return he receives the friend's promise to repay the loan. The notation for this could be

Cash	—$200
Loans receivable	+$200

A double entry was used this time because two different items on the balance sheet were affected.

Another example of a transaction that does not increase or decrease net worth is the repayment of a liability. For example, one might record

Cash	—$2000
Bank loan	—$2000

This transaction leaves net worth unaffected because the reduction in an asset has been cancelled out by a reduction in a liability.

In the traditional accounting system all transactions require a double entry. If wealth is changed as a result of the transaction, one notation of balance sheet change and one notation of flow needs to be made. If wealth is left unchanged by the transaction, two notations affecting the balance sheet must be made.

Single entry "shortcut" systems

Many record-keeping systems that are suggested for families require only one entry for many transactions. For example, a household account book may contain sections entitled Food or Rent, in which expenses for these items are to be listed. These systems work very well for most household expenses that are paid in cash and by check. In fact, they are not basically different from the double entry system, for every time an entry is made in one of the expense columns, the record keeper *understands* that the expense has been accompanied by decrease in his cash balance of the same amount.

On the other hand, when transactions that involve other items besides money expenses (or income) are undertaken, the single entry system will have limitations. Suppose, for example, that a family buys an airplane ticket on a time payment plan. The cost of the ticket, purchased for a trip in December 1970, is $400. The ticket is to be paid for at $50 per month with payments starting in January 1971. If the expense is recorded in 1970, when the family consumed its travel, the family would want to note that this expense was different from other expenses recorded in 1970 because no cash was used. If the expense is recorded in 1971, the family would also like to note that, though 1971 was the year in which the money was paid out, 1970 was the year when the consumption was obtained.

This type of noncash transaction may be handled more effectively with double entries. In 1970 the family may record

Travel expense	+$400
Liability for travel	+$400

to show that the consumption has occurred but has not been paid for. Then, each time a payment is made in 1971, it may record

Liability for travel	—$50
Cash	—$50

to show that cash is being used to reduce a debt owned by the family.

There is no reason why a single entry system cannot be used for most transactions with double entries reserved for the more complicated transactions that are not simply cash received as income or paid out for consumption.

Preparing statements: the relationship between stocks and flows

Suppose that someone wanted to begin keeping a set of personal financial records. On the date that he began he would prepare a balance sheet by recording all of his assets and his liabilities in accordance with the principles of traditional accounting discussed earlier. Then, as he carried out various transactions, he would make notations, or entries describing each transaction. (These could be made on scratch pads or in a notebook, but more commonly a record book would be bought for the purpose.) At the end of a time period, such as a month or a year, he could prepare a savings statement on the basis of the entries that described income and expense flows. The net savings shown on this statement would also show the change in his net worth position during the period for which he prepared the statement.

He could also prepare a balance sheet for the end of the same period. He would start with his balance sheet from the beginning of the period and make changes in it according to the transaction entries that affected assets and liabilities. He would then have his balance sheet prepared, except for one more important change. If his savings statement showed that income exceeded expenses so that saving took place, he would have to add this amount to the net worth amount in the original balance sheet to obtain a net worth value for his ending balance sheet. (If dissaving had occurred, the amount would be subtracted.)

The result of all these changes would be a completed balance sheet for the end of the period. If all his transaction notations and changes in the balance sheet had been recorded correctly, the balance sheet equation would be borne out in the new balance sheet; that is, the assets would be equal to the sum of the liabilities and the net worth. If the "books did not balance," a recheck of work would be in order.

Accounts

One practical method for recording accounting information involves the use of a separate record for each of the individual items that appear on the balance sheet and in the income or savings statement. These individual records, or accounts, could, for example, be kept on separate sections or pages of a record book. (Such a book of accounts is usually called a ledger.) An original value is entered in the account when the record keeping begins and then other transactions are recorded as they occur. The sum of the last item recorded (or entry) and all previous entries is called the balance in the account. An account might look something like this.

Accounts Receivable

Date	*Description*	*Plus*	*Minus*	*Balance*
Jan. 1, 1971	Original balance			$2000
Jan. 7, 1971	Extended credit to Sam Luce	$200		2200
Jan. 15, 1971	Collected money from R. C. Stewart		$500	1700
Feb. 5, 1971	Collected money from Roy Kline		300	1400

There is no "one right way" for keeping an account; in fact, it does not have to be formally kept at all. However, it is a convenience and all but the simplest personal record systems usually include the keeping of individual accounts. As noted previously, it is often convenient to keep some of these accounts in single entry form.

A justifiable estimate: depreciation

Suppose that an individual bought a new car in 1967 for $4000. At the time he purchased the car he would have made the notation

Car	+$4000
Cash	—$4000

This entry would have resulted in a change in the next balance sheet that he prepared. Now suppose that he sold the car in 1971 and at that time it was worth only $1000. He would now have to make an entry to show that he had received $1000 in exchange for the car. This notation would be

Cash	+$1000
Car	—$1000

A question now arises. The car was originally entered in the balance sheet at $4000. When it was sold, the amount of Car in the balance sheet was reduced by $1000, the sale price. This would mean that there would still be a $3000 balance in the Car account. Since the individual does not own the car any longer, we would have to conclude that this $3000 represented the amount of Car he had used up during the period that he owned it. One method we could use for making a notation to remove the $3000 of Car from his balance sheet would be to record, in 1971

Car	—$3000
Car expense	+$3000

This entry would show that the car had been used up, that it was part of his consumption.

The difficulty with this approach is that the $3000 would appear in his records as car expense in 1971, even though he had been using the car in other years. In 1968, for example, when he was using the car, he would have shown no indication in his records that the car was being used and was, in effect, being consumed.

To overcome this difficulty, an estimate is admitted into the accounting process. Suppose that he buys the car on January 1, 1967 and at that time he estimates that he will keep the car five years. He also guesses that at the end of five years the car will be worth $500. Therefore he has estimated that over the five-year period, the car will drop in value from $4000 to $500 or by $3500. This is the amount of Car he will be consuming during the five-year period. He now divides the $3500 by 5 and obtains the estimate that his consumption of Car will be $700 per year during the time that he owns it. This estimate of the using up of an asset during a time period is usually called an estimate of *depreciation.*

When he uses the concept of depreciation, he would use the following accounting entries to describe his Car experience. At the time of purchase he would record

Car	+$4000
Cash	—$4000

At the end of 1967 after he had used the car for a year, he would record

Car	—$700
Depreciation expense: Car	+$700

In this way he would show in his records for 1967 that he owned a car which was gradually being consumed. (A more extended discussion of depreciation is included in an appendix at the end of the chapter.)

A marginal approach to accounting

Even though personal systems are often quite simple, they still require effort. Elaborate accounting systems of businesses are often expensive to develop and maintain. Because of these costs, it is appropriate to apply the same type of marginal analysis suggested for other expenditures to the development of accounting information. It is only necessary to refine an accounting system to the extent that marginal benefits from improvement exceed the marginal costs of that improvement. Although marginal costs and benefits are not very easily identified, by keeping this concept in mind, we can explain why any accounting system is likely to contain shortcuts, estimates, and "easy" solutions to problems.

Consider an example of the admission of imperfection into an accounting system. Sometimes one deliberately decides to ignore the temporary accumulation of assets. Suppose that the housewife buys food for her family every week. At the time she comes back from the store she has a stock of groceries on hand. Most of these will be consumed during the week, but some, such as spices or baking powder, might last for a much longer period. To develop a perfectly accurate accounting system, it would be necessary to record all the weekly purchase as an asset (perhaps groceries inventory) and then record flows out of this inventory each time some of the groceries were eaten. This would require the making of accounting entries at the time of every meal or snack.

Rather than carry accuracy to this ridiculous extreme, the housewife would almost certainly want to leave groceries inventory out of her balance sheet and make the assumption that groceries were consumed at the time they were purchased. In this way she would just have to make a note of food expense every time she shopped. The only disadvantage of this simplification would be the failure to record grocery inventory on the family balance sheet. The understatement of personal wealth by this amount, probably less than $100, is not likely to have very serious consequences.

We noted earlier that there was no one correct way to prepare financial statements, since different degrees of simplification would be desirable for different types of financial statement readers. Similarly, there is no one correct way of maintaining an accounting system. Since accuracy and precision in an accounting system cost money or effort to achieve, the achievement of unnecessary perfection is wasteful. This second observation helps explain why businesses are developing much more detailed accounting information now than a decade ago. Computers have made data handling so cheap that the marginal cost of a more finely tuned accounting system is becoming much lower. Therefore it now pays for businesses to gather and use more accounting information.

Following the same line of reasoning, if one individual likes to keep records he may wish to develop a rather elaborate personal accounting system. Another, who dislikes bookkeeping, will be likely to rely on a simpler form of information since he must either undergo personal displeasure to maintain his records or pay someone else to maintain them.

Keeping the record straight: business versus personal

We have been talking about an accounting system which could be applied to either personal or business use. Some individuals not only conduct personal affairs but also are directly connected with business operations. It is desirable to keep business records distinct from personal records. To do this, someone who owned his own business would want to have balance sheets and income statements that reported the affairs of the business only. Then, when he developed his personal accounting records, he could include the net worth of the business (or his share of the net worth if there were other owners) as one of his assets in his personal balance sheet. Income (or loss) from the business could be included as earnings in his personal savings statement. The advantage of this distinction is that a business can now be evaluated independently; otherwise, its performance might be concealed among personal affairs. For example, an individual might own a very profitable business, but if he did not keep separate records on it, he might think it was unprofitable, whereas in fact he was short of money because he maintained a high level of consumption expenditures. On the other hand, an individual who received a high salary and also had a small business might not notice that the business was a losing proposition.

Accounting as a tool for personal decisions

We have spent some time investigating how records are kept under the traditional accounting system. However, no one would want to keep records unless he could see some benefits derived from his information. As mentioned earlier, accounting information can serve as an aid in evaluating past performance. Although events that have already taken place cannot be changed, an analysis of what has happened in the past may lead to a change in the pattern of future decisions. For example, a family with a rapidly rising income might look back over its personal savings statements and decide that it had been saving more money than it now feels is necessary. Such a family might then decide to reduce its future level of saving, either by increasing its leisure and thereby reducing its money income or by spending more money on consumption purchases. In a more typical example, a family might wish to enlarge its expenditure on some consumption item, such as entertainment, and might examine its records of past expenditures to see from where the money could come.

In addition, accounting information can be used directly for planning. An examination of the balance sheet should give a family some idea of the state of its current resources. This, in turn, should help it to decide whether or not it can provide for future needs out of its stock of existing wealth. Statements should also enable the evaluation of various individual assets, and thus provide a guideline for possibly replacing some assets with more beneficial ones. For example, suppose that the family is offered the chance to buy a house as "income property." The house costs $10,000 and will return net income of $600 per year. The family statements could show whether or not $10,000 is available for the purchase and also provide a standard for gauging its prospective benefits. If the $10,000 can be made available only by selling claims that are now earning interest at the rate of $700 per year, the family has a basis for rejecting the house purchase opportunity.

To plan for the future we want to consider additional statements beyond the income or personal savings statements and the balance sheet. Statements in the form of budgets and projections are useful. These statements are not directly developed from information on the past or present, but instead are built from estimates of future happenings. The discussion of budgets and projections is left for a later chapter. Let us now turn more specifically toward constructive criticism of the use of traditional accounting statements for evaluation and planning purposes.

Accounting statements as a measure of performance

Several difficulties are associated with the use of traditional statements for evaluating past performance. One of these, as noted previously, is that they do not account for the accumulation of human capital. If this were to be admitted to the accounting records, it would probably need to be done with an entry such as

Earnings (wealth inflow) in the form of human capital from attending college	+$400
Human capital (asset)	+$400

Both this "earnings" account and balance sheet account would have to be valued on an opportunity cost basis. In the above example the individual must have given up the opportunity to earn $400 elsewhere during a period of time when he was undergoing education.

One of the serious practical difficulties associated with human capital is a matter of depreciation. What is the expected life of a stock of human capital? Does it last the lifetime of the individual or only a few years until he has forgotten what he learned; does it last longer than his lifetime in the sense that educated parents pass on their knowledge to children?

We will not try to solve this problem of accounting for human capital. A venturesome individual may wish to include dollar amounts of human capital in his accounting system when evaluating his past performance. Even if one does not want to go this far, he should certainly, when he appraises his past record, consider informally the change that has taken place in his stock of human capital.

Similarly, traditional accounting makes no record of flows of leisure or nonmoney services. An individual may receive the same income in each of two time periods, spend the same amount of money on consumption, and accumulate the same amount of wealth, but in one period he may have worked 50 hours a week and in another period 30 hours a week. Has he not made some improvement in his state of well-being in the second period? Very few people would argue that he has not. However, leisure is again very difficult to measure and therefore is something that most people will probably only want to consider informally.

Traditional accounting also does not normally include recognition of increases in the value of assets that have not been "proved" by money transactions. For example, a lot owned by a family may be rising in value at the rate of $1000 per year. Unless the lot is sold, the traditional accounting would not record it. The family, in evaluating its performance, may wish to take note of the fact that it has been making some gains by holding the lot. If it wishes to record this gain, the entry would be

Earnings from gain in value of land	+$1000
Land (asset)	+$1000

If these increases in value seem to be of significant amount, it should be desirable to recognize them in evaluating past performance. Similarly, one should also periodically examine his assets to see if any of them have decreased in value unexpectedly. (When the decrease in value is expected, a depreciation allowance or some similar procedure will most likely have been employed.) If, for example, an individual has bought ten shares of common stock for $100 each and he now finds that similar shares are selling for $75 each, he would probably wish to record

Loss (expense) on share	+$250
Share (asset)	—$250

In later chapters we touch on other accounting problems associated with the evaluation of performance. At the present, however, we proceed with the idea that traditional accounting will serve as a measure of performance if we keep these important limitations in mind. It does not measure human capital, leisure, or nonmoney services, and it usually does not recognize increases in the value of unsold assets.

Accounting statements and planning

In addition to pointing out desirable policy changes on the basis of their description of past performance, financial statements may also be used directly in the planning process. An extensive discussion of the development of financial plans appears later. Right now, however, it is useful to make one comment about the limitation of the traditional balance sheet as a planning aid. First, recall again that there is no one right way to record economic information. A statement that is exactly right for evaluating past performance may have serious limitations for guiding future policy.

The balance sheet, prepared according to traditional accounting, contains a list of assets that are valued at historical cost. If we had decided to try to improve on traditional accounting, we might have added some human capital to the physical capital and claims that were recognized by the traditional method. We also might have wanted to revalue some of the assets above historical cost to show that they had been subject to increases in value as time passed. We would have done this in an attempt to create a balance sheet that described, as effectively as possible, the success of the individual, or business, in the accumulation of wealth.

For planning purposes a balance sheet prepared in this way might not be very useful. For example, a family may have a strong desire to own a home that has a floor plan in the shape of an ice cream cone. There would be nothing wrong about building a home this way, but it would be a rather unusual form of construction. Suppose such a home is constructed at a cost of $40,000. The family moves into the house with the anticipation of living in it. However, perhaps this is a family that often makes other investments. It is therefore interested in the possibility, if a good enough investment opportunity comes along, of selling the house and investing the proceeds. How should the house be shown on a balance sheet?

After the house is constructed, it is probably worth at least $40,000 to the family as a residence. (Otherwise, why would it have been built?) On the other hand, since most other people probably do not prefer to live in a cone-shaped house, it might be rather difficult to sell such a house. Perhaps the house could be sold to someone else for $20,000. If the family considers disposing of the house, it would have a much lower value than if it were to be used as the family's residence. For planning purposes this second value, which may be called a liquidation value, is more useful than the $40,000 cost figure. If the family considers switching from the house to another investment, they will only have $20,000 to invest alternatively. Any time one is planning, he contemplates the possibility of various courses of *action*. Since one of his courses of action is selling the house, he is interested in the liquidation value. Once the house is built, the fact that it cost $40,000 is, for planning purposes, really only an irrelevant incident in history.

Thus we can see the possibility of using two balance sheets. For examining performance, a revised version of the traditional balance sheet is probably suitable. For evaluating courses of future action, a balance sheet based on liquidation values would be more useful. This second balance sheet would, on the other hand, not be very useful in evaluating performance, since many assets have a value to their owner in excess of the amount that others are willing to pay for them. The owner, in evaluating his performance, ought to be more concerned with the success he has had in meeting his own standards rather than those of others.

There does not appear to be a convenient compromise possible between these two statements. An individual who keeps his records in the traditional way (with perhaps some revisions) will need to sit down and develop another balance sheet for planning purposes. This will consist of converting the values that assets have to him or his family (an appropriate measure of the family's achievements) to values that the assets have to others (the liquidation values needed for decisions about whether to dispose of the assets).

Summary

Income taxes and business records are customarily based on the traditional system. Traditional accounting does not recognize human capital; the traditional balance sheet includes physical assets and claims and may be described with the following equation.

$$\text{Assets} = \text{liabilities} + \text{net worth}$$

The income statement deals with flows. For a business flows are classified as revenues or expenses, depending on whether they increase or decrease the business' net worth. Net income is calculated by subtracting expenses from revenues. The income statement can be modified into the form of a personal saving statement in which consumption expenses are subtracted from earnings to yield savings.

Accounting systems customarily use a double entry for each transaction; however, there are ways of simplifying parts of a double system into a single entry process without losing the logic of the double entry method. Accounts are records of various classes of transactions.

Depreciation is an estimate used to recognize the using up of an asset over time.

Accounting systems should be subject to marginal analysis; an individual's record keeping should usually be kept as simple as possible. Business records should be kept separate from personal records.

Accounting should be regarded as a tool. Accounting statements prepared for some purposes may not always be useful for other purposes. Personal judgment is required in the interpretation and application of any accounting statement.

SUGGESTED READINGS

Financial institutions provide a variety of personal record-keeping material. Consult your local bank, finance company, insurance agent, credit union, or savings and loan association.

There are many university textbooks that deal with the topic of accounting. One very popular elementary text used is *Accounting: The Basis for Business Decisions* by Walter B. Meigs and C. E. Johnson (New York: McGraw-Hill, Inc., 1967). Another somewhat more advanced general textbook is *Accounting in Business Decisions*, 2d ed., by Homer A. Black, John E. Champion, and R. Gene Brown (Englewood Cliffs, N.J.: Prentice-Hall, Inc., 1967).

QUESTIONS

1. How would you identify the cost of an automobile that you have purchased several months ago? Could you "prove" to someone else that the automobile had cost you this much?
2. How would you identify the cost of the human capital that you have acquired within the last year? Would it be easy to "prove" to someone else that your human capital had cost this amount?
3. List the assets you own that could be included in a traditional balance sheet. (Group smaller assets into classifications such as clothing and personal articles, or books and school supplies.) What assets do you own which would not be included in a traditional balance sheet?
4. Including only traditional assets, prepare your personal balance sheet.
5. Prepare your own personal savings statement for the preceding month. Also, prepare one for the preceding year.
6. What is the purpose of the double entry accounting system? Why do personal accounting systems often make use of a single entry method?
7. Suppose that you buy a used car at a price of $1000. You make a $300 down payment and the remaining part of the purchase price is to be paid by a series of monthly payments. Prepare accounting entries to describe this action.
8. Why are depreciation figures necessarily only estimates?
9. For your own situation discuss the marginal costs and marginal benefits that would result if you decided to adopt a system of personal record keeping. If you already have a personal record-keeping system, answer this question with respect to proposed improvements in that system.

10. Why should business records be kept separate from personal records?
11. Distinguish between using accounting information for planning and as a measure of performance.
12. Examine the personal balance sheet you prepared in Question 4. What would this balance sheet look like if you include human capital as well as traditional assets? How suitable would this balance sheet be for planning purposes?

PROBLEMS

1. A student notes the following information about his personal financial condition. He has about $40 in cash and about $400 in a bank account. He recently purchased a car for $1200. He estimates that his clothing and personal assets are worth $500. He also owns a $1000 bond. He owes $800 on his car and also has borrowed $1500 on student loans to meet his college expenses.
   (a) Prepare his balance sheet in the traditional manner.
   (b) Can you imagine a situation where an individual's assets were less than his liabilities? For example, suppose the student did not own the $1000 bond. How would you then show his balance sheet?
2. Joe Brown operates a small clothing store. He sells about $10,000 worth of clothing each month. His cost of purchasing this clothing is about $6000. He employs two sales persons who each earn about $800 per month. His rent is $500 per month and his other expenses are about $200 per month. Prepare his monthly income statement.
3. A car was purchased new for $4000. Its owner estimates that he will keep the car five years and at the end of that time his car will be worth about $500.
   (a) How much does he estimate that the car will depreciate per year?
   (b) Using this depreciation estimate, what would you estimate the value of the car to be at the end of the second year?
   (c) Does this mean that the owner would necessarily be able to sell his car for this amount at the end of the second year? If not, what is the purpose of preparing this estimate?
4. Prepare accounting entries to describe the following transaction:
   (a) The purchase of a new dress
   (b) The receipt of a $600 salary check
   (c) The sale of a $10,000 house
   (d) Buying a $3000 car by trading in a $1000 car, paying $1000 in cash, and borrowing the remaining $1000.

Appendix: depreciation

The usual way of recording the events in this chapter's depreciation example differs slightly from the method just presented. Because depreciation is an estimate, it has been considered desirable to have it shown as an estimate in the records being maintained. Therefore, rather than deduct $700 directly from the balance in the asset Car, as shown previously, it would be customary to enter a negative $700 under a separate heading, "depreciation allowance" or some similar title. The individual would then, in preparing his balance sheet at the end of 1967, show among his assets

Car	$4000
Minus depreciation allowance	$ 700
Net value of car	$3300

Suppose that he repeats this process in 1968, 1969, and 1970. At the end of 1970 he will then show on his balance sheet

Car	$4000
Minus depreciation allowance	$2800
Net	$1200

Now let us say, in November 1971, he sells the car for $1000. He records the sale of the car as

Car	—$1000
Cash	+$1000

This leaves a $3000 balance remaining in Car. The depreciation allowance balance was built up to $2800 during 1967 through 1970; hence the net value of Car is $200 after the car is sold. This $200 may be treated as consumption in 1971 and recorded as

Allowance for depreciation	—$200
Depreciation expense: Car	+$200

With this last entry, the Car account's $3000 balance is matched by the balance in depreciation allowance. Since the car is no longer owned, a final notation can be made, canceling the balances off the balance sheet.

Depreciation allowance	+$3000
Car	—$3000

Observe that this method of estimate caused the individual to record a $700 expense item in each of the first four years of the car's life, but in the year that the car was sold only a $200 expense item was recorded. This difference can be explained by the fact that the original estimate of the amount that he would get for the car (this is normally called salvage value) was too low. He thought he would get $500 when he sold the car, but he actually got $1000; therefore his depreciation did not perfectly distribute his recording of consumption on Car over the period in which the car was being used. Other results might also have taken place. If, for example, he had actually received $1500 when he sold the car, he would have in the fifth year been selling a car for $1500 that was valued in his balance sheet at $1200, net of depreciation. In this case, he would either have to go back and correct his earlier depreciation allowances or resort to the practical expedient of saying that in 1971 he sold the car at a profit. Because of its simplicity, this last procedure would probably be the one most typically employed.

Depreciation expenses, which are recorded in almost all published financial statements, are always estimates. Thus the reader should remember, when he sees numbers down in "black and white" on a financial statement, that some of these numbers are based on estimates and that sometimes these estimates may be wrong.

chapter three

Compound interest and the effect of time on plans

The timing of consumption is important to families. Most people would not wish to go from feast in one year to famine in the next. Furthermore, a family has the power to change timing of its consumption. By denying itself consumption in one period so that it can acquire assets, the family can build up its potential for consumption in later periods. For example, an individual who makes a decision to go to medical school usually has to spend ten or more years going to college and working in low paid training-type jobs (internship and residency), and during this period he may have to accept a very low standard of living. Later he receives a payout from his decision when, as an established doctor, he commands a high income and can live very well. In contrast, an individual who accepts a job requiring less training may find himself at age 25 enjoying a much higher level of consumption than his medical counterpart, but a much lower level at age 40.

Borrowing represents another possibility of

changing the pattern of consumption over time. An individual can borrow to improve his present standard of living with the knowledge that the required repayment will constitute a drain on his future consumption. To complicate matters further, sometimes an individual may accumulate assets such as human capital which postpone consumption and at the same time engage in borrowing to accelerate consumption. For example, the typical college student is often both accumulating human capital and living in part off the proceeds from loans.

To make sense out of decision making in this area, we need a way of comparing money or consumption at present with money or consumption in the future. Our first step in this process is to try to describe the extent to which present acts produce future consequences. For this description we use variations of a measure that is already in everyday use: the interest rate.

Interest rate

An *interest rate* describes the compensation given by the borrower to the lender in an agreement in which the lender has provided the borrower with the use of some money. For example, if Joe lends Bill $1000 for one year at an interest rate of 10% per year, Bill must at the end of the year repay the original $1000 (principal) plus an additional 10% of that amount, or $100 (interest). If we were to look at this transaction from the standpoint of Bill's consumption in different time periods, we could say that Bill received the opportunity to consume $1000 at the time the loan was made in return for giving up the opportunity to consume $1100 a year hence when he had to repay the loan. Thus from the borrower's viewpoint the 10% interest rate can also be regarded as a ratio that describes the amount of extra consumption that must be given up next year in order to obtain consumption now. Similarly, from the standpoint of Joe, the lender, 10% represents the rate at which consumption can be increased by waiting since Joe can consume $1100 next year by giving up the $1000 now.

With this very limited introduction we can observe how interest rates might be used in one very simple decision. Suppose Bill has decided that he must repair his home's roof next year and he has been told that the normal price for this job is $1200. However, Bill's neighbor, Jack, is a carpenter. Jack now comes to Bill and tells him that he is unemployed and that if Bill will immediately hire him to fix the roof, he will only charge $1000. Bill reasons that by giving up $1000 in consumption now to add an asset, his house, he can avoid giving up $1200 worth of consumption next year. Thus he can say that by fixing the roof now and delaying some consumption for a year, he can gain 20% ($200) in extra consumption.

The next step is obvious. Bill can gain 20% in consumption by buying an asset (better roof). He will lose 10% in consumption if he borrows \$1000. Since the gain from fixing the roof early exceeds the cost of borrowing, it will be advantageous for him to employ Jack now. He may be quite satisfied to simply reduce his consumption by \$1000 this year, but if he is not, he can borrow, consume the same amount this year as he would have without fixing the roof, and in fact find himself with an extra \$100 available for consumption for next year. The decision is illustrated in detail.

Alternative A: Wait to fix roof

This year	Next year
No change in consumption	Give up consumption to fix roof \$1200

Alternative B: Borrow and fix roof

This year	Next year
Pay Jack \$1000 for improvement	Give up consumption to repay Joe, \$1100
Borrow \$1000 from Joe	
No change in consumption	

Net difference

This year	Next year
A and B yield same consumption	B yields \$100 extra consumption

Conclusion

B is better than A; hire Jack and fix the roof now.

Compound interest

Interest is usually expressed in the form of a rate per year. When one speaks of 6% interest, he refers to the fact that on a loan of \$100 interest is accumulating at the rate of \$6 per year. Thus, if the 6% loan ran for three months (one-fourth year), 6% interest on \$100 would mean a \$1.50 interest payment. It is also possible to express interest in terms of other time periods. If, for example, one expressed the interest rate as ½% per month, he would be saying the same thing as 6% per year. In the ½% per month case, interest on a \$100 loan for three months is again \$1.50.

Although the time period in which the rate of interest is expressed does not matter, the time period over which interest is calculated may be important. Suppose that we consider two possible loans, both bearing interest at the rate of 6%. In one interest is calculated at the end of each six-month period and in the other interest is calculated at the end of each year.

In the first alternative the interest that accumulates on a loan of \$100 at the end of six months is \$103 (6% per year is the same as 3% per half year). At the end of six months the lender has an extra $3 available for investment. He can take this $3 and use it to earn more interest. This process of investing interest to obtain more interest is called *compounding.*

It is very common for loan contracts to specify the payment of compound interest. The loan on which interest was to be calculated each six months might not require any actual payment of interest until the end of the year, but if the calculation was made on a twice a year basis, the borrower would have to pay interest on $103 during the second half of the year. At the end of the year his payment to the lender would be fully calculated as

Original amount of loan	$100.00
Interest for six months	3.00
Amount of loan at the end of six months	$103.00
Interest for second six months ($103 × 3%)	3.09
Amount of loan at the end of second six months	$106.09

On the other hand, if interest had been calculated on a once a year basis, the amount of loan at the end of the year would have been $106. The period over which interest is calculated is sometimes called the *compounding interval.* Ordinarily, however, the compounding interval would be denoted by such expressions as "compounded yearly," or "compounded monthly," with these expressions implying one year or one month compounding intervals. On a $100 loan the compounding interval does not make much difference, but if the loan in the example had been for $10,000, the annual difference would have been $9 in the first year and much greater if the loan had been made for several years.

Thus, in calculating interest, one must be sure to identify the compounding interval. However, to simplify later discussion, any rate of interest used in this book will be a rate per year, compounded annually, unless an exception is noted.

The concept of compound interest can be applied to a variety of personal economic problems. To approach these problems in a systematic way, it is useful to have a notation system that will aid in identifying the common elements of differing planning problems. Therefore we introduce

P = a present amount of money
F = a future amount of money
r = a rate of interest (per year, unless otherwise stated)
n = the number of compounding intervals (years, unless otherwise stated)

Using this notation, we can express a simple formula for finding the amount that must be repaid on a one year loan.

$$F = P(1 + r)$$

This says that the amount to be repaid (future amount F) is equal to the amount borrowed now (present amount P) multiplied by the sum of 1 + the rate of interest r. The use of the factor $(1 + r)$ expresses the fact that the present amount plus interest must be repaid.

It is now easy to extend this formula to a longer term loan. Suppose that X lends \$1000 to Y for two years at 6% compound interest. The calculation would be \$1000 (1+.06) for the first year, resulting in \$1060. At the beginning of the second year the amount owed will be \$1060 and this amount, compounded again by (1+.06), will be \$1123.60. This whole calculation could have been expressed as

$$F = P(1 + r)(1 + r)$$

or

$$F = \$1000(1.06)(1.06) = \$1123.60$$

To make the formula applicable to any number of time periods, we may write it as

$$F = P(1 + r)^n$$

Notice that this formula is not inconsistent with the previous examples of calculations for one and two years.

Interest tables

Let those who dislike mathematics take hope. There is a way around the use of formulas or other rather laborious methods of interest calculation. In situations in which more than one time period is involved, most persons working with interest make use of tables. One type of interest table available is the "Compound Sum of \$1" table, a "future value" table. A detailed table of this type is given in the Appendix at the end of this book (Table A.1). A simplified sample of such a table is presented here.

COMPOUND SUM OF \$1 *(F)*

	Rate of Interest *(r)*				
Number of time periods *(n)*	4%	5%	6%	8%	10%
1	1.04	1.05	1.06	1.08	1.10
2	1.08	1.10	1.12	1.17	1.21
3	1.12	1.16	1.19	1.26	1.33
4	1.17	1.22	1.26	1.36	1.46
5	1.22	1.28	1.34	1.47	1.61

To use this table one must first identify the nature of his problem. If one is borrowing \$500 for three years at 8% compound interest, he may set up his problem as follows.

$$\begin{aligned} P &= \$500 \\ r &= .08 \text{ or } 8\% \\ n &= 3 \\ F &= \text{unknown} \end{aligned}$$

He then goes to the table, which tells him the value of F when $n = 3$, $r = 8\%$, and $P = \$1$. (The table provides answers for only this single value of P.) He uses the table by reading down the 8% column until he is on the same line as 3 in the n column. He finds the number 1.26. His reading of the table may be illustrated.

Number of time periods (n)	Rate of interest (r) 4%	5%	6%	8%	10%
1				↓	
2				↓	
3 →				1.26	
4					
5					

This tells him that for every \$1 borrowed now at 8% he must repay \$1.26 three years later. Since he is actually borrowing \$500, he multiplies the value of F for \$1 by 500.

$$1.26 \times \$500 = \$630$$

Where $P = \$500$, $n = 3$, and $r = 8\%$, he finds $F = \$630$, the amount he will have to repay. The table can be used just as readily by a lender (or the purchaser of an asset) as by a borrower (issuer of a liability). For example, if someone deposits \$200 in a savings account (such an account is, in effect, a loan by an individual to a financial institution) and expects to receive 5% compound interest, he may wish to know the amount he will accumulate in his deposit after five years, if he leaves his \$200 there, as well as any interest earned. This situation can be expressed as

$$\begin{aligned} P &= \$200 \\ n &= 5 \\ r &= 5\% \\ F &= \text{unknown} \end{aligned}$$

Using the table, he finds that where $n = 5$ and $r = 5\%$, the amount given is \$1.28. Each dollar will build up to \$1.28, so he can solve for F.

$$\begin{aligned} F &= \$200 \times 1.28 \\ &= \$256, \text{ the amount available in five years} \end{aligned}$$

An Interesting Rule of Thumb

One simple calculation may be of some interest to the reader and certainly illustrates the power that compound interest has to make money grow. This rule is not perfectly accurate, but it will usually do for a rough approximation. To find how long it will take money to double, divide the annual percentage interest rate into either 70 or 72, whichever is more convenient. Your answer will be the approximate number of years required for doubling your money. For example, if you can invest at 6% per year, dividing 6 into 72 will give you the answer 12 and will tell you that $1 invested for 12 years at 6% will increase in value to $2. Similarly, money invested at 10% will double in about seven years, and money invested at 14%, in about five years. Later we will explore this relationship with more precision.

Present value

Suppose that an interest rate of 7% is available on savings accounts and that a person is offered the opportunity to buy a piece of land which he is convinced will be worth $10,000 at the end of ten years. He now wishes to determine what would be an appropriate price to pay for the piece of land. We can approach this issue by reasoning in the following way.

At 7% interest, using the rule in the preceding section, money placed in the savings account now can be doubled in ten years. Therefore, if he had $5000 now he could receive $10,000 in ten years through the savings account. From this fact he can reason that the privilege of receiving $10,000 from the sale of a lot at the end of ten years is worth no more to him than $5000 now, since $5000 would grow to $10,000 in ten years via compound interest. We could also say, using the term employed previously, that a future value of $10,000 has a present value of $5000, given that 7% interest is available and that he is dealing with a ten-year period.

To decide whether or not to purchase the piece of land the prospective purchaser would simply see if he could buy it for less than its present value. If he could, he would probably regard it as a bargain; if not, he should decline the opportunity to buy it.

Certainly few real investment decisions can be made in such an uncomplicated way. In the above example, one would have to be concerned about such issues as whether or not the land would really be worth $10,000 at the end of the ten years and whether 7% interest would actually be available on another asset during the total ten-year period. However, we will draw again on the principle of simplification and consider the present value approach first. Complications can be examined later.

A formula for present value can be developed from the future value formula discussed previously, which was

$$F = P(1 + r)^n$$

This same formula can be rearranged into

$$P = \frac{F}{(1+r)^n}$$

The Present Value Table

Again, direct use of the formula can be avoided by a variation of the compound interest table, called a "Present Value of $1" table. A detailed table is given in the Appendix (Table A.2) and a simplified version is shown here.

PRESENT VALUE OF $1

	Rate of Interest (r)				
Number of time periods (n)	4%	5%	6%	8%	10%
1	0.96	0.95	0.94	0.93	0.91
2	0.92	0.91	0.89	0.86	0.83
3	0.89	0.86	0.84	0.79	0.75
4	0.85	0.82	0.79	0.74	0.68
5	0.82	0.78	0.75	0.68	0.62
10	0.68	0.61	0.56	0.46	0.39
20	0.46	0.38	0.31	0.21	0.15
30	0.31	0.23	0.17	0.10	0.06
40	0.21	0.14	0.10	0.05	0.02

Let us try this table on a personal problem. Suppose a 25-year-old individual is interested in providing some money for use during his retirement period, and he is offered an asset called an endowment policy by an insurance salesman. This policy will pay him $20,000 at age 65. (This amount would probably be paid to his heirs if he died, but let us simplify the problem and not worry about that contingency yet; two later chapters are devoted to insurance.)

Suppose he is confident that he can earn 5% by putting money in a savings account. To find out how much he would be willing to pay, he can find the present value of $20,000 to be received 40 years later. The problem can be expressed as

$$\begin{aligned} F &= \$20{,}000 \\ n &= 40 \\ r &= 5\% \\ P &= \text{unknown} \end{aligned}$$

Going to the table, we find that the present value of $1, where n and r are 40 and 5%, is 0.14. Therefore the present value of the endowment policy is $20,000 × 0.14 or $2800. Unless he could buy the endowment policy for $2800 he would not find it desirable, at least in this simplified situation.

Using the Present Value Table: Discounting

One of the purposes for which the present value table is employed is the process of discounting. Suppose that X has made a loan of $1000 to Y for three years at a generous 2% interest. Y is to pay the interest in cash at the end of each year and is to repay the original amount (principal) of the loan at the end of three years. X discovers after he has made the loan to Y that he is short of money and he offers to sell his receivable (Y's promise to pay) to Z.

Z does not wish to buy X's receivable unless he can make 10% interest on any money he pays X. To find out the amount he can afford to pay X, he proceeds in three steps.

1. He identifies the amounts of money that he will receive from the receivable and the times these amounts will be received. The receivable being offered for sale consists of the following future amounts: at the ends of years 1 and 2, $20 interest will be paid; at the end of the third year, $20 interest plus the original $1000 will be paid.

2. He now calculates the present value of these three amounts. To obtain the present value of the $20 to be received at the end of the first year, he sets $r = 10\%$ to represent his required interest rate; $n = 1$ since the $20 will be received one year hence. The present value of $1 where $r = 10\%$ and $n = 1$ is shown in the table to be 0.91. $20 $\times$ 0.91 = $18.20.

His calculation for all three years is

n	F	Present value of $1 ($r$=10%)		Present value of F
1	$20	0.91		$18.20
2	20	0.83		16.60
3	1020	0.75		765.00
			Total	$799.80

3. He now adds the three present values, as shown, and concludes that the receivable has a present value of about $800. Z therefore would be willing to pay X this amount, but no more, for his receivable.

Discounting is a very common business practice. For example, an individual may buy a used car from a dealer on an installment plan and then find out that he is required to make his payments to a finance company, which is entirely separate from the car dealer. The car dealer has sold his customer's promise to pay to the finance company, and the price for which the promise is sold will be determined by discounting.

(Sometimes this type of transaction does not work out very well from the customer's standpoint. Suppose the car dealer has guaranteed the car and then refuses to fulfill his obligations under the guarantee. The customer is not able to force him to honor his guarantee by withholding payment, for he does not make payments to the dealer but to the finance company, which in turn has no legal obligation to fulfill the guarantee.)

The term discounting, incidentally, relates to the conversion of future values into present values, and does not imply that a receivable will be valued at less that its original principal. (The present values of $1 read from the table are often called *discount factors* and the table itself is often called a discount table.) It is possible for a receivable to be discounted and still sell for more than its original value. For example, suppose that A has (not too generously) lent $1000 to B for one year at 10% annual interest. Immediately after lending the money to B he decides to sell the receivable to C, who requires an 8% annual return. The receivable will return $1100 at the end of one year. C identifies from the table that the appropriate discount factor, where $n = 1$ and $r = 8\%$, is 0.93. $1100 multiplied by 0.93 is $1023; therefore C would be willing to pay A $23 more than the amount of the original loan, after discounting it.

More Uses for the Present Value Table: Finding r *and* n

Either the present or future value tables (we shall use the present value table) can be used for finding r or n. Let us first consider a problem where one might wish to find r. Suppose an individual bought a building for speculative purposes in 1965. The rent he received on the building was just enough to pay the taxes, maintenance, insurance, and other expenses associated with holding the building. He paid $5000 for the building and sold it in 1970 for $7000. He would like to know the rate of return that he earned on the building.

We can describe his experience with the building by saying that in 1965 he gave up the present value of $5000 in order to get the future value of $7000 five years later. Expressing this in the terms we have been using, we have

$$\begin{aligned} P &= \$5000 \\ F &= \$7000 \\ n &= 5 \\ r &= \text{unknown} \end{aligned}$$

Since we know that he gave up 5000 present dollars to receive 7000 future dollars, we can say that he gave a present value of $5 for every $7 future value he received or that present value of a future $1 was 5/7 of $1, or $0.71. Now we know the present value of a future dollar (discount factor); $P = 0.71F$.

We can go to the table, read down the "Number of time periods" column to 5, and then read across looking for a discount factor of 0.71.

We do not find that figure, but we find some near it, 0.75 and 0.68. If the rate of interest is 6%, the discount factor for five years is 0.75. If the rate of interest is 8%, the discount factor is 0.68. With a discount factor of 0.71 we conclude that the rate of interest must have been between 6 and 8%, or approximately 7%. The investment proposition described actually returned about 7% even though no interest rate was actually expressed in the proposition itself. An interest rate found in this way is often referred to as an *implicit rate* or an *internal rate.*

A very useful application of the technique for finding an internal rate, and one we discuss in much greater detail later, is to find the actual rate of interest on time payment transactions. For example, suppose a store advertises "Wait three months to pay" and also advertises "10% off for cash." What the store is really saying is that it will sell merchandise priced at $1 for $0.90 now or for $1 paid three months later. Expressed this way, the credit extended by the store does not sound quite so free.

To find the rate of interest actually being charged by the store, let us use a monthly compounding interval. We now identify these values.

$$\begin{aligned} P &= \$0.90 \\ F &= \$1 \\ n &= 3 \\ r &= \text{unknown} \end{aligned}$$

The discount factor (P/F) is 0.9; for a solution, we go to the present value table (A.2) in the Appendix and find that where the discount factor is 0.9 and $n = 3$, the monthly interest rate is between 3 and 4% (by interpolation, 3½%). Under the "truth-in-lending" law, discussed in a later chapter, the retailer could make this calculation and state, in his advertisement, that the yearly rate was 12 times this monthly rate, or approximately 42%.

It may also be useful to find n where the other values are known. For example, a family might decide to put $100 into a savings account and let it grow at compound interest until it reached the price of a set of china dishes. Let us imagine that this price was $200 and that the savings account returned an interest rate of 6%. The problem set up as follows.

$$\begin{aligned} P &= \$100 \\ F &= \$200 \\ r &= 6\% \\ n &= \text{unknown} \end{aligned}$$

The discount factor (P/F) is 0.5; we go to the present value table and read down the 6% rate of interest column until we reach a discount factor that is approximately 0.5. Since this discount factor is reached at the 12th time period, we can conclude that the family will be able to buy a $200 set of dishes in about 12 years with the accumulated amount of its $100 investment. Incidentally, we observe that this exact calculation of how long it would take the family to "double its money" coincides with the "rule of thumb" rule discussed earlier; in that rule 6% would have been divided into 72 to obtain 12 years as the approximate amount of time needed to double the investment at 6% interest.

Present value of flows: annuities

Some aspects of personal planning are more readily approached by considering money flows. For example, someone might decide that, in addition to any pension and other income he might have, he would like to provide himself with $200 per month extra income after retirement. He will be satisfied if he can have this income for ten years (say from age 65 to 75) and wants to know how much money he would have to have in his 5% savings account at age 65 to provide this income.

For simplicity we can express $200 per month as $2400 per year. Payments which are received each year are called *annuities*. Let the symbol A denote an annuity. We can now identify a problem as

$$\begin{aligned} A &= \$2400 \\ n &= 10 \\ r &= 5\% \\ P &= \text{unknown} \end{aligned}$$

We want to find the amount at the beginning of a ten-year period (present) which will be sufficient, if invested at 5%, to provide $2400 a year during the period.

A third table (Appendix Table A.4), entitled "Present Worth of Annuity of $1," is available for this type of calculation.

A simplified version is presented.

PRESENT WORTH OF ANNUITY OF $1

Number of time periods (n)	Rate of interest per time period (r) 4%	5%	6%	8%	10%
1	0.96	0.95	0.94	0.93	0.91
2	1.88	1.86	1.83	1.78	1.74
3	2.78	2.72	2.67	2.58	2.49
4	3.63	3.55	3.47	3.31	3.17
5	4.45	4.33	4.21	3.99	3.79
10	8.11	7.72	7.36	6.71	6.14
20	13.59	12.46	11.47	9.82	8.51
30	17.29	15.37	13.77	11.26	9.42
40	19.79	17.16	15.05	11.93	9.78
Perpetual (Forever)	25.00	20.00	16.67	12.50	10.00

In the table we find the present value of a $1 annuity ($n = 10$, $r = 5\%$) to be $7.72. For every dollar provided *per year* in the ten-year period,

\$7.72 must be placed in a savings account at the beginning of the period. Since \$2400 per year is required, \$7.72 × 2400, or about \$18,500, must be placed in the account. (This calculation is only an approximation. For it to be exact our retired individual would have to make withdrawals from his account at the end of each year, rather than at the end of every month. We discuss a way of improving this estimate later.)

Now consider a simpler example to illustrate the nature of the present value of a flow of payments more fully. Suppose that one wished to find the present value of a payment of \$100 a year for three years at an interest rate of 10%. Reading from the table and multiplying by \$100, we find $P = \$249$. To prove this result, consider what would happen if \$249 were invested at 10% to obtain three future annual payments of a \$100 per year. This amount would draw approximately \$25 in interest during year 1. At the end of one year the accumulated amount would be \$249 plus \$25, or \$274. From this amount an initial \$100 payment is made; there is \$174 left to provide for future payments. Calculations for the three-year period are the following.

Year	Beginning balance	Interest	Beginning balance plus interest	Annuity	Ending balance
1	\$249	\$25	\$274	\$100	\$174
2	174	17	191	100	91
3	91	9	100	100	0

When the third payment is made, there will be nothing left in his fund. Perhaps this arithmetic illustration makes it easier to appreciate that the present value figures from the table actually represent the amount that must be presently invested at the given interest rate in order to duplicate the particular future payments.

An Application of the Annuity Table: Time Payment Plans

Consider the following problem. X sells his car to Y for \$1500. Y makes a down payment of \$500 and wishes to pay the balance in three equal annual installments with 8% interest. Since only \$1000 of the purchase is being financed, the value of P in this problem is \$1000. A full statement of the problem is

$$\begin{aligned} P &= \$1000 \\ n &= 3 \\ r &= 8\% \\ A &= \text{unknown} \end{aligned}$$

X needs to know the annual payments that Y must be required to make if the loan is to be fully paid, with interest, at the end of three years. To find this amount, the Present Worth of \$1 Annuity table can be employed.

If we look for the discount factor given in the table where $r = 8\%$ and $n = 3$, we find \$2.58. Since X is providing an original amount of credit of \$1000, he can divide \$1000 by 2.58 to find out how many dollars per year Y must pay. \$1000 ÷ 2.58 = about \$338; therefore, if Y pays \$338 per year, he will pay for the car in three years with interest. (The interested reader could verify this amount by doing a calculation like the one in the preceding section, if he begins with a \$1000 receivable rather than a \$249 deposit and uses 8% instead of 10%.)

Of course, most installment payments are made by the month rather than by the year. However, a calculation by the year can serve as a useful approximation of monthly payments that will be required; putting the preceding problem on a monthly basis we could estimate that required monthly payments would be about \$338 per year divided by 12 months, or a little less than \$30 per month.

Installment problems can also be of another form. Suppose A contemplates buying a house and borrows \$20,000 to pay for it. He thinks he can borrow the necessary amount at 8% interest and also feels he can afford to make \$200 per month payments on this debt. (In addition, he will have to be able to meet other homeowner's expenses, such as property taxes; these complications are discussed in Chapter 8.) He wants to find out about how long it will take him to pay for the house.

$$\begin{aligned} P &= \$20{,}000 \\ A &= \$2400 \text{ per year} \\ r &= 8\% \\ n &= \text{unknown} \end{aligned}$$

Since he knows P and A, he can find a discount factor, P/A, of \$20,000/\$2400, or 8.33. Going to the Present Worth of \$1 Annuity table, he can read that, with $r = 8\%$ and a discount factor of 8.33, n is between 14 and 15 years.

A third application of the table in the installment plan area lies in finding r, the rate set forth under "truth-in-lending" laws. Suppose that an installment plan advertisement reads, "No money down, 24 months to repay," and a person finds that he can buy a \$50 appliance by paying monthly payments of \$3 per month. He can now solve for a monthly interest rate by using his annuity table on the basis of monthly compounding intervals.

$$\begin{aligned} P &= \$50 \\ A &= \$3 \\ n &= 24 \\ r &= \text{unknown} \end{aligned}$$

The discount factor (P/A) is 16.67. Reading in the detailed annuity table in the Appendix, we find that with $n = 24$, a discount factor of 16.67

implies an monthly rate of interest of about 3%. Therefore the interest rate is approximately 36% annually.

Future value of payment flows

The Present Worth of \$1 Annuity table enables us to solve for the values of any one of P, A, r, and n when the other three are known. However, one may also wish to solve for the future value of an annuity F. This value would be desired in "how much will accumulate?" type of problems. For example, if someone saves \$1000 per year for ten years and invests his savings at 6% compounded annually, how much will he have at the end of the period? He now has the following values:

$$\begin{aligned} A &= \$1000 \\ r &= 6\% \\ n &= 10 \\ F &= \text{unknown} \end{aligned}$$

To solve for F in such a situation, a fourth table is presented in the Appendix, "The Sum of an Annuity of \$1 for N years" (Table A.3). From this table we find that $F = \$13{,}180$.

Yearly versus monthly calculations

Up to this point, in analyzing flows, we have been making liberal use of the principle of simplification by assuming that flows occur at the end of the year. In practice, these flows may occur throughout the year. For example, when we discussed paying for a house at \$2400 per year, payments actually were not made in a lump sum at the end of the year, but instead at \$200 per month over the entire year. In many calculations one is working with rather rough approximations, and the error introduced by assuming that all flows are paid at the end of the year (or alternatively, received) is not very serious.

If an individual, however, did want to correct for this, he could make the correction by either of two routes. He could make his whole analysis more precise by analyzing the flows that were expected each month rather than each year. Unless he were working with quite high annual interest rates, this might require a special set of tables. In the tables in this book, the lowest interest rate given is 1%; therefore the table can be readily used on a monthly basis only if the annual interest rate involved is 12% or more. Banks and other institutions that deal in installment payment arrangements have tables available which will enable them to work with monthly interest rates such as 7/12% (7% annual rate), or ¾% (9% annual rate).

There is another simple method of approximately correcting for the error caused by treating monthly payments as end-of-year payments. The person can make the assumption that payments occur not at the end of the year but at the middle of the year. To obtain the present value of the flows that are received in the middle of the year, he can make a calculation assuming that they are received at the end of the year and then make another calculation assuming they are received at the beginning of the year. He can average the present values of the two different calculations to arrive at the approximation of the true present value of the earnings flows.

For example, suppose one wished to correct that house financing problem posed earlier in which \$20,000 was to be borrowed at 8% and paid off at \$200 per month. We previously asked, how long would it take to pay off this amount at \$2400 per year (end-of-year payments). Now let us ask, how long would it take to pay off the \$20,000 if payments were at the beginning of each year? This would mean that as soon as the loan was made, \$2400 would be paid. (Remember, this situation is part of a correction and does not have to be realistic.) That would mean that actually only \$20,000 − \$2400, or \$17,600, was being used by the borrower. Thus another problem can be set up.

$$\begin{aligned} P &= \$17{,}600 \\ A &= \$2400 \\ r &= 8\% \\ n &= \text{unknown} \end{aligned}$$

When payments are made at the beginning of the year, n is now found to lie between 11 and 12 years, instead of the 14 to 15 years time associated with end-of-year payments. By averaging we can now estimate a payout time, when payments are made *throughout* the year, of about 13 years.

Solving problems

The writer's experience has shown that reading material about financial problem solving or listening to lectures about this subject will not enable the student to become a proficient problem solver. Individual practice seems to be almost inevitably required. One cardinal rule can be laid down for the solution of problems. Identify, in a systematic way, what you know and what you do not know. For any set of circumstances write down the value P if you know it, r if you know it, and any other values. Also indicate specifically which values are unknown. Once a problem is reduced to familiar symbols, it usually can then be solved easily. When difficulty ensues in the solution of a problem in financial mathematics, it almost always seems to arise in the area of classification and arrangement of information.

Application to overall financial planning

Let us consider a very simple type of planning situation. Suppose a married couple makes the following estimates about their future.

	Expenses
Next ten years (1971–1980):	Children in school; heavy expenses Total consumption needs $700 per month
1981–2000:	Lower expenses, $550 per month
Remaining lifetime (estimated 2001–2015):	Retirement period; expenses $500 per month.

	Income from Job
1971–1980:	$600 per month
1981–2000:	$750 per month
2001–2015:	$350 per month pension

The family has $2200 in the bank at the beginning of 1971 when it starts to plan for the future. Its outlook for the future can be summarized as

	Income minus expenses
1971–1980	−$1200 per year
1981–2000	+$2400 per year
2001–2015	−$1800 per year

At first it might appear that the family is going to be in serious difficulties very soon, when its $2200 runs out. However, we recall from Chapter 1 that families may be able to dissave by borrowing, as well as by using up previously accumulated assets, such as the $2200. Suppose the family assumes that it can borrow at 8% interest and that it can also get 6% interest on any money that it can put in a savings account.

Let us now check and see if it will be possible for the family to stay with its estimated spending plans. To do this we must inquire into whether savings generated in the 1981–2000 period will be sufficient to both repay previous borrowing and to provide the "nest egg" necessary to cover the family's estimated dissaving during retirement.

We can divide our work into several steps.

1. Find how long the $2200 will last.
2. Find the amount the family will owe by 1980.
3. Find how long it will take the family, after 1980, to get out of debt.

4. Find the amount of savings the family will build up by 2000.
5. Find whether these savings will be adequate for retirement.

Each of these steps can be approached with a technique from this chapter. (For simplicity, end-of-year saving and dissaving will be assumed.)

1. $P = \$2200$, $A = \$1200$, $r = 6\%$, $n =$ unknown. \$2200 is available to provide for annual dissavings of \$1200 per year. This discount factor is $P/A = \$2200/\$1200 = 1.8$. Using the Present Worth of \$1 Annuity table, and the savings account interest rate of 6%, we find n is about *2 years*.
2. $A = \$1200$, $r = 8\%$, $n = 8$, $F =$ unknown. The family must start borrowing in 1973, after its original \$2200 is used up, and borrow for eight years. It needs to know how much it will owe by 1980, at the end of the eight-year period. Using the Sum of \$1 Annuity for N years (Appendix Table 3), it finds that \$1 per year for eight years will accumulate, where $r = 8\%$, to \$10.63. Since it must borrow \$1200 per year, its indebtedness by the end of 1980 will be \$1200 × 10.63, or about *\$12,800.*
3. $P = \$12{,}800$, $A = \$2400$, $r = 8\%$, $n =$ unknown. The family will owe \$12,800 and it wants to know how long it will take to pay this amount off, with 8% interest, when it can pay in installments of \$2400 per year. A discount factor of \$12,800/\$2400, or 5.33, can be found. It can now go to the Present Worth of \$1 Annuity table, and find, where $r = 8\%$, that \$1 per year would pay off \$5.33 in slightly less than eight years, or that \$2400 per year will also pay off \$12,800 in about *eight years.*
4. $A = \$2400$, $n = 12$, $r = 6\%$, $F =$ unknown. The family will be out of debt by 1988 and can therefore put \$2400 per year into a savings account for the next 12 years, until retirement at the end of year 2000. It can read from the Compound Sum of \$1 Annuity for N Years table that \$1 saved every year and invested at 6% will accumulate to \$16.87. Therefore \$2400 per year will grow to \$2400 × 16.87, or about *\$40,000.*
5. $P = \$40{,}000$, $n = 15$, $r = 6\%$, $A =$ unknown. The family will have \$40,000 at the beginning of 2001. It wishes to dissave \$1800 per year for 15 years. It finds, in the Present Worth of \$1 Annuity table, that it is necessary to invest \$9.71 at 6% to obtain \$1 per year for 15 years. Since it has \$40,000 in its savings account, it will be able to make withdrawals of \$40,000 divided by \$9.72, or over *\$4000 per year.* Thus it can more than provide for its \$1800 per year needs.

This example has been significantly simplified. (What would happen if the husband died in 1990? If income was much better than expected? And so on.) However, it illustrates the usefulness of this chapter's analysis in the planning of households. This family has found one way of answering the question: Are we spending beyond our means? In this case, the answer was "No."

Before we return to a more careful consideration of long range planning, it will be useful to do two things. First, since taxes are such an important part of our lives, their effect must be considered in any plan. We devote the next chapter to a consideration of taxes. Then several chapters are spent on assets, since assets provide a way in which, as the savings account in the preceding example illustrates, income in one period can be converted into consumption in a future period.

Summary

Many personal decisions involve switching consumption from one time period to the next. Because interest rates exist, total consumption can be increased by waiting or decreased if it is moved toward the present.

To make decisions which compare consumption in different periods, tables which employ the concept of compound interest are extremely useful. Four basic tables are presented in this chapter.

The *Compound Sum of $1* table tells how much money (or consumption) can be obtained at a given time in the future if $1 is invested ($1 consumption given up) at present.

The *Present Value of $1* table tells the amount that must be given up now to obtain $1 at sometime in the future.

The *Present Worth of Annuity of $1* table tells the amount of money that must be given up now to provide $1 per year for a given period.

The *Compound Sum of Annuity of $1* table tells the amount of money that will accumulate if $1 per year is invested for a given period.

These tables have a variety of uses. They can be used to estimate the value of property to predict how long it will take them to pay a loan, to find a true annual interest rate, or to find how much savings a family will accumulate. These tables are applied extensively in later parts of the book.

SUGGESTED READINGS

The reader who is interested in advanced readings on this topic will have to turn to material that discusses problems that are related to business rather than personal situations. One widely used textbook on the topic is *The Capital Budgeting Decision* by Harold Bierman and Seymour Smidt (New York: Macmillan, 1966), especially Chapters 1 through 7.

QUESTIONS

1. How can an asset purchase change the timing of consumption? How can borrowing change this timing? job choice?

2. What is compound interest? If one borrows $1000 for three years at 6%, would it make any difference whether the interest is compounded yearly or semiannually, or not at all?
3. What is meant by the expression, "I expect to inherit $40,000 in 20 years. The present value of this amount is $5000."
4. Have you ever been involved, directly or indirectly, in a discounting transaction? If so, describe the transaction.
5. Why do you think lenders are required to disclose the actual interest rate they are charging on credit transactions?
6. Why does one sometimes use a present value table and at other times a separate present worth of an annuity table? Could the present value table ever be used to find the present value of an annuity?
7. Try to give an example of a situation where you might personally wish to find a future value with the use of one of the "compound sum" tables.

PROBLEMS

1. You place $1000 in a savings account that pays 5% compounded annually. To what amount will the $1000 accumulate with interest by the end of five years?
2. Joe borrows $1500 from a bank at an 8% annual interest rate. He repays the loan after four months. How much interest must he pay?
3. J executes a contract in which he promises to repay a $10,000 loan to L in two years. The interest rate is 9% with interest payable at the end of each year. L immediately sells J's promise to M, who discounts it at a rate of 12%. What amount will M pay to L?
4. Every year the Johnson family spends about $300 on renting a boat. It is now thinking about buying a boat which it expects will last about ten years.
   (a) If it uses a 6% discount rate, what is the present value of the rent that it will save over the estimated life of the boat?
   (b) If the Johnsons could buy a boat for less than this present value, would you recommend that they do so or would you suggest that they also consider some other factors?
5. The Leer family would like to buy a house in about five years and it thinks that during the next five years it can put about $1500 a year into a savings account to be used for a house down payment. The savings account bears 6% interest. How large a down payment will it be able to make?
6. Peter buys a car for a full price of $4000. He pays $1000 down and agrees to pay $100 per month for 42 months.
   (a) Estimate the interest rate that Peter is paying on his car loan.
   (b) Will your estimate be slightly too high or slightly too low? Explain by using the appropriate table.
7. How long will it take to repay a loan of $10,000 with 8% annual interest in monthly payments of $150 per month? $100 per month? $50 per month?

chapter four

Income taxes and their effect on planning

After-tax income

If a student ran a beach concession as a summer occupation, he might obtain revenues of, say, $4000 over the summer and incur $2500 expenses. If he were thinking about the money income he would have available for consumption or other personal uses, we would agree that $1500 rather than $4000 would be the appropriate figure for him to consider. Similarly, if he had to pay $200 income tax on the $1500, he could regard himself as having only $1300 available for personal use. For planning, when we consider how money can be used for personal consumption, purchase of assets, or repayment of debts, we need to know the amount of money that we will actually be able to use. This after-tax money income is often called *disposable income.*

Tax consideration is complicated by two factors. First, not all benefits received by a family are subject to income tax. Second, not all dollars received by a family and subject to income tax are taxed by the same amount; some types of income are given special tax treatment, and, in general, as the size of taxable income increases, the tax *per dollar* of taxable income increases. Therefore it is necessary to examine the way income taxes are applied before we can proceed with economic planning.

A word of caution

Any brief examination of the nature of income taxes and their effect on personal financial decisions must begin with a note of caution. Whereas the basic logic of the income tax is rather simple, many specific income tax issues are complicated. Income tax laws and their interpretations by the courts and government tax collection agencies also change as time passes. Therefore many families will require professional assistance in filing their income tax forms and in incorporating income tax factors into detailed financial planning. This chapter is not developed to replace the services of lawyers, accountants, and tax advisory firms, and the reader is strongly advised not to become overconfident about his ability to grapple with income tax details.

On the other hand, general knowledge of the income tax laws is essential to economic planning. Unless an individual wants to turn over all his decisions to an outside consultant, he has to think about tax effects. He can check out details or questionable issues with a consultant and certainly ought to consider employing outside help for filing all but the simplest of income tax returns. However, before the individual can even ask intelligent questions of outside tax advisors, he must have a basic understanding himself.

Which taxes should be considered?

For most families there is one type of income tax that is more important than others. This is the tax called the ordinary Federal income tax, which is levied on all personal income unless that income is exempted. Social security taxes are also levied against income by the Federal Government, and state and local governments sometimes levy income taxes.

Individuals also pay other taxes besides income taxes. Property tax is sometimes charged on certain types of physical assets and claims. These are usually levied every year as a proportion of the asset's appraised value (a value estimated for tax purposes by a governmental body). In many places sales taxes are charged as a proportion of the purchase price of certain consumption goods or assets at the time these items are purchased. Death taxes are also common; these are applied as a proportion of assets owned by an individual at the time of his death (his estate) and/or a proportion of assets received by living individuals from the estate of a dead person (inheritances).

However, these other taxes are not associated with the earning of income and can be considered in indirect ways. When one considers making any expenditure, sales taxes on the expenditure should be included in the total cost of the item on which the expenditure is to be made. When wealth is to be held in the form of property that is subject to tax, the return on this property should be reduced by the amount of the property taxation. These are quite uncomplicated matters in the form which they affect most personal financial decisions and we do not give them further treatment. As for death taxes, we discuss these taxes on the disposal of assets briefly in a later chapter.

The ordinary federal income tax

The single most important principle in understanding the Federal income tax is that it is built on traditional accounting. Ordinary income, as determined on the Federal income tax forms (which are really just special types of financial statements), is determined in much the same way as the income in the traditional business income statement. All revenues received by the individual, whether in the form of interest, wages and salary, rental income, or income from business interests, must be declared on the form or on supporting documents that may be required. Then expenses associated with the earning of the income are subtracted and the difference, corresponding to net income on the business income statement, is taxable ordinary income. A copy of the basic Federal income tax form, Form 1040, is depicted in Figure 4.1. Virtually all families must fill out this form and send it to the Internal Revenue Service once a year. Sending required tax forms in is often called *filing a tax return*. The information in the return normally covers a calendar year (for example, January 1, 1970 to December 31, 1970), and the return must usually be filed on or before April 15 of the following year (the 1970 return must be filed by April 15, 1971). Tax forms are usually mailed out, but those who do not receive forms in the mail (such as persons filing returns for the first time) may pick up forms at their post offices. Instructions for filing are included with the forms.

The tax forms are numbered, and we can make use of this numbering in referring to the forms. On Form 1040 (Page 1) the first 11 items numbered refer to information about the taxpayer and his family. We can summarize all of the various numbered items.

Form **1040** US Department of the Treasury / Internal Revenue Service **Individual Income Tax Return** **1970**

For the year January 1–December 31, 1970, or other taxable year beginning ...., 1970, ending ...., 19....

Please print or type

Your social security number

Spouse's social security number

Occupation: Yours / Spouse's

Filing Status—check only one:

1 ☐ Single; 2 ☐ Married filing jointly (even if only one had income)

3 ☐ Married filing separately and spouse is also filing. If this item checked give spouse's social security number in space above and enter first name here ▶

4 ☐ Unmarried Head of Household

5 ☐ Surviving widow(er) with dependent child

6 ☐ Married filing separately and spouse is not filing

Exemptions Regular / 65 or over / Blind — Enter number of boxes checked ▶

7 Yourself . . . . . . ☐ ☐ ☐

8 Spouse (applies only if item 2 or 6 is checked) ☐ ☐ ☐

9 First names of your dependent children who lived with you .... Enter number ▶

10 Number of other dependents (from line 34) . . . ▶

11 Total exemptions claimed . . . . ▶

Please attach Copy B of Form W–2 to back

Income

12 Wages, salaries, tips, etc. (Attach Forms W–2 to back. If unavailable, attach explanation) .	12	
13a Dividends (see pages 5 and 9 of instr.) $........ 13b Less exclusion $........ Balance . ▶ (Also list in Part I of Schedule B, if gross dividends and other distributions are over $100)	13c	
14 Interest. Enter total here (also list in Part II of Schedule B, if total is over $100) . . .	14	
15 Income other than wages, dividends, and interest (from line 40)	15	
16 Total (add lines 12, 13c, 14 and 15)	16	
17 Adjustments to income (such as "sick pay," moving expense, etc. from line 45) . . .	17	
18 Adjusted gross income (subtract line 17 from line 16)	18	

● *See page 2 of instructions for rules under which the IRS will figure your tax and surcharge.*
● *If you do not itemize deductions and line 18 is under $10,000, find tax in Tables. Enter tax on line 19.*
● *If you itemize deductions or line 18 is $10,000 or more, go to line 46 to figure tax.*

Tax and Surcharge

19 Tax (Check if from: Tax Tables 1–15 ☐, Tax Rate Schedule X, Y, or Z ☐, Schedule D ☐, or Schedule G ☐)	19	
20 Tax surcharge. See Tax Surcharge Tables A, B and C in instructions. (If you claim retirement income credit, use Schedule R to figure surcharge.)	20	
21 Total (add lines 19 and 20)	21	

Please attach Check or Money Order here

Payments and Credits

22 Total credits (from line 55)	22	
23 Income tax (subtract line 22 from line 21)	23	
24 Other taxes (from line 61)	24	
25 Total (add lines 23 and 24)	25	
26 Total Federal income tax withheld (attach Forms W–2 to back) . 26		Make check or money order payable to Internal Revenue Service.
27 1970 Estimated tax payments (include 1969 overpayment allowed as a credit) 27		
28 Other payments (from line 65) 28		
29 Total (add lines 26, 27, and 28)	29	

Bal. Due or Refund

30 If line 25 is larger than line 29, enter BALANCE DUE. Pay in full with return . . . ▶	30	
31 If line 29 is larger than line 25, enter OVERPAYMENT . . . . ▶	31	
32 Line 31 to be: (a) Credited on 1971 estimated tax ▶ $; (b) Refunded ▶	$	

Under penalties of perjury, I declare that I have examined this return, including accompanying schedules and statements, and to the best of my knowledge and belief it is true, correct, and complete.

Sign here

▶ Your signature .... Date ▶ Signature of preparer other than taxpayer, based on all information of which he has any knowledge. .... Date

▶ Spouse's signature (If filing jointly, BOTH must sign even if only one had income) .... Address

16—81168-1

Figure 4.1 U. S. Federal Income Tax Form 1040 (Page 1)

Items	*Description*
1–11	General information
12–18	Income received (corresponds to revenues in a business income statement)
19–21	Amount of tax owed
22–29	Credits: Various items which reduce amount of tax owed
30–32	Amount of money left to be paid by taxpayer or amount of money to be refunded to taxpayer

These items are explained in more detail in the material that follows.

It is useful to examine Page 2 of Form 1040 (Figure 4.2) which includes some supporting information for figures supplied on Page 1 and also contains the computation of the amount of tax owed.

When Pages 1 and 2 are considered together, the similarity of the tax return to a business income statement is apparent. In fact, we can construct the following statement by referring to Form 1040 (money amounts for an imaginary taxpayer are included).

Personal Income Statement
for Tax Determination

Gross taxable income		
Wages, salaries, etc. (Item 12)	$9000	
Dividends and interest (13, 14)	300	
Other income (15)	0	
Total (18, 46)		$9300
Deductions		
Deductible expenses (47)	$ 930	
Exemption from tax (49)	1800	
Total		2730
Net taxable income (50)		$6570

Other items on Form 1040 refer either to information needed for determining deductions, adjustments for special purposes which are explained in the instructions that accompany the tax form, or the calculation of the amount of tax owed including social security taxes.

Personal revenues or gross taxable income

We have seen that revenues (gross taxable income) received by the individual are reported on Form 1040 in determining ordinary income. Again, there are exceptions. If property held by an individual rises in

Page 2 Form 1040 (1970) — Attach Copy B of Form W–2 here. ►

Foreign Accounts (check appropriate box) ► Did you, at any time during the taxable year, have any interest in or signature or other authority over a bank, securities, or other financial account in a foreign country (except in a U.S. military banking facility operated by a U.S. financial institution)? . . . . ☐ Yes ☐ No. If "Yes," attach Form 4683. (For definitions, see Form 4683.)

PART I.—Additional Exemptions (Complete only for other dependents claimed on line 10)

33 (a) NAME	(b) Relationship	(c) Months lived in your home. If born or died during year write "B" or "D"	(d) Did dependent have income of $625 or more?	(e) Amount YOU furnished for dependent's support. If 100% write "ALL"	(f) Amount furnished by OTHERS including dependent.
				$	$

34 **Total number of dependents listed above.** Enter here and on line 10 . . . ►

PART II.—Income other than Wages, Dividends, and Interest

35 Business income (or loss) (attach Schedule C) . . .	35	
36 Sale or exchange of property (attach Schedule D) . . .	36	
37 Pensions and annuities, rents and royalties, partnerships, estates or trusts, etc. (attach Schedule E) .	37	
38 Farm income (or loss) (attach Schedule F) . . .	38	
39 Miscellaneous income (state nature and source)	39	
40 **Total** (add lines 35, 36, 37, 38, and 39). Enter here and on line 15 . . . ►	40	

PART III.—Adjustments to Income

41 "Sick pay" if included in line 12 (attach Form 2440 or other required statement) . . .	41	
42 Moving expense (attach Form 3903) . . .	42	
43 Employee business expense (attach Form 2106 or other statement) . . .	43	
44 Payments as a self-employed person to a retirement plan, etc. (attach Form 2950SE) . . .	44	
45 **Total adjustments** (add lines 41, 42, 43, and 44). Enter here and on line 17 . . . ►	45	

PART IV.—Tax Computation

46 Adjusted gross income (from line 18) . . .	46	
47 (a) If you itemize deductions, enter total from Schedule A, line 22 (b) If you do not itemize deductions, and line 46 is $10,000 or more, enter $1,000 ($500 if married and filing separately) . . .	47	
48 Subtract line 47 from line 46 . . .	48	
49 Multiply total number of exemptions claimed on line 11, by $625 . . .	49	
50 Taxable income. Subtract line 49 from line 48. (Figure your tax on this amount by using Tax Rate Schedule X, Y, or Z unless the alternative tax or income averaging is applicable.) Enter tax on line 51	50	
51 **Tax.** Enter here and on line 19 . . . ►	51	

PART V.—Credits

52 Retirement income credit (attach Schedule R) . . .	52	
53 Investment credit (attach Form 3468) . . .	53	
54 Foreign tax credit (attach Form 1116) . . .	54	
55 **Total credits** (add lines 52, 53, and 54). Enter here and on line 22 . . . ►	55	

PART VI.—Other Taxes

56 Self-employment tax (attach Schedule SE) . . .	56	
57 Tax from recomputing prior-year investment credit (attach Form 4255) . . .	57	
58 Minimum tax. See instructions on page 7. Check here ☐, if Form 4625 is attached . . .	58	
59 Social security tax on unreported tip income (attach Form 4137) . . .	59	
60 Uncollected employee social security tax on tips (from Forms W–2) . . .	60	
61 **Total** (add lines 56, 57, 58, 59, and 60). Enter here and on line 24 . . . ►	61	

PART VII.—Other Payments

62 Excess F.I.C.A. tax withheld (two or more employers—see instructions on page 7) . . .	62	
63 Credit for Federal tax on gasoline, special fuels, and lubricating oil (attach Form 4136) . . .	63	
64 Regulated Investment Company Credit (attach Form 2439) . . .	64	
65 **Total** (add lines 62, 63, and 64). Enter here and on line 28 . . . ►	65	

☆☆☆☆ U.S. GOVERNMENT PRINTING OFFICE:1970—O-398-203 (E.I. 13-5568295) 16—81168-1

Figure 4.2 Form 1040 (Page 2)

value, he may choose to recognize this increase as income in his own personal accounting system. However, the tax accounting methods are based on traditional accounting which does not recognize increases in the value of assets held by the individual. Thus it is possible for someone to become very wealthy through property appreciation without paying any Federal income tax on the wealth accumulation.

On the other hand, income does not have to be received in the form of cash to be subject to inclusion in a tax reckoning. For example, A works for B. B gives A a car instead of money wages. The tax laws require that the value of the car be estimated and included in A's gross income.

Other exceptions in determining gross income should also be noted. If an individual makes a profit on the sale of property that he has held for over six months, it is quite likely that such income will not be included in determining ordinary personal income. Instead this type of income will be classified as a capital gain and subjected to a different, and less rigorous, income tax.

Certain types of investment income are completely exempt from Federal taxation. Because of the interpretation that the Supreme Court has placed on the United States Constitution in an effort to preserve the relative rights of Federal and state governments, income received on bonds issued by state and local governments is not subject to Federal income tax. To avoid harming citizens of the United States who live outside the country, some income earned and taxed in other countries is exempt from American taxation. To avoid compounding the hardships suffered by individuals who are disabled or ill, "sick pay" is not regarded as income for tax purposes.

Withholding and other advance tax payments

Most taxpayers receive most of their income in the form of wages and salaries. Tax laws provide that before employers pay out wages and salaries, they must turn over a portion of these wages and salaries to the Federal Government. This process is called *withholding*. The amounts of income withheld during the year will *usually* be about equal to the income tax owed on the wage or salary. Thus, in effect, most income taxes are collected before the tax return is filed.

When persons receive income from sources other than wages and salaries, most taxes on this income must also be paid in advance. Anyone earning a significant amount of income from which taxes are not withheld should find out, by studying the text material received with his tax form or by asking someone, whether he should arrange to pay some taxes in advance of filing.

Supplementary Forms

When someone has received wages or salary from which taxes have been withheld, he will receive an official statement from his employer stating the amount of his wages and salary from that employer during the year, the amount of tax withheld, and other information. This statement is called Form W-2 and a copy of it must accompany the tax return.

In addition, the tax instructions provide for the filing of other supplemental forms in some situations. Figure 4.3 illustrates one of these forms. However, any individual who receives income from sources other than wages and salaries will need to check to see if he is required to file a supplemental form. Note that the total amounts of interest and dividends from the form illustrated are transferred to Form 1040. Thus Schedule B provides more detailed information to explain the total that appears in Form 1040.

The nondeductibility of consumption expenses

We have noted that in determining ordinary taxable income, certain types of expenses can be deducted from the revenues received by an individual. However, most of the expenses incurred by the individual cannot be deducted. In general, consumption expenses are nondeductible. If one takes a pleasure trip, he normally cannot deduct this as an expense even though he could deduct expense for a business trip. (This particular aspect of tax law gives rise to many disputes because it is sometimes difficult to distinguish between trips that are for business and for pleasure.) Food expenses, entertainment, and rent on housing used by the family are normally regarded as nondeductible consumption expenses.

Again, there are many intricate and sometimes curious rules that affect the classification of expenses. For example, if the family pays rent on its home, this rent is a nondeductible expense. However, if the family borrows money and buys a home, the interest payment on the borrowed money is deductible. And, of course, if a family rents a building for business purposes, such rent would be deductible as a business expense. There are other examples of difficulty of classification. Educational expenses are sometimes regarded as personal expenses, but in certain instances these costs are regarded as associated with the earning of income and are deductible.

Sometimes the tax laws make use of the principle of simplification. Many people incur expenses in getting to work in the form of bus fare, car ownership costs, and so forth. However, because nearly every taxpayer incurs some of these expenses, the tax rules make this particular type of expense nondeductible in most instances. If everyone were allowed

Schedules A & B (Form 1040) 1970

Schedule B—Dividend and Interest Income

Page 2

Name(s) as shown on Form 1040 (Do not enter name and social security number if shown on other side) | Your Social Security Number

Part I Dividend Income

Note: If gross dividends and other distributions on stock are $100 or less, do not complete this part. But enter gross dividends less the sum of capital gain distributions and non-taxable distributions, if any, on Form 1040, line 13a. (see note below)

1 Gross dividends and other distributions on stock. (List payers and amounts—write (H), (W), (J), for stock held by husband, wife, or jointly)

2 Total of line 1

3 Capital gain distributions (see instructions on page 9. Enter here and on Schedule D, Part I, line 7.) See note below

4 Nontaxable distributions (see instructions on page 9)

5 Total (add lines 3 and 4)

6 **Dividends before exclusion** (subtract line 5 from line 2). Enter here and on Form 1040, line 13a

Part II Interest Income

Note: If interest is $100 or less, do not complete this part. But enter amount of interest received on Form 1040, line 14.

1 Earnings from savings and loan associations and credit unions (list payers and amounts)

2 Other Interest on bank deposits, bonds, tax refunds, etc. (list payers and amounts)

B

3 **Total interest income.** Enter here and on Form 1040, line 14

Note: If you received capital gain distributions and Schedule D is not needed to report any other gains or losses or to compute the alternative tax, you need not file Schedule D. Instead, enter 50 percent of capital gain distributions on Form 1040, line 39, under "Miscellaneous Income," and identify the source as "50% of cap. gain dist."

☆ U.S. GOVERNMENT PRINTING OFFICE: 1970—O-370-042 16—81169-1 GPO

Figure 4.3 Schedule B

to deduct this type of expense, a great deal of extra work would be involved, both for taxpayers in determining the amount of their expenses and for the tax collectors in verifying the accuracy of the individual expense statements. If everyone deducted the expense, the tax rates would have to be set a little bit higher to compensate the Government for the lost tax revenues. Most people would not gain anything anyway. Therefore it has been simpler to rule them nondeductible. (Of course, in special situations, exceptions are made; this reinforces the statement that careful study or professional consultation is often necessary on individual tax issues.)

Deductions

We said earlier that consumption expenses are usually not deductible in the determination of taxable income. There are a few exceptions. In addition to interest expense which was mentioned previously, some medical expenses and charitable contributions are deductible. The payment of state and local taxes, even if for personal purposes, may also result in a deduction. To avoid the processing of many small personal deductions, the tax laws provide that an individual may elect to take a standard deduction, which is a general deduction for personal expenses that does not need to be supported by any evidence. This deduction can be taken even though no deductible personal expenses have been incurred. If the deduction is taken, however, no additional deductions can be made for personal expenses. The individual has to consider his personal circumstances when he decides whether to use the standard deduction or to give up this deduction and instead itemize his actual deductible personal expenses. The determination of the amount of the standard deduction is described on Page 2 of Form 1040.

Each individual is also allowed to claim a personal deduction which allows him to avoid tax on some of the income used to purchase bare necessities. Since this deduction was $625 per person in 1970, a family consisting of a husband, wife, and two dependent children could have subtracted $2500 for personal deductions in addition to the personal expense deduction discussed earlier. (There are exceptions to this rule too; for example, persons over 65 and blind people can claim larger personal deductions.)

Evidence

As a general rule income tax deals with revenues and expenses that are easily measured. All revenues in the form of cash or items with readily apparent cash value must be shown unless they are specifically exempted. Similarly, expenses are usually recognized only if they are in a form recognized by traditional accounting and if they can be supported by some kind of evidence. The individual can be asked to prove that the expenses he lists on his tax forms have in fact been incurred; items such as cancelled checks, invoices, and receipts are normally part of this proof. Again, there are exceptions to the general rule and, in some instances, well-explained estimates of expense items or well-kept personal accounting records are acceptable.

Federal ordinary income tax rates

The ordinary Federal income tax is progressive in nature. This means that higher ordinary incomes are taxed at a higher rate than lower incomes. This is accomplished through the use of marginal tax rates. The rates prevailing in 1970 are shown in Table 4.1. Note the application of higher and higher tax rates on steps of additional income.

TABLE 4.1
ORDINARY PERSONAL INCOME TAX RATES, 1970
(JOINT RETURNS FOR MARRIED TAXPAYERS)

Total taxable income	Tax on column 1	% on excess
$ . . .	$ . . .	14
1,000	140	15
2,000	290	16
3,000	450	17
4,000	620	19
8,000	1,380	22
12,000	2,260	25
16,000	3,260	28
20,000	4,380	32
24,000	5,660	36
28,000	7,100	39
32,000	8,660	42
36,000	10,340	45
40,000	12,140	48
44,000	14,060	50
52,000	18,060	53
64,000	24,420	55
76,000	31,020	58
88,000	37,980	60
100,000	45,180	62
120,000	57,580	64
140,000	70,380	66
160,000	83,580	68
180,000	97,180	69
200,000	110,980	70
300,000	180,980	70
400,000	250,980	70

It is useful to make a distinction between a household's average tax rate and its marginal tax rate. Suppose that a married couple have a taxable income of $9000 per year. According to the tax schedule, since their income falls into the $8000 to $12,000 bracket, the tax is $1380 plus 22% of the amount over $8000. Since their $9000 income is $1000 more than $8000, the total tax is $1380 plus 22% of $1000 ($220) or a total of $1600. If we think of their income in steps of $1000, their ninth step of income, from $8000 to $9000, was taxed at the rate of 22%; we may call this the *marginal rate*. We can also find the rate that the couple paid on their total amount of income. Their total tax was $1600 and their total income was $9000. $1600 is 18% of $9000; this overall rate which the couple pay on all taxable income may be called their *average tax rate*. We observe that the average tax rate is lower than the marginal rate. The average rate is never higher than the marginal rate for any individual and, except for persons with very low incomes, the marginal rate is always higher than the average rate.

We can also observe in the tax schedule that the marginal tax rate applied to the highest level of the individual's income can never exceed 70%. Therefore we know that no matter how high an income an individual has, he can always earn more and have something extra left after taxes. Many of us have heard someone tell about an individual he has known who is earning so much money that, if he earned any more, he would get into a higher tax bracket and actually have less after-tax income. These stories are always erroneous. Higher tax rates are levied only on additional amounts of income. When a person gets into a higher tax bracket, a higher marginal tax applies to income within that bracket, but he still has something left over from the additional income. There is no change in the tax levied on his previous level of income.

Joint Returns

A husband and a wife are given the choice of filing separate returns or of filing a return that lists the income that both of them are earning. This second type of return is called a joint return and is usually advantageous for a married couple. The effect of the use of the joint return is to divide the combined income of the husband and wife into two equal parts for purposes of tax rate determination. If, for example, the husband earns $10,000 a year and the wife earns nothing, the joint tax return automatically enables the family income to be treated as two $5000 incomes. Because the tax rate is less on a $5000 income than on a $10,000 income, the result of the joint return is to diminish the tax rate and hence the total amount of taxes paid by the husband and the wife.

Single persons cannot take advantage of the joint return. There is an intermediate option, called "head of household" status, which may reduce the tax rates of some single individuals, although these rates will still not be as low as the rates that would prevail if the person were able to use a joint return. Again, since the tax laws in this area of choice of returns are complicated in some aspects, the individual is advised to study the tax instructions and to seek expert opinion if he has doubt about his status.

In the event that a husband and wife file a joint return, they do not need to go through personally the task of dividing up their total income into two parts and determining the rate on these parts. This calculation has already been made in the schedules of tax rates for joint returns as shown in Table 4.1. In material sent to the taxpayer when he receives his tax forms, schedules of tax rates are listed both for joint returns and persons filing under a single or "head of household" status.

Marginal Tax Rates and Decisions

We have placed considerable emphasis on marginal tax rates because these are the rates that matter when the individual makes financial decisions. If an individual decides to earn some additional income, that income will be taxed at the marginal rate. If an individual is choosing between two possible investments, only one of which will produce taxable income, again the after-tax income that he derives from these projects will be affected by his marginal tax rate. This is the rate that always applies when an individual acts in such a way as to change his taxable income. Nearly every financial decision has some effect on an individual's taxable income and we often use these marginal tax rates in later chapters.

The capital gains tax

So far the ordinary Federal income tax has been discussed. Another important Federal income tax is the *capital gains tax.* If an individual holds property longer than a specified time period, normally six months, and sells at a profit, the excess of what he receives over what he paid may be classified as a capital gain. If it is classified as a capital gain, instead of ordinary income, it is taxed at a lower rate than ordinary income. There are two ways of calculating a capital gain tax. For most people, the method used is to take the amount of capital gain, reduce it by one-half and pay ordinary income tax on half of the capital gain. This is a perfectly legal operation; in effect, capital gains are subject to tax at one-half the marginal ordinary income tax rate.

If an individual has a very high income, he can use another method for calculating capital gain tax. He may take the amount of his capital gain and pay 25% income tax on the entire amount. Obviously, if a person's marginal ordinary tax rate is over 50%, it is to his advantage to simply pay a 25% capital gain tax rather than to pay his ordinary income tax on half of the capital gain.

The classification of income as capital gain instead of ordinary income is not a simple matter. For example, an individual may buy a house, sell it a year later at a $10,000 profit, and have the $10,000 treated as capital gain. On the other hand, if the individual is in the real estate business and buys the house as part of his regular business operations, the gain on the house would probably be treated as ordinary income. Therefore expert advice is sometimes needed in determining whether revenue obtained from the sale of property is classified as a capital gain. We take up this subject again when we consider personal investment in a home, corporation common stocks, and some other types of assets.

We should note that capital gains taxes are payable only when property is sold. An individual may hold property which increases in value tenfold and as long as he does not sell it, there is no tax levied against this. At first it appears that an individual could receive no benefit from the increased value of his property, in terms of increasing his standard of living, unless he did sell it. However, it is often possible to borrow money in larger amounts if one holds property of high value. Therefore, it is possible for an individual to increase his standard of living by borrowing increasingly high amounts as his property rises in value, and thus obtain benefit from the increase in property value without paying any tax. (Money that is borrowed is not counted as income either.)

The relevance of the capital gains tax can be summarized by the general statement that if a family can receive income in the form of capital gains, this income is worth more to them than money received in the form of ordinary income because of the difference in tax expense in earning the two forms of income.

Social security taxes

A third form of income tax is also collected by the Federal Government. In order to provide for payment of old age benefits, payments to widows, and other types of social assistance payments, a social security tax is levied currently on the first $7800 of ordinary income that an individual earns each year. This tax is payable on income earned from wages and salaries or from personal business enterprises.

It is sometimes contended that this tax is a form of savings since individuals receive benefits from social security. However, the tax differs greatly from what we normally conceive to be personal savings. The individual cannot control the wealth that is accumulated through the tax process; for example, he cannot use some of these savings at age 55 even if he wants to; instead, he must wait until an age prescribed by law, presently 62 years. Furthermore there is not a precise relationship. between the amount of social security tax an individual pays and the amount of transfer payments that he receives as part of the social security system. An individual can have a very low income most of his life. If he happens to raise his income during the last few years that he is employed, he pays social security tax at a higher rate during those years and, as a result of this short history, becomes eligible for a high level of social security benefit payments upon retirement. We will not dwell further on this issue, but accept the idea that social security as a form of saving was probably originated to convince the public of the desirability of financing a program which provided benefits to older persons and other beneficiaries deemed worthy of public support.

Although the social security tax is a form of income tax, it is not as important as the ordinary income tax in financial decision making. First, it is not as large as other income taxes. (Rates are increasing nearly every year; when this book was written, they were 5% for employees and 7% for self-employed individuals.) Second, it is only payable on a given amount of income; when an individual earns more wage and salary income than this amount, the marginal social security tax becomes zero. In addition, no social security tax is applied against such items as rental income or interest. Therefore, in many investment decisions and for many individuals with moderately high incomes, marginal social security tax is zero. Still, as a family plans the future uses for its salary and other income, it will have to deduct the social security tax in determining its after-tax income.

State and local income taxes

This text does not contain a description of the wide variety of income taxes that are levied by states and cities. Some of these are very closely related to the Federal income tax (these are sometimes called "Federalized" taxes), whereas others are somewhat different. The general idea of the state and local income taxes, though, does not differ greatly from the Federal income tax arrangements. When an individual is making financial decisions, he will need to consider whether he will be subject to state and local income taxes (this depends on where he lives) and include the effect of these taxes in his financial planning.

An example of decision making with taxes considered

To illustrate the effect of taxes in individual planning, let us consider an example of a farmer, 40 years old, who is considering the possibility of selling his farm and moving to the city. To make the example simple, assume that the farmer does not particularly care where he lives and is making the decision only on the basis of the amount of wealth he will be able to accumulate by the time he is 60 years old. Also assume, for simplicity, that the farmer's cost of living will be the same whether he stays on the farm or moves to the city.

If the farmer leaves the farm, he will be able to sell his farm and invest the proceeds at interest of 6%. Suppose that he can currently sell his farm for $40,000. If the farmer remains on his farm, he visualizes that he can accumulate wealth in two ways. Traditional accounting shows his farm income as $9000 per year; he actually receives this much in cash each year from his farm. In addition, he expects that his farm will increase in value at a rate of 3% per year, because as population increases land values usually go up.

If the farmer moves to the city he can earn $8000 per year, but in addition, he will be able to invest his $40,000 and receive interest on this. Let us suppose that the farmer estimates that his marginal tax rate will be 25%. He also estimates that he will require an $8000 before-tax income to provide for his living expenses. Thus, if he stays on the farm, he can save $1000 of before-tax income; since this is taxed at the marginal rate of 25%, this amounts to a $750 a year saving rate. In addition, of course, the value of his farm is increasing and this will contribute to the amount of wealth that he can accumulate at the end of the 20-year period.

If he moves to the city, he will not be able to save anything out of his wages, but he will be able to save all the interest that he earns on his $40,000. Because the farmer is able to invest at 6% and because we know that any interest will be taxed at the marginal rate of 25%, the farmer will earn a 4½% interest rate after taxes. Now some of the analysis from Chapter 3 can be employed to solve for the amount of wealth that the farmer will accumulate.

If the farmer stays on the farm, his land, currently worth $40,000, will increase in value by 3% per year for 20 years. Because the farmer is holding his land, none of this increase in value will be subject to tax unless he sells it. To find the value of the farm at the end of the 20-year period, one can set up the following problem.

$$\begin{aligned} P &= \$40{,}000 \\ r &= 3\% \\ n &= 20 \\ F &= \text{unknown} \end{aligned}$$

When this problem is solved, one finds that the farm will be worth about $72,000 at the end of 20 years. If the farmer sells the farm at the end of 20 years, he will have realized a capital gain of $32,000 over the farm's original value of $40,000. This capital gain will be taxed at one-half the farmer's marginal tax rate, so it will be taxed at 12½%. Thus the tax on the $32,000 capital gain will be $4000. After the farmer has paid the tax, he will have $68,000 remaining from the sale of his farm.

In addition, if the farmer stays on the farm, he can save \$750 per year. If he invests this at 4½% after-tax interest, one can set up the problem.

$$A = \$750$$
$$r = 4\tfrac{1}{2}\%$$
$$n = 20$$
$$F = \text{unknown}$$

Solving, F is approximately equal to \$23,500. Thus, if the farmer stays on the farm, he will be able to accumulate \$23,500 plus \$68,000, or a total of about \$91,500 at the end of the 20-year period.

If he goes to the city, the wealth he will accumulate will be based on the future value of his \$40,000 invested at compound interest of 4½%, after tax. Thus still another problem can be identified.

$$P = \$40{,}000$$
$$r = 4\tfrac{1}{2}\%$$
$$n = 20$$
$$F = \text{unknown}$$

Solving for F, we obtain approximately \$97,000. The farmer would be somewhat better off by selling his farm and moving to the city.

It would be possible to construct much more complex examples. For example, the farmer might have expected that if he moved, his salary would go up during the period. If he stayed on the farm, he might have been able to invest his \$750 annual saving in additional land, which might both increase his current income and also go up in value; the increase in value would be subject to only the capital gains tax. With our general understanding of tax and with our knowledge of financial mathematics, we would be able to solve much more complicated problems. These solutions might take a great deal of time, but some major personal economic decisions are important enough to warrant many hours of calculation.

Summary

Not all income received by individuals is theirs to dispose of as they wish; a substantial part is immediately required for the payment of income taxes.

The most important tax paid by Americans is the ordinary Federal income tax. Most individuals pay this tax gradually throughout the year because amounts of money are withheld from their paychecks by their employer. However, every individual earning more than \$600 per year must annually file a tax return in which he makes a final accounting with the Government for the year's income taxes.

Income tax regulations are very complex, yet the basic principles of the tax are simple. On the tax form an individual first sets forth all the income he has earned during the year, unless some of this income is specifically exempt from taxes. He then reduces this amount by his personal exemption and by any deductible expenses. The amount left over is taxable income which is subject to tax according to a schedule of rates provided with the individual's tax forms.

Income received from capital gains is given special tax treatment. In addition to paying Federal income taxes of the ordinary and capital gains types, individuals are responsible for paying social security taxes. Additional, although usually much smaller, income taxes are imposed by some states and cities.

American income taxes are progressive; that is, the ratio of tax to income becomes higher as income becomes higher. An individual's marginal tax rate is that rate which he will pay or save if he increases or decreases his income from its present level. His average rate is determined by dividing the amount of income tax he must pay by his income. In a progressive tax structure, marginal rates are higher than average rates.

Taxes are important in the making of personal economic decisions. It is not the income that one gets from some course of action that is important but the after-tax income that he will receive. For example, unless a college graduate going on to his first job has explicitly looked ahead at the effect of taxes, he is often surprised at the discrepancy between the salary he is being paid per month and the amount of the paycheck that he actually receives after income taxes (and some other items that we discuss later) have been withheld.

SUGGESTED READINGS

Instructions accompanying the income tax form provide a great deal of information and are worth careful study.

Two widely used publications which describe the Federal income tax are J.K. Lasser's *Your Income Tax* (New York: Simon & Schuster, Inc.) which is normally available on newsstands or in bookstores, and the annual *Master Tax Guide* published by the Commerce Clearing House of Chicago.

The instructions that accompany the tax forms also note some low-priced sources of supplemental information that may be ordered from the U.S. Government.

QUESTIONS

1. What other major types of taxes, besides the income tax, are likely to affect you?
2. Does your state have an income tax? If it does, see if you can find out something about its rates and its deductions and exemptions.

3. Why is after-tax income rather than before-tax income used for planning purposes?
4. When individuals' incomes are subject to withholding for the personal income tax, why are some individuals required to pay extra taxes at the time they file their tax returns, whereas others are eligible for refunds?
5. Which of the following are likely to be deductible expenses?
   (a) Car expenses incurred by a traveling salesman
   (b) Car expenses incurred by a factory worker who commutes long distances to work
   (c) House rent (or a portion thereof) paid by an insurance agent who maintains an office in his home
   (d) Medical insurance premiums paid by a family
6. What is a standard deduction? Why do some families make use of a standard deduction, whereas others do not?
7. You hear the following rumor: Bill Brown, a wealthy independent businessman, now only works nine months out of the year because if he earned any more money, he would get into a higher tax bracket and actually have less after-tax income. Can you explain why this rumor is false?
8. By looking at Table 4.1, it is possible to observe that high income people are subject to very high tax rates. Can you think of any reason why it would be possible to earn $400,000 or $500,000 per year or more and still not be subject to such high tax rates? (*Hint*: Taxes are levied on *taxable* income.)
9. What is a joint return? Why is the use of a joint return especially advantageous to a family when the family earns a high income and the wife earns no taxable income?
10. What is the difference between a marginal tax rate and an average tax rate? Why are marginal tax rates important in many decisions?
11. Can you think of any transactions in which you are likely to be involved where income will be received in the form of capital gains?
12. Why are marginal social security tax rates often zero? Why is an individual's average social security tax rate lower if his income is $20,000 per year than if it is $10,000?

PROBLEMS

1. Charles receives pay of $10,000 from his job. Mary, his wife, earns another $3000 in part-time work. Charlie and Mary earn another $500 per year in interest. They have three children and use the standard deductions. What is their taxable income and how much income tax will they have to pay?
2. The Williams family earns $13,000 per year. The family consists of a husband, wife, and one child; the family pays $800 per year in tax-deductible interest. It makes tax-deductible charitable donations of about $150 per year and also normally incurs about $300 in tax-deductible medical expenses. It is also entitled to about $200 in tax deductions for state and local taxes it has paid. Should it use the standard deduction?

3. X considers two possible investments. One is a piece of land which he can buy for $5000 now and which he expects he can sell for $10,000 at the end of six years. The gain on this transaction will be treated as a capital gain for tax purposes. His second alternative is to buy a bond which pays 10% interest. This interest is fully taxable.

   Using techniques from Chapter 3, what is the internal rate of return on each of the assets before taxes are considered? after taxes are considered?

4. Taxable income of the Gould family is $12,000 per year. What is its marginal ordinary personal income tax rate and its average rate?

5. How much social security tax will be paid by an individual earning $5000 per year? by an individual earning $15,000 per year?

chapter five

General principles of asset choice

We may begin a discussion of assets by considering them as a part of a larger choice process. To do this, first recall the nature of the personal balance sheet and its equation.

$$\text{Assets} = \text{liabilities} + \text{net worth}$$

From the balance sheet equation, three major financial issues may be drawn. These issues, incidentally, are not only relevant to families but also to the decisions of businesses and to government-owned enterprises.

1. *What should the composition of the assets be?* The personal balance sheet can contain a variety of assets including various types of human capital, physical capital, and claims. Different families maintain different types of assets in varying proportions. Each family has to attempt to decide what is its correct mixture of assets.

2. *What total amount of assets should be held?* Some families may wish to accumulate many valuable assets, whereas others, even though they could build up large stocks of

assets, elect to have few possessions. Each family must choose the total amount of assets that is best suited to its own circumstances.

3. *How should the assets be financed?* A family may pay for assets out of personal resources that are built up through saving or through the receipt of transfers such as inheritances. Assets may also be acquired by borrowing from a variety of sources. Some families prefer not to go into debt at all; others feel it is to their advantage to maintain liabilities that are equal to a rather high proportion of their total assets. A family must try to choose the amount and kind of borrowing that is best for it.

This chapter and Chapters 6 to 9 are primarily concerned with Issue 1, the choice among alternative asset holdings. Some discussion of Issue 2 is also included in these chapters but principally Issues 2 and 3 are discussed in a later part of the book.

A general unit of measure

The objective of the personal asset selection process can be stated quite simply. From a given amount of assets, whether obtained by savings, transfers, or borrowings, the individual wants to obtain the greatest possible amount of personal benefit. This statement in itself, however, does not tell very much about choosing among asset alternatives. In the first place, benefits are received from assets in many different forms. Some assets, such as receivables, are promises of fixed money payments. Others, such as shares in business enterprises, offer the possibility of money payments, but these payments are not fixed in nature; the payments will depend on the success of the business in which the share is held. Many other personal assets do not offer direct money returns; for example, a dishwasher may offer returns in time saving, improved washing quality, or even in pride of ownership. Other assets, such as investments in human capital, may offer a mixture of money returns in the form of improved earning power, and nonmonetary returns such as the satisfaction of being a more well-informed citizen.

Unless a benefit measure is used that applies to all types of assets, systematic asset selection will be difficult. Because many of the returns on assets are directly in money form, we shall use money as a common measuring unit for the evaluation of asset alternatives. This will mean that money values will have to be estimated for the nonmonetary benefits that are conferred by assets. In the case of the dishwasher it is necessary to put some money value on the time saved, and, with much more difficulty, on the more sanitary dishes and the pleasure of displaying the shiny new machine. This is not an attempt to impose a materialistic standard of values on personal asset selection; we simply need a common unit of measure and the dollar is the most widely used measure of value.

The marginal approach

In considering asset possibilities, we want to return to the marginal concept introduced in Chapter 1. Many assets can be bought in varying quantities; remember the example of the automobile in Chapter 1 in which we consider increasing the value of the automobile in $300 steps. In asset analysis it is useful to use the term *marginal benefit*, defined as the amount of benefit obtained on a marginal step of asset purchase. We know from the discussion in the previous section that money values are involved in the measurement of marginal benefit, but a later section of this chapter expresses this measure in a more complete way.

The form of benefits

The benefits received from holding assets are subjective by nature; that is, they depend on the personal viewpoint of their holder. An individual may receive satisfaction simply by "having" a large stock of assets. Such a preference, however, does not need to enter into the asset *selection* decision as long as it is not a preference for a particular type of asset. If it is, the individual will have to identify a money value he attaches to this preference. For example, an individual might say that it was worth $100 per year to him to keep a $1000 hoard of cash on hand. As long as the individual had strongly made up his mind about this preference, it would be then quite rational for him to turn down the opportunity to put his money to work at 8% interest. If he invested in an asset bearing 8%, he would get only $80 per year, which would be less than the benefit he received by knowing that his money was still in his mattress.

This book does not attempt to treat the matter of personal preference for different investment types in very great detail, although we have more to say about individual attitudes toward one characteristic of various investments (their riskiness) in later chapters. At present we want to emphasize that a return on personal assets is a personal matter and an individual, to obtain the greatest possible benefit from a collection of assets, must consider his own preferences.

Most people, of course, will probably not have strong preferences for particular types of assets themselves and will go about identifying benefits from alternative assets in a fairly straightforward way. If a person contemplates the acquisition of human capital, for example, he will probably examine increased earnings and then make some additional approximation of a value of the personal satisfaction to be obtained from the education.

Sometimes, too, the identification of all benefits from the potential investment can be omitted. Consider the example of buying an automatic clotheswasher. Perhaps the time saving from a new clotheswasher will be 100 hours per year and the housewife considers that her opportunity cost of time is $2 per hour. Suppose she can buy the appliance for $250. She can now already see a $200 a year return from a $250 investment; this is probably already far superior to any of the family's other investment alternatives. Therefore perhaps the clotheswasher can be selected without bothering to identify the value of the benefits that it confers beyond time saving.

There is another point of view also which can simplify the identification of benefits. This is discussed at greater length in the next section, but its general tone is that it may be better to make a few mistakes in the asset selection process than to spend too much time worrying about small details in this process.

Marginal analysis of asset selection procedures

It is imperative in developing the techniques for personal asset selection that one follow the same line of reasoning described in the development of accounting systems. We cautioned against the development of too perfect an accounting system because the marginal cost and difficulty associated with attaining the final degrees of near perfection would probably not be worth the marginal benefit of this extra refinement in record keeping. Similarly, one must look for opportunities to employ the principle of simplification in selecting assets.

There are at least two methods of simplification in asset selection. One of these is *approximation.* When estimating the benefits associated with an asset, it is necessary to keep this estimation procedure in proper perspective. If the asset under consideration is low cost, the consequences of an estimating error are not very severe. It may be better to make a few mistakes on small assets than to use so much time on these decisions that more important matters are neglected. Of course, on large financial decisions such as the example in Chapter 4 in which an individual considered selling his major asset, a farm, and buying receivables with the proceeds, a very careful study of expected future benefits from the asset alternatives is desirable.

A second method of simplification is by *delegation.* An individual may want to hire some specialized investment management for part of his asset collection. He may decide that it is better to pay someone to help with his investments than to spend excessive time managing his own investment position. Admittedly, this will mean that he will have to trust someone else's opinion on many details of investment decision making. In some situations, however, it may be more productive to make a major decision about whose opinion one can trust rather than make many complicated individual decisions about, for example, which shares of corporation common stock should be purchased.

The timing of benefits

We have already mentioned the necessity of placing money values on the benefits that are expected from a particular asset. However, we observed from Chapter 3 that a particular sum of money could be valued differently, depending on the time period in which it was expected to occur. If one were to choose between $100 to be received now and $100 to be received ten years from now, we could invariably expect that he would choose the $100 now. This $100 has a full $100 present value, whereas the present value of the $10 occurring ten years from now would be less than $100; how much less would depend on the rate of interest used in determining the discount factor. Thus it follows that an asset may or may not be desirable depending on the time periods in which its benefits are expected to be conferred.

To fully set forth the nature of the benefits expected from an asset, it is useful to prepare a simple financial statement, called a *benefit projection.* This statement identifies the monetary benefits expected from an asset and also indicates the time period in which they are expected to occur; the following is an example.

Estimated cost of dishwasher, installed—$400
Estimated benefits

	1971	1972	1973	1974	1975
Estimated annual labor saving, in hours	150	150	150	150	150
Estimated value of labor per hour	$1.50	$1.50	$1.50	$1.50	$1.50
Benefit from dishwasher	$225	$225	$225	$225	$225

It is obvious that this type of statement could deal with much more complex data. One refinement that would be immediately desirable would be to include the concept of net benefits. The dishwasher will not be an unmixed blessing; it will use extra hot water (above that used in the hand dishwashing method) and electricity. It will also probably require some maintenance. Suppose that the housewife estimates that the extra hot water and electricity will cost $30 per year, that there will be no maintenance in the first two years, and that maintenance costs after that will run $20 per year. On the basis of this information she can amend her benefit projection into a net benefit projection.

Estimated cost of dishwasher, installed—$400
Estimated net benefits

	1971	1972	1973	1974	1975
Benefit from dishwasher	$225	$225	$225	$225	$225
Hot water and electricity	30	30	30	30	30
Maintenance			20	20	20
Estimated net benefit	$195	$195	$175	$175	$175

We observe that now she not only deals with a reduced stream of benefits but also with a stream that is not uniform over time.

Observe that in the housewife's benefit projections, she included projections for only five years. Presumably, she has estimated that the dishwasher will have no further usefulness after this period. If she thought the dishwasher would be used after that time, she should have included more years in the projection. If she thought that it would have a trade-in value at the end of that time and that she would be disposing of it then, she should have estimated this trade-in value and counted that as one of the benefits to be received in the final year of the dishwasher's net benefit projection.

One might ask why she did not include a figure for depreciation expense along with electricity, hot water, and maintenance in determining net benefits. If she had, she would have been guilty of confusing a statement prepared for planning with one prepared for the evaluation of performance. A benefit projection is an attempt to compare the benefits conferred from the dishwasher with its initial costs. The prospective buyer is not interested in measuring the performance of the dishwasher investment in any particular time period, but instead she is considering the whole life of the dishwasher in determining whether or not to purchase it. Therefore she does not need to make depreciation estimates which are intended to evaluate performance in a particular time period.

Depreciation is a useful measure of the success of a past decision. It is a reminder to us not to forget about the original cost that was incurred in acquiring assets that are currently in use. However, one does not need this reminder when directly comparing original cost and expected benefits as he does in the decision of whether or not to purchase an asset.

Rate of return

Since the original cost of an asset is known and the net benefits have been projected, it is possible to identify a rate of return on the asset. This may be done by finding r along the lines described in Chapter 3 when other values are known. In the dishwasher example, the buyer knows the cost of the dishwasher, $400, that must be currently expended.

In return for spending \$400, she receives a stream of net benefits which are future payments in different time periods. If she assumes for simplicity that the benefits from the dishwasher occur at the end of each time period, she can proceed to summarize the benefits in terms of values of F and n. For example, since a net benefit of \$195 is expected in the first year of the dishwasher's life, she would for that year identify:

$$F = \$195$$
$$n = 1$$

She can do the same for subsequent years and summarize her findings in the following schedule.

n	F
1	\$195
2	195
3	175
4	175
5	175

She can then find the correct value of r by experimentation ("trial and error"). To do this she tries to find an interest rate that will satisfy the equation

$$P = \text{cost}$$

She first guesses an interest rate (say, $r = 10\%$) and, discounting the above schedule, finds $P = \$666$. She could pay this amount for the dishwasher and still receive a 10% return on the investment. Since she must pay only \$400, she concludes that r must be greater than 10% and therefor experiments with 20%. This and a third experiment with 36% are shown.

		$r = 10\%$		$r = 20\%$		$r = 36\%$	
n	F	Discount factor	P	Discount factor	P	Discount factor	P
1	\$195	0.91	\$177	0.83	\$162	0.74	\$130
2	195	0.84	158	0.69	121	0.54	105
3	175	0.77	120	0.58	104	0.40	70
4	175	0.71	110	0.48	86	0.29	51
5	175	0.65	101	0.40	70	0.22	39
	Total P		\$666		\$543		\$395

Since an r of 36% results in a P of \$395, only slightly lower than the cost of \$400, she concludes that 36% is the approximate return on the dishwasher.

Mixture of assets, again

Now that we have considered the identification of costs and benefits on individual assets, let us apply this identification in a broader context A technique is needed for selecting the assets that will cause a given amount of wealth to yield as much benefit as possible. A number of techniques can be used for this purpose, but the one that we will use is the method of ranking assets by rate of return.

Ranking by Rate of Return

Suppose that a family has $5000 in accumulated savings to be apportioned among various asset possibilities. One of these possibilities might be the dishwasher mentioned which yielded an after-tax return of almost 36%. Suppose that the family considered another physical asset investment, trading in its car on a new model at a cost of $2000. On this investment through items such as increased satisfaction and reduced repairs, an after-tax return of 10% is estimated. Other uses may also be considered. Perhaps $1000 could be considered for use in taking a "short course" to increase the individual's earning power. Suppose the estimated increase in earnings, net of associated extra income taxes, cause this investment prospect to yield 12%, after tax. No doubt there would be many possibilities for investment in claims, such as common stocks, that would confront the individual. After identifying the after-tax rate of return on the differing alternative assets, it is possible to rank the assets in the order of their rate of return. For the assets mentioned, the ranking would look like this:

Rank	*Asset*	*Rate of return*	*Amount*	*Cumulative amount*
1	Dishwasher	35%	$400	$400
2	"Short course"	12%	1000	1400
3	Car	10%	2000	3400

One could imagine a much longer list with the cumulative amount (the sum of a given asset and all preceding assets) running to much more than the $5000 available. The asset selection problem would then consist of going down the rank list and selecting assets until the cumulative amount of the assets was just below $5000.

The need for a marginal approach

The basic rule for selecting a "best" collection of assets is a simple one: A dollar should never be used in a particular asset if it can yield a higher return when used in another asset. However, it is easy to fall into an error that violates this principle when the ranked rate of return method is applied to assets that are divisible (capable of being purchased in varying amounts). The following example illustrates this point.

Suppose an individual has $400 to spend and considers two asset possibilities: buying a dishwasher or putting the money in a 5% savings account. If the dishwasher situation was like that in our previous example, the dishwasher would seem to be the obviously superior investment, since it yielded nearly 36%.

However, he would have to ask himself, "Is $400 the least amount I could spend on a dishwasher?" Suppose he knows that a lower priced machine is available and could be installed for $300. Now he can raise still another question: "I know that a dishwasher is desirable, but is the marginal $100 difference between a $300 and a $400 dishwasher a good purchase?"

Suppose he decides that the $400 dishwasher will perform the same as the $300 one, but that the $300 machine will require $20 per year in extra maintenance. Now he can ask the question, "What is the return on the marginal $100?" It is $20 per year (expense saved) for five years, the estimated life of the dishwasher. However, $20 marginal benefits per year for five years would only total $100, the same amount as the marginal cost of buying a better dishwasher. Thus the marginal rate of return on the marginal step from a $300 to a $400 dishwasher is zero. (No excess of marginal benefit over marginal cost.)

Accordingly, he can conclude that, although buying a $400 dishwasher seems advantageous, buying a $300 dishwasher and putting $100 in a savings account are better.

This example is oversimplified (the higher priced dishwasher might wash better or last longer, for example), but it illustrates the possible advantage of breaking down the purchase of an asset into marginal steps. Obviously, some assets can be bought in so many different quantities that it would be a hopeless task to identify marginal returns for all possible steps in which the asset could be purchased. However, one needs to think, at least to some extent, about divisibility. If a homeowner is dissatisfied with his house he may view the opportunity to acquire a much larger and better house as a sound investment. A more careful analysis may reveal to him that, in fact, most of the benefit associated with upgrading his housing could be obtained from only a slightly more expensive home than the one he presently occupies. In this case, his analysis would show a very high marginal return on the possibility of upgrading his housing by one step but a much lower marginal return associated with upgrading the housing by a second step. The individual might still want to acquire the second step of housing improvement, but by treating the decision in steps he will make sure that the second step is superior to other assets which he could buy with the marginal money.

The Marginal Approach: A Note of Caution

We should note one chance for nonsensical application of the marginal approach. Suppose someone was again considering a choice between a $300 and a $400 dishwasher. This time the $300 model was markedly inferior (less labor saving because more heavily soiled dishes had to be hand washed, higher repair costs, and so forth.) Perhaps one might identify a 5% return on the $300 model and a 35% return on the $400 model. One might, if he was thinking only about the marginal approach, note that the marginal return on the extra $100 between the $300 and $400 models would be very great. However, whereas one can *avoid spending* an extra $100 on a dishwasher, he cannot *spend* the extra $100 without first spending an original $300.

Thus, if larger expenditures lead to greater returns, the marginal approach on "extras" is not helpful. In the above case it would be pointless to talk about receiving a marginal return on the extra $100; the marginal return on a $400 investment would simply be 35%, the return on all the dollars that must be spent to achieve the 35% return. The marginal return needs to be calculated separately on "extras" only when the extra expenditure on an asset yields a lower return than a smaller amount spent on the asset.

Asset interrelationships: the need for judgment

Most personal asset selection is likely to be an informal matter even though the methods propounded in this book appear to be rather neat, precise ways of obtaining answers. These methods will normally function best when used not as answer-generating oracles but as guidelines for thinking or approaches toward economic planning problems. They are not intended to be systems which relieve the decision maker of the need for thought and judgment.

Consider one of the pitfalls of the ranked return approach, a deficiency so obvious that no thoughtful person is likely to be ensnared by it. The value of an asset may be based on the absence of a similar asset. For example, an individual without a home freezer might consider two possible solutions to his problem. He might trade in his existing refrigerator for a combination refrigerator-freezer or he might buy a separate freezer unit and keep his old refrigerator. He should be able to determine the rate of return for either of these undertakings. However, even if his budget permitted, it might be foolish to undertake both alternatives. Part of the return estimated on the refrigerator-freezer would be based on the absence of an existing deep-freeze facility; similarly, part of the return on the freezer would be based on the same absence. If one of these appliances were acquired, that absence would be remedied and the benefit accorded by a second appliance would be greatly reduced. In general, one must be careful to avoid including assets that do similar tasks in a ranked return listing, unless the benefit identification for the second asset listed has taken into consideration the fact that the first asset would be available. (Some people *do* buy freezers even though they already have refrigerator-freezers, and for some families the additional benefits may be justified.)

If one failed to consider the preceding interrelationship between assets, he would make the error of acquiring too many of a particular type of asset. An opposite type of error can also be introduced—too few assets might be acquired. This type of error can occur when an individual is considering two assets which support one another; for example, a family might consider building a new patio and acquiring outdoor barbecuing facilities. If the patio were viewed independently, it might not seem to convey many benefits because entertainment would be limited by lack of food-preparing facilities. The outdoor barbecue viewed independently might appear to offer limited benefits because of the inadequacy of the area in which food could be served. If these two assets were viewed jointly, as an outdoor entertainment and recreation facility, the return on the combined projects might be much higher than the return on each of the projects considered individually.

Another example of this mutual reinforcement of assets could be two different night classes. The first of these might enable the student to take the second, and the second might enable the student to apply some of the material in the first toward practical purposes. Still another example: several pieces of living room furniture purchased at once might confer significant benefits, whereas each of these might accentuate the shabbiness of the old pieces if purchased separately.

There is no substitute for judgment in seeking out these asset interrelationships. The decision maker can usually avoid the error of considering assets whose functions overlap, but it is sometimes quite easy to overlook ways of combining assets. When we consider the topic of asset risk later, we return to the topic of asset interrelationship and the problem of choosing assets in a manner that attempts to avoid "putting all the eggs in one basket."

Evaluation of assets already held

Some assets once acquired cannot be readily resold. Investments in human capital usually fall into this category; there is no way of transferring college educations, for example. On other assets the purchase decision is quite easily reversed. For example, a ready market exists for some types of housing; often a house can be resold at nearly the same or a higher price than that for which it was acquired. In between these extremes are assets which can be resold but only at a price considerably less than the original purchase price.

Because many assets can be resold, it is possible and may be desirable to rearrange an existing asset collection. Assets that have been acquired must be occasionally reevaluated to see if they should be sold to acquire different assets. In evaluating existing assets the same type of evaluation techniques may be employed as are used for new assets with one important difference. When one considers a new asset, he compares the benefits from the asset with the cost of the asset. After the asset has been acquired, however, the cost of the asset is only history. Already-owned asset benefits should be compared with the price that can be realized if the asset is sold.

Suppose, for example, that a homeowner builds a garage not attached to his house and after owning it for a time decides that he does not utilize it very much. He finds that he usually does not bother to put his car inside and that the garage serves only as a storage facility, conferring benefits which he values at $100 a year. The original cost of the garage was $2000, but because it is difficult to move a garage, and some portions of it, such as the floor and the electrical wiring leading into it, cannot be moved, the resale value of the garage is only $1000. Benefits of a continuing $100 a year constitute a 5% return on the garage valued at historical cost but a 10% return on the resale price. Comparing the garage with other investment opportunities, the resale figure of 10% should be used. This is the rate that will have to be earned, if the $1000 from the sale of the garage is invested elsewhere, in order for the homeowner to realize $100 a year.

With the use of the resale value instead of historical cost, rate of return can be calculated for old assets. This should be done periodically, especially for major assets that can be readily resold without much loss. Also note that if existing assets can be resold at an amount greater than the original price, this resale value should still be used, rather than historical cost, in evaluating the asset. Once a rate of return has been determined for an old asset, the return on the old asset can be compared with new asset opportunities that are currently being rejected because of lack of funds. If new assets yielding 12% after tax are being passed up because of inadequate funds and if a garage yields only 10%, it would be wise to consider selling the garage and using the proceeds in an alternative way.

Another short note is in order here. If one did not think much about the matter, he might ask, "Does not the homeowner subject himself to a loss when he sells a $2000 garage for $1000?" The answer to this question is "No." The homeowner incurred the loss when the garage turned out to be less productive than he thought it would be. When he sells it, he is simply making the best of a situation that resulted from his original purchase of the garage. To repeat—the loss arises because of the *original* decision and not because of the *resale* decision.

Rate of return ranking: a summary

Before briefly considering other methods of asset selection, let us review the steps associated with asset selection by rate of return ranking.

1. Identify the cost of each of various possible assets. The cost on divisible assets may be divided into steps.
2. Identify the amount and timing of after-tax benefits expected from each asset for each of its marginal steps.
3. Identify the rate of return on each asset or step of an asset. If assets are evaluated in steps, use the rate of return on each marginal step as long as the marginal return on each step is less than the previous step. (If returns are increasing from step to step, use only the largest amount of investment possible and the return on the entire asset rather than any marginal step.)
4. Remember to consider interrelationships between assets. Are two of the proposed assets doing the same job? If so, use the one with the highest rate of return; if it seems practical, benefits for the second best asset can be recalculated on the assumption that the first asset will have been acquired, to produce a second independent asset proposal. Can two assets possibilities be grouped to provide a more productive total package? If so, consider them as a single project and recalculate benefits.
5. Rank projects according to their rate of return.
6. Select projects until the cumulative total of the projects has exhausted the money available for asset purchase.

Alternative proposals for asset selection

Another commonly used method of asset selection involves the use of what is called the *net benefit cost ratio.* The first two steps in this method are the same as in the rate of return method. After the future benefits from the project have been identified, they are discounted to a present value with the use of an interest rate. (A discussion of the correct interest rate for this purpose is not included.) For instance, someone considers the purchase of a vacant lot as a real estate speculation and anticipates selling it in five years. The cost of the lot is \$3000 and the estimated selling price is \$6000. An interest rate of 6% is to be used in his calculation. The benefit that we have identified from the lot is, again, \$6000 to be received five years hence, and the present value of this benefit (using 6%) is about \$4500.

The net benefit cost ratio for the project is determined as

$$\frac{\text{present value of benefits} - \text{cost}}{\text{cost}}$$

In the example, this fraction is ($4500 — $3000)/$3000, or 0.5. Instead of using a rate of return this ratio would now be used in the ranking process. Beyond this the technique is the same, including the necessity for sometimes considering marginal steps and the need for applying judgment to the consideration of asset interrelationships.

Both the ranked rate of return and the net benefit cost ratio methods are widely used procedures for asset selection in government and business, and both are considered by experts to be generally sound. Usually, the techniques will lead to the same results when properly applied. In this text, however, we continue to use the ranked rate of return method, since it is the one that probably relates more closely to everyday thinking about asset acquisition decisions.

Other procedures for selecting assets are sometimes employed, but they are of much more questionable desirability. We mention only a quite common one, *the pay-back method*, but the reader should be cautioned that if he encounters other methods, he ought to scrutinize them very carefully before selecting them in preference to either the ranked rate of return method or benefit cost ratio method. (Sometimes, of course, these two methods appear under other names and are still basically the same as the procedures set forth here.)

The pay-back method is attractively simple. It evaluates an asset on the basis of the time it takes for the total benefits received from the project to equal the cost. For example, if an asset is yielding returns valued at $500 per year and if the initial cost for the asset is $2000, the pay-back period on the asset would be four years. The serious drawback of the pay-back method is that it does not consider what happens after the initial cost of asset has been recovered. If two projects each cost $2000 and if one will return $500 per year for five years, whereas another will return $500 for ten years, these projects will not be differentiated by use of the pay-back ratio. In both cases the pay-back period will be four years. Therefore, we must reject this method as being less sound than the two methods previously discussed.

Conclusion

The writer again wishes to stress that the enunciation of arithmetic or mathematical techniques for choice among assets is not done in an attempt to transform the personal decision maker into a calculating machine. These techniques are completely invalid unless the individual has given careful thought to his estimates of benefits that will ensue from his various assets (and expressing these benefits in money terms is often not a very easy or precisely executable task). Additional judgment has to be applied in considering asset interrelationships and as we see later in considering risk. The rate of return technique is really only part of the asset choice process, a skeleton around which material for the complete decision can be assembled.

Summary

A family needs to decide the amount of assets that it should acquire, the amount of borrowing it should undertake, and the type of assets that it should select. Chapters 5 to 9 deal with the problem of selecting the right mixture of assets from the three categories available: human capital, physical capital, and claims.

An individual needs a systematic method of looking at his asset selection process. The method will try to ensure that an individual will not accidentally purchase one asset when, with the same amount of money, he could purchase another that would provide him with greater benefit.

To compare the benefits to be obtained from various assets it is first necessary to determine the amount and timing of net benefits from each of the assets. Even though many assets acquired by the household will provide nonmoney benefits, it will be necessary for comparison to express the money value of these nonmoney benefits.

The net benefits from an asset can be compared with its associated cost by calculating an internal rate of return. This calculation follows the method presented in Chapter 3. Assets can then be ranked by their marginal internal rate of return.

SUGGESTED READINGS

At the end of Chapter 3, a section in Bierman and Smidt was suggested as a possible advanced reading; that selection is also related to the issues in this chapter.

QUESTIONS

1. What are the three major choice issues that arise from the balance sheet equation? Try to think of examples of these choices for your own personal situation.
2. To compare benefits from various asset alternatives, a common measuring unit is necessary. Why is money usually used for this measuring unit?
3. Discuss some nonmoney benefits that you receive from assets and attempt to estimate the money value of these benefits.
4. What general means of simplification in asset selection are suggested in the chapter? Try to provide specific examples of simplification that are appropriate for your own situation.

5. When the purchase of an asset is being considered and its costs are being projected to determine net benefits, why is depreciation omitted?
6. Why is a marginal approach essential in asset selection? Present an example of differing marginal returns on a type of asset with which you have been personally involved.
7. Provide an example of two assets that are substitutes for each other and two other assets that are mutually reinforcing. (Do not use the examples given in the chapter.)
8. In calculating the return on an asset already owned, why is resale value more appropriate than historical cost as a basis for the calculation?
9. What is a net benefit:cost ratio?
10. What is the major disadvantage of the pay-back method?

PROBLEMS

1. The price of a house is $20,000. The estimated net benefits from ownership of the house are valued at $2000 per year. The estimated life of the house is 30 years. Estimate the rate of return on the house.
2. An individual considering the house in Problem 1 also considers another house priced at $35,000. It also has an estimated life of 30 years and it will provide annual benefits with an estimated value of $3000 per year. Find the marginal rate of return obtainable by selecting the $35,000 instead of the $20,000 house.
3. An individual contemplates taking two different night classes. Each of these classes requires that the individual give up $1000 of part-time income that he could otherwise earn and that he pay $400 in tuition costs. On each of the classes the individual estimates that he can increase his earnings by $200 per year over the next ten years.
   (a) What is the rate of return on each of the classes?
   (b) Suppose that by taking both classes, the individual feels that he will qualify for a job entirely different from his present one and that moving to this job will increase his earnings by $500 per year over the next 20 years. What is the rate of return on these classes if *both* are taken?

chapter six

Claims: common stocks

This chapter and Chapters 7 to 9 consider three types of assets that are available and which were identified in Chapter 1: physical capital, human capital, and claims. Claims are treated first, but in actual asset selection decision, all three types should be considered as alternative ways of giving up present consumption in exchange for future consumption.

Two important types of claims are discussed in later sections of the book. These are (a) money and moneylike assets, including accounts in banks, savings and loan associations, and credit unions, and (b) various types of insurance policies. These groups of claims are set aside because of some distinctive purposes which they fulfill (or are expected to fulfill) —ready availability in the first category and protection from various financial hazards in the second.

Claims include common stocks in corporations, bonds, and mutual funds plus several other categories. This chapter is devoted to one type of claim, common stocks, not because common stocks are exceptionally important in personal economic planning but because this asset possibility is likely to be least familiar to the reader. Since a common stock is a claim to ownership of part of a corporation, it is necessary to first consider the nature of a corporation. In turn, to do this it will be useful to contrast the corporation with two other forms of business which are not corporations.

Forms of business organization: proprietorship and partnership

The simplest form of business organization is a single proprietorship. If a family owns a house, we say that the family is the proprietor of that house. Similarly, if an individual owns a store or other business property, he is the proprietor of that property. The assets of the business are purchased and held in his name and any net worth shown on a balance sheet prepared for his business belongs to the owner, or the owner and his wife.

Sometimes two or more individuals want to join forces to own a business, since businesses must often be maintained on a scale beyond the financial and other capabilities of the sole owner. Partnership differs from the single proprietorship only in that two or more owners (with a married couple counting as one owner) are involved. Although a partnership may be established formally with the help of lawyers and elaborate legal documents, it can also be formed in a very casual way. Sometimes people become partners without realizing that they are occupying the role of partner and, as we shall note in the following paragraph, this accidental membership in a partnership can have quite unpleasant consequences. (If the reader plans to own a business in association with someone else, he should, through study of a standard text on business law and/or consultation with a lawyer, make himself fully aware of the legal characteristics of the partnership.)

There are several disadvantages to conducting business in a partnership. Probably the most formidable of these drawbacks is the matter of *unlimited liability*. When persons are partners in a business, each person is usually treated under the law as if he were fully responsible for all the debts of the business and all the actions of the other partners. Thus it would be possible for a family to have only a minor interest in a partnership and, after another partner had incurred large debts on behalf of the partnership, to find itself held responsible for these debts, even up to the point at which the family would have to sell its house and other nonbusiness assets to cover the obligations of the partnership. (One can now sense the unpleasantry that may be associated with accidentally becoming a partner.)

Another limitation of the partnership is the matter of transferring ownership. If a partner wishes to sell his interest or if a partner dies, a new partnership must be formed. Thus, if a business were large enough to require the resources of a great many partners, say, in the hundreds, the business might have to be frequently reestablished as a new partnership, a process with many attendant legal problems.

There is another problem shared by partnerships and proprietorships that relates to taxation. Earnings of proprietorships and partnerships belong directly to the owners of the business and are taxed accordingly. When one of these forms of business makes a profit, that profit must be immediately included in the personal income tax returns of the owner(s). We have more to say on this issue later in the chapter after corporation taxes are considered.

The corporation

To overcome the difficulties of the proprietorship and partnership, the corporation has evolved as a separate and very widespread form of business organization. A corporation is distinct in that the business assets in this form of business organization are not owned directly by individuals, but, instead, are owned by the corporation itself. When a corporation is created through a prescribed legal procedure (for small corporations this procedure can often be quite simple), the corporation takes on an identity of its own. When a corporation buys an asset, it buys in its own name.

The corporation in turn is owned by individuals who have supplied the money to form the corporation's net worth. The individuals who own the corporation have only indirect ownership in the corporation's assets. In the proprietorship or partnership, individuals own assets; in the corporation, individuals own the corporation and the corporation owns assets. When, as is often the case, the corporation has many owners, each of these owners owns a fraction of the corporation. Evidence of this ownership is created by *stock certificates* that are issued by the corporation. A corporation can be divided into a few shares or into millions of shares. If, for example, the ownership is divided into 1000 shares, an individual owning one share owns 1/1000 of the corporation's net worth. If an individual owns ten shares, he owns 10/1000, or 1% of the corporation.

There are several advantages to this arrangement. First, an individual can sell or transfer all or part of his shares in the corporation, including transfers that take place upon the death of the shareholder, without having any effect on the corporation itself. A new stock certificate is issued to acknowledge new ownership of shares, but the corporation goes on just as before.

Second, since the corporation has an identity separate from its owners,

owners are not responsible for the liabilities of the corporation; thus, unlike the participant in a partnership, the part owner of a corporation (stockholder) need not fear that he will have to sell his personally owned assets to discharge debts incurred by the business in which he is participating.

A third major difference, again arising from the separate identity of the corporation, is that income earned by the corporation is subject to a corporation tax. Then, *if* corporate net income (after the corporation tax has been deducted) is transferred to stockholders, those stockholders are also required to pay personal income tax on the amount received. This transfer of money from a corporation to a stockholder is called a *dividend*. The corporation that earns income and declares dividends is subject to double taxation. Consider, for example, the simplified income statement of X Corporation.

X Corporation
Income Statement
1971

Revenues	$500,000
Expenses	−400,000
Net income	100,000
Corporation tax	−40,000
Net income after tax	$ 60,000

The corporation now provides its stockholders with a $30,000 dividend. Suppose stockholder A owns 1% of X Company's stock; he will receive 1% of the total dividend, or $300. If X's marginal tax rate is 20%, he will pay an additional $60 tax on the dividend.

In spite of the possibility of double taxation, which occurs only when the corporation pays dividends to its stockholders, there may still be a tax advantage from the corporate form of business organization. (Depending on the circumstances, there may also be a tax disadvantage.) The effect of this tax treatment on stockholders is discussed later.

A share of common corporate stock

The type of corporate stock discussed so far, a share of ownership in the business, is called *common stock*. There is another form of stock, in much less frequent use, called *preferred stock*; it is perhaps misnamed inasmuch as it is usually associated with a quite restricted type of ownership interest in the corporation (which is discussed in the next chapter). To make sure that we understand what is involved in a share of common stock, let us consider a corporate balance sheet.

Acme Corporation
Balance Sheet
January 1, 19__

Assets	$250,000	Liabilities	$100,000
		Net worth (1000 shares outstanding common stock)	150,000
Totals	$250,000		$250,000

According to the records of this corporation, the $150,000 net worth is divided into 1000 shares; thus each share, according to the accounting of the corporation, has a value of $150.

Many rights are included in the ownership of stock, but two of these are ordinarily of greatest importance to the individual stockholder. One is the right to receive dividends declared by the corporation; the other is the right to share in any growth in the value of the corporation's net worth. When a corporation earns income from its business operations, the directors of the corporation, who constitute a governing body for the corporation and who are elected by stockholders, may declare a dividend and pay all or part of these earnings to stockholders. In this case, each stockholder is entitled to receive his proportionate share of the dividend. In the corporation exemplified in the preceding balance sheet, the individual who owned one share of the corporation would receive one-thousandth of the total dividend paid.

The directors are not required to declare a dividend even though the corporation earns income and could well afford to pay the dividend. It is very common for a corporation to hold back part of its income for use within the corporation and pay only a portion of the corporate income out to shareholders. At first this may seem a disadvantage to share owners, but it should be remembered that the corporate earnings which are not paid out in dividends (retained earnings) still belong to the corporation and hence, indirectly, to the stockholders.

An individual who wishes to accumulate claims and who is not concerned much with immediate consumption might prefer the corporation's tax arrangement. Consider an example. A wealthy individual, X, owns a small business among other things. X considers transferring ownership of this business to a corporation that he also owns. The individual's marginal tax rate is about 60%. He expects that the small business will earn $20,000 next year. The corporation's marginal tax rate is 50%. Furthermore, X does not wish to use any of the small business' earnings for consumption.

If the earnings belong to the corporation, the net worth of the corporation will increase by $10,000 during the year ($20,000 earnings − $10,000 taxes). Thus at the end of the year, X will note a $10,000 increase in his assets from these earnings, since he will regard the corporation's net worth as one of his own assets. On the other hand, if the earnings belong to X personally, he will pay a 60% tax, and hence will be able to increase his assets by only $8000 ($20,000 earnings — $12,000 tax).

Thus for some individuals with high marginal tax rates and no desire for dividends, the corporation may confer tax advantage. For most individuals, however, purchase of corporation stock is not made because of tax advantage, but because this enables an individual to participate in the ownership of a business. Without corporations large business ventures could be undertaken only by wealthy individuals or groups of wealthy partners. With the existence of corporations, there does not need to be any fixed relationship between the size of the business being undertaken by the corporation and the amount of participation in this business by any stockholder.

Also note that the corporation may, either by good fortune or good judgment, acquire assets which themselves rise in value and increase the value of the corporation's net worth. Since corporations follow traditional accounting, this increase in the value of assets owned by the corporation will normally not be recorded in the corporation's financial statements unless the assets are sold. Thus a corporation whose assets have been increasing in value is likely to understate the value of its net worth on its published financial statement.

Of course, the corporate net worth can also fall. Even when corporations retain some earnings the assets acquired with these earnings may not be great enough to offset the decline in value of other corporate assets. As in the case of proprietorship and partnerships, when the corporate business is less than successful, the loss is borne by the owners, in this case the stockholders. If the value of the corporation's net worth declines, this represents a shrinkage in the value of the assets of those who hold its stock.

In addition to the right of participation in dividends and in any growth (or shrinkage) of the corporation's net worth, stockholders have other rights which may or may not be important to the individual stockholder. Since the stockholder is an owner of the corporation, he is entitled to attend annual stockholder meetings held by the corporation, to vote for the corporation's board of directors, and to participate in other discussions and votes on corporate business. However, the small stockholder is likely to feel that his vote will be relatively unimportant and also that he is too uninformed about the details of the corporation's operations to participate usefully in its decisions. Usually, when a small stockholder is dissatisfied with the conduct of a corporation's affairs, his recourse will be to sell his stock in that corporation.

Buying and selling stock

One can distinguish between stock that is being issued and sold for the first time by corporations that are either being formed or adding new owners in order to acquire additional net worth, and stock that is being sold "second hand" by stockholders who want to dispose of part or all of their shares in already existing corporations. Because secondhand (or secondary market) transactions are much more common than new stock issues (primary market transactions), the secondary market for stock is discussed first. The key element in buying and selling stock in the secondary market is the securities firm, often called by the general term of stockbroker, or just broker. Securities firms buy and sell stock and act as an agent (broker) for individuals wishing to buy and sell stocks.

If someone wishes to buy ten shares of stock in the General Motors Corporation, for example, he can engage a securities firm for a fee to obtain the stock for him. To do this the securities firm must find another individual who is willing to sell ten shares of General Motors. To seek out another buyer, the securities firm will normally make use of another institution called a stock exchange, where brokers representing prospective buyers and sellers of stock "match up" those persons wishing to buy with those willing to sell. The shares of most large, well-known corporations can be bought and sold with the aid of a stock exchange; those that can are said to be *listed* on a stock exchange.

The individual engaging the services of the broker can assume that when he wishes to buy or sell listed stock, a corresponding seller or buyer will be found. However, to have this confidence, he must give his broker directions for buying or selling in the form of an "at the market" order. This type of order does not specify a price at which the transaction is to take place. If, temporarily, orders are placed for more shares of a stock than the number of shares being offered for sale, a shortage of stock will exist in the market. This will cause the price of the stock to rise in the market. The rising price, in turn, will normally cause some prospective buyers to change their minds about buying and some individuals, who had not thought of selling, to offer shares for sale because of the high price. Thus an individual can rely on being able to buy or sell shares of major companies as long as he is prepared to buy or sell at the prevailing market price.

The individual does not need to give his broker an "at the market" order. Instead he may specify the lowest price he is willing to accept if he is selling a stock or the highest he will pay if he is buying a stock. However, with this type of instruction to the broker, he cannot be sure that his order will be executed. His specified price may not coincide with that currently available on the stock exchange.

An individual does not have to buy or sell stock through securities firms. He may attempt to search personally for someone who is willing to buy or sell shares in the corporation in which he is interested. However, because of his limited contacts, this would usually be a time-consuming and costly task. Normally individuals rely on securities firms. The fees charged by them depend on the size of the transaction in which they assist; a schedule of fees (commissions) charged by major securities firms is given in Table 6.1. (The schedule is given only as an example since there is no assurance that these rates will not change with the passing of time.)

TABLE 6.1
SCHEDULE OF BROKERS' COMMISSIONS
NEW YORK AND AMERICAN STOCK EXCHANGES[a]

Amount of Money Involved	Commissions
Under $100	As mutually agreed
$ 100 to $ 399	2% + $ 3
$ 400 to $2399	1% + $ 7
$2400 to $4999	½% + $19
$5000 and above	1/10% + $39

In addition a charge of $15, or 50% of the commission determined above, is levied as a service charge on all transactions involving less than 1000 shares.

[a] At the time the book was completed, security exchanges, brokers, and regulatory bodies were seriously discussing proposals to drastically change these commission schedules or to eliminate them entirely and let each broker set his own rates.

Stock price information

When an individual contemplates buying or selling stock, he will want to know the current price of the stock. Most daily newspapers provide data about recent stock transactions that usually enable a person to predict the approximate price that will prevail on transactions carried out in the next day or two. Sometimes a stock price will change very rapidly so that any published records of previous prices, no matter how recent, are only a guide to the price that can be expected to prevail when the individual carries out his own stock transaction. Below is a sample price quotation from a financial section.

High	Low	Stocks	Sales, in 100s	Open	High	Low	Close	Net Change
49¼	39½	TimesMir	13	43½	43⅞	42½	42½	−1½

The stock prices recorded are those of the Times Mirror Corporation, abbreviated Times Mir. Names of companies are normally abbreviated and one may have to ask his broker about the abbreviation for a stock before it can be found in the newspaper. Prices are all quoted in dollars and fractions of dollars. Thus we can read that during a recent period, whose dates will be specified on the financial page, this stock has sold for as high as $49.25 and as low as $39.50. We also read under the caption, "Sales, in 100s," that during the day in which trading is currently being reported, 1300 shares of the stock were sold. The first stock sold during the day was sold at a price of $43.50 (we see this under the heading "open"). During the day the stock sold as high as $43.87½ per share and as low as $42.50 per share. The last transaction of the day (shown under "close") was at $42.50. The right-hand figure, net change, indicates that today's close was $1.50 lower than yesterday's close; therefore the last transaction on the previous day must have been for $44.00. Thus, from this very brief report, we not only find out the last price for which the stock has been sold but also learned something about the range of the stock's price over a longer period, the current daily amount of fluctuation in the stock's price, and the direction (upward or downward) that the stock's price took during the last day.

Return on stocks

The arithmetic procedure for identifying the rate of return on a common stock is quite simple. However, the estimates on which the arithmetic must be based are extremely difficult to make. Let us first examine the arithmetic. Two benefits may ensue from the ownership of a stock: the receipt of dividends and appreciation in the stock's market value. Neither of these benefits are sure; dividends may not be paid and the stock may depreciate in price rather than appreciate. However, when one buys a stock he does so in anticipation of either or both of these benefits occurring.

The two benefits are accorded different income tax treatment. Dividends are subject to ordinary personal income tax, but appreciation in price, provided the stock has been held six months before it is sold, is treated as capital gains and thus is normally taxed at only half the ordinary income rate. This relationship, incidentally, explains why stockholders often do not wish to have corporations in which they own stock pay large dividends. Instead they prefer to have the corporations retain earnings in an attempt to increase the value of the shares. Then, if a stockholder wishes to realize money from his stock, he can sell some of these shares and be taxed at a lower rate than if he had received extra money in the form of dividends.

Suppose that a stock is currently selling at $100 per share and an individual anticipates that this price will not change for the next few days. Suppose also that he anticipates a \$2 commission to the broker, making the total cost \$102 per share, that he expects to hold this stock for a year, and that he expects, on the basis of what he has learned about the corporation, to be paid a \$3 per share dividend during the year. He also predicts that the stock will reach a price of \$110 per share at the end of the year. He estimates that his marginal income tax rate is 33%.

His expected returns at the end of the year can be summarized as follows:

Expected dividend	\$ 3	
Tax on dividend at 33%	−1	
After-tax dividend		\$2
Estimated selling price	\$110	
Brokerage fee on sale of stock	−2	
Selling price after brokerage fee	\$108	
Original cost of stock	−102	
Gain on sale of stock	\$ 6	
Capital gains tax (33% × ½)	−1	
After-tax gain on sale		\$5
Total gain for holding stock for 1 yr		\$7
Approximate rate of return \$7/\$102 cost = about 7%		

The same method of finding the estimated rate of return can also be applied to problems of greater complexity in which longer periods of time are involved, although present values tables would then be needed for finding r.

If stock is expected to be held for a rather long period of time, a simplified estimating technique is

$$\text{Estimated after-tax return} = \text{current after-tax dividend rate} + \text{estimated after-tax growth rate}$$

$$\text{Current after-tax dividend rate} = \frac{\text{current annual dividend} \times (1 - \text{marginal ordinary tax rate})}{\text{price of stock}}$$

$$\text{Estimated after-tax growth rate} = \text{estimated annual percentage increase in stock price} \times (1 - \text{marginal capital gains tax rate})$$

If an individual is in a 40% marginal tax bracket (20% capital gains rate), if he can buy a share of stock for a net price of \$160, if the current dividend on this stock is \$5 a year, and if he expects that the stock will rise in price by 4% per year, he can calculate as follows:

Current annual dividend	$5	
Less tax at 40%	−2	
After-tax dividend	$3	
Market price	$160	
Current after-tax dividend rate ($3/$160)		1.9%
Estimated annual percentage increase in price	4.0%	
Less capital gains tax at 20%	−0.8%	
Estimated after-tax growth rate		3.2%
Estimated after-tax return		5.1%

To repeat, the arithmetic of obtaining a projected return on stock is uncomplicated, but the estimates required are difficult to obtain. Even the current dividend rate may not be known for sure, since some corporations pay dividends in a rather erratic manner, and any projections of price movement in the stock are inevitably difficult for built-in reasons that are discussed in the following sections.

Estimating stock price changes

One often reads advice of the following type, which at first may appear rather appealing:

> The careful investor avoids making heavy commitments in the stock market during periods of high stock prices and will often wish to dispose of part of his stock holdings during these high-price periods. He then watches for periods when stocks are generally depressed in price and concentrates his purchases at these periods.

This and similar advice can be abbreviated into the expression "buy low, sell high." It must be regarded as worthless information. Obviously, one would be attracted to stock if its price was low; that is, if it was expected to rise in price rapidly. The trick is to know whether a stock is "low" and about to reverse its direction of price movement or whether it will go still lower. Buy low, sell high advice is tantamount to advising to buy assets on which very high returns are expected. Everyone knows this is desirable, but it is not always very easy to find assets of this type.

There is another bit of counsel that may be more useful to the person contemplating the purchase and sale of stocks: There are two parties to every transaction. Whenever anyone buys a stock, he buys it from someone who has decided to sell it; often the seller feels the stock is "overpriced" and has little appreciation potential. Furthermore, the buyer is paying a higher price than the seller receives since both must pay broker's commissions. Therefore, when one makes predictions of appreciation in the stock which he plans to buy or lack of appreciation in the stock that he plans to sell, he is advised to proceed cautiously in the formulation of these predictions. He should always ask himself if he thinks his predictions are superior to those made by the other party in his proposed transaction.

To consider the problem of predicting stock price movement, it will be useful to recall again the nature of stock market price movements. Stocks rise in price when there are fewer shares offered for sale at the previous price than the number that people are trying to buy. However, past prices were also determined by the interaction of buyers and sellers and were based on their expectations. There does not appear to be any very easy way of predicting whether tomorrow some of today's sellers will turn into buyers and push the market up or whether some of today's buyers will turn into sellers and drive the market down.

Two market strategies

Although predicting price movement, which is essential to identifying the return on stock, is a difficult task, it need not be so discouraging that it drives the individual away from the stock market. To the author it seems that one can participate in the stock market in a rational way by employing either of two viewpoints, which we may label the *dart* theory and the *extra information* theory.

The first line of reasoning holds that it is difficult if not impossible for the investor to select one stock as being superior to others. On the other hand, the stock market as a whole has over the years treated investors reasonably well—although, of course, this general statement does not apply to all time periods or to all investors. Several careful academic studies have been made of returns on common stock and have shown that the average after-tax returns on stocks have been around 7%. (The return, of course, differs for persons in various tax brackets.) Thus an individual may have reason to invest in stocks because of their overall performance, but he may have no basis for preferring one stock over another. Hence the name of this theory: The investor could select the particular stock or stocks he is going to buy by throwing darts at a financial page and buying the stocks hit by his darts.

Although it is not likely that anyone would choose stocks quite this way, some investors choose stocks about as haphazardly and may show rather spectacular market successes with stock selection based on hunches, "hot tips," and other dartlike selection processes. (There are also spectacular failures; both successes and failures of dartlike methods are usually attributed to other causes by the practitioners of these methods—shrewdness for the successes and inflation, creeping socialism, foreign intrigues, and so forth, for the failures.)

The advantage of the dart method is the avoidance of a costly and often futile process of analysis. The buyer does not try to carefully estimate how particular stocks are going to behave, but relies on the action of market forces. He assumes that companies with unsatisfactory prospects have already been found out by other participants in the market and therefore these stocks are likely to be priced at such low levels that they still have as much chance for appreciation as any other stock. Similarly, he assumes that the so-called growth companies with very attractive prospects are also known about and have been priced so high in the market place that they now have no greater prospects for appreciation than other securities. He also assumes that if there are dividend prospects on some stocks that are superior to others, these prospects are also reflected in the current prices of the stocks.

The dart method can also be adapted to individual preferences. If some stocks have desirable tax features (a low ratio of dividends to earning may, for example, especially appeal to high income taxpayers), dartlike selections can be made from these stocks only. Or if some stock returns seem especially hard to predict (for example, very new companies), these types of companies may be avoided by the dart practitioner who does not like taking risks.

The dart approach has a disadvantage. The stock market participant following this approach might not bother to look for extra information available to him which would enable him to outguess the market. For many amateur investors, however, the possibility of extra information may be an unjustified hope, and the dart method, or a modified version of this method, does allow an individual to venture into the stock market without trying to become a market expert.

The extra information method involves more work. Following this strategy, the stock market participant needs to seek out information that enables him to know more about a particular stock than other market participants. If he sees favorable prospects in the stock that others have not seen, he will then be able to buy the stock while it is still priced low because of its unattractiveness to others. There appear to be two ways of having better information about a stock. One of these is through extremely careful study of the prospects of a particular firm. The second is through inside information such as some personal knowledge about the competence of a particular corporation's managers.

The extra information strategy should, on the average, yield no worse results than the dart method, since there is no reason to believe that an individual trying to carefully select stocks will be likely to select them less successfully than one who is not trying to follow a careful selection process. On the other hand, the search for information is costly. Ordinary information is not enough. The strategy rests on better information than that available to others. One must balance the marginal cost of acquiring extra information against the possible marginal gain that this method provides over the dart method. This choice must be left to the individual.

Sources of Information

If the individual elects the extra information method, he would normally wish to be familiar with standard sources of information. A careful scrutiny of these standard sources may put him ahead of some of his competitors in the market, and study of these sources may put him on the track of additional information. Many magazines are published for the prospective stock market investor. (*Barrons* and *Forbes* are examples). The *Wall Street Journal* is an example of a daily newspaper that is oriented toward the needs of stock market investors. Securities firms often maintain small libraries and accumulate much information that can be useful to the investor. Some general magazines such as *Time* and *Newsweek* contain sections on business that often provide some investor information. *Fortune* Magazine maintains a personal investment section that often contains thoughtful commentary. The investor should, of course, either through a securities firm or by writing to the company, obtain at least a present financial statement and preferably previous ones issued by any company in which he is interested.

A note should be added here about advice provided by securities firms. These firms often have large stores of information and very competent personnel. However, the stock market participant needs to be cautious in one respect in acting on their advice. These firms derive their livelihood from commissions that are earned when stocks are bought and sold. Therefore, there is some incentive for the firm to encourage the stockholder to continually rearrange his collection of stocks. The person following the extra information method will occasionally want to make changes in his stock collection and ought to review it periodically. He should also be advised that switching stocks is not done without cost—both selling and buying commissions are involved.

Another note on stock values

In previous sections we have been discussing evaluation of a stock in a fairly advanced way. We need to stop for a moment and reject a very simple method of stock evaluation, the method referred to as *book value*. Earlier in this chapter a sample corporation balance sheet was presented. It was possible on the basis of this balance sheet to calculate a value per share by dividing the company's net worth by the number of shares outstanding. The value obtained, however, is entirely a creature of traditional accounting. It does not include extra value for assets held by the firm that have appreciated in price but which have not been sold. In general it is subject to all the difficulties of the traditional accounting method discussed in Chapter 2. Therefore the reader is cautioned against relying on the book value of the stock as an indicator of its "correct" value. There is no reason to believe that a stock priced above book value in the stock market will eventually decline in price or that one priced under book value will rise in price. The two types of valuation involved, the market's appraisal versus historical accounting, are so different that comparisons are very dangerous.

It is appropriate to make another comment about valuation at this point. Sometimes corporations *split* their stocks; when they do this they exchange, for example, three new shares for one old one and because every stockholder receives the same exchanges of shares, the proportionate shares of each stockholder in the company are unchanged. An individual's claim on the company does not change if he owns one of the 1000 shares or three of 3000 shares outstanding. The result of such a stock split in terms of book value is to reduce the book value of each share by one-third; with three times as many shares the total book value of any individual's stock will remain unchanged. Similarly, since the company itself is not changed, one can expect that with a three for one split of the type above, the market price of each share will drop to approximately one-third of the old price at the time the split occurs.

A process very similar to a split is the *stock dividend.* Sometimes a company, instead of paying dividends in cash, will issue one new share of stock for, say, every ten shares of old stock outstanding. The result of this issuance of stock is again the same as in the case of the stock issued by a stock split. Since each stockholder receives the same fractional increase in the number of shares, his proportionate interest in the company remains unchanged. In the case of the 10% stock dividend the book value of 11 shares after the dividend will be the same as ten shares before the dividend was declared and the market value of the 11 shares after the dividend will also probably be about the same as the value of the ten shares before the stock dividend.

Extra information for sale

One alternative to either the dart method or careful searching for extra information is to engage the services of an individual or business that specializes in providing extra information in return for a fee. Bank trust departments and independent investment counselors will undertake to select stocks for the individual, although these services are usually too costly for the very small investor. A more common way for small investors to obtain expert assistance is through participation in an institution called a *mutual fund.* A subsection will be devoted to mutual funds in Chapter 7, but basically they constitute opportunity for an individual to buy a small fraction of a large professionally managed collection of stocks. Market advisory letters and other information frequently advertised on financial pages purport to offer extra information in return for a fee.

Although there is another advantage to mutual fund participation which we discuss later, the extra information service provided by these firms can be considered in the light of marginal analysis. One has to ask himself whether or not he thinks the information he is buying will improve his chances for better returns over the return that he can obtain through the dart method. Do these marginal returns from the purchase of extra information justify the marginal cost of acquiring the information? This is a decision that the purchaser of stocks will have to make for himself, but the author notes that the academic studies on mutual fund performance do not yield any clearcut evidence that buying their extra information constitutes a superior tactic to the application of the dart method.

Margin purchases and short sales

This section attempts to answer two questions that may occur to the individual thinking about stock market activity. The first is: Is financing available for stock purchases or must they be paid for in cash? The answer is that financing is usually available through a type of arrangement called "buying on the margin." An individual may arrange a loan through his broker to finance part of his security purchase. The fraction of the purchase that can be borrowed is regulated by the Federal Government (Federal Reserve Board) and varies from the occasional stipulation of no borrowing being allowed to sometimes about half the purchase price. Note that if one does buy on the margin and the stock price goes down in price, the borrower will be asked to provide additional cash to repay part of the loan so that the loan is brought down to its original relationship with the price of the stock. For example, if a stock is bought at a price of $80 and it is financed at a time when the maximum allowable amount of borrowing is 30%, $24 might originally be borrowed on the purchase of the stock with the remaining $56 being paid in cash at the time of purchase. If the stock subsequently declined in price to $60, the maximum allowable amount of borrowing at 30% would be only $18. Therefore the individual would have to provide $6 to his broker to reduce the loan balance from $24 to $18. If an individual fails to keep his loan amount in conformity with the "margin requirement" by providing additional cash as necessary, the broker will sell his stock, repay the loan, and give him the check for the remaining balance less commissions.

Margin loans are convenient and are usually offered at a favorable interest rate, but an individual can also finance stock market operations by indirect borrowing. If he was planning to buy both some stock and a car, he could borrow for his car to release more of his own money for stock market activity. In general there is no point in separating borrowing for stock purchases from other types of personal borrowing, and we therefore defer further discussion of this topic until we discuss the general issue of personal borrowing in Chapter 14.

The second question that might arise is: If I have extra information that makes me feel that a stock is going down in price, is there any way that I can profit from this information? Of course, if one owned some of the stock, he could sell it. Beyond this, however, there is a device for profiting from declining stock values which is called the *short sale.* We do not discuss the technicalities of the short sale here, but the substance of the arrangement is that one can arrange with his broker to "buy stock in reverse." To do this he pays the broker the market price of the stock. Then if the stock declines in price up to the time when he wishes to withdraw from activity in this particular stock, he requests his broker to close his transaction. When the broker does this, he will pay the short seller the original purchase price *plus* the amount that the stock has *declined* in price less commission. On the other hand, if the stock has gone up, the broker will subtract the amount of the price rise plus commissions from the original purchase price when he closes the transaction.

Although short sales are less common than conventional purchases and sales of stock, there is no reason why the extra information stock market participants should not consider this form of activity. Short sales should not be used by the dart strategist, because over a long time period stocks are more likely to go up in price than down. These sales, however, enable someone approaching the market with an extra information strategy to take advantage of his information in certain types of situations where he might not otherwise be able to use it.

Over-the-counter markets and primary issues

The secondary market for the stock of major corporations is largely carried on through securities firms with the use of stock exchanges. The secondary market for the stock of smaller companies is normally on an *over-the-counter* basis. When stock is marketed over the counter, securities firms act as dealers rather than brokers; that is, they buy and sell stock themselves rather than as representatives for others. If an individual wishes to sell the stock that is traded over the counter, the dealer will buy it from him or arrange to have the stock bought by another securities firm who is dealing in it. In this type of marketing securities firms also offer stock for sale.

Instead of charging commissions for these over-the-counter transactions, the securities firms profit from them by buying stock at one price, which is called the *bid* price, and reselling at a higher price, which is the *ask* price. The difference between the bid and ask prices is called the *spread.* This is the securities firms' gross profit for an over-the-counter transaction. For example, X stock price may be quoted Bid 16 and Ask 18. This price quotation informs us that if we have X stock to sell, a security firm will pay $16 per share for it; if we wish to buy, we can do so for $18. When the securities firm buys and then sells a share at those prices, it receives a *spread* of $2 for undertaking these transactions.

When stock is originally issued by a corporation and is being sold to the public, this stock is also not traded through the stock exchanges. Securities firms conduct a primary market for securities by arranging the sale of stock by the corporation to interested individuals. If an individual is interested in purchasing newly issued stocks, he should discuss arrangements for this with a securities firm. Advance notice of forthcoming stock issues is often given by advertisements and in a more detailed way by a descriptive brochure called a *prospectus.*

Stockholdings summarized

It is difficult for the individual to assess the return that he will receive on a particular stock even though studies have shown that, on the average, stocks have yielded returns that compare quite favorably with many other assets. Most stocks have the advantage of being readily marketable; therefore it is easy to dispose of stocks if cash should be required for some other purpose. Stocks may also confer a tax advantage on their purchaser, especially if they are issued by corporations that retain earnings and hence give the stockholder more chance of receiving returns in price appreciation, taxed at the capital gains rate, rather than in dividends which are taxed at ordinary income tax rates. Another tax advantage is also associated with holding at least a small amount of stock. To encourage more widespread stock ownership, current tax laws exempt $100 in annual dividends, per taxpayer, from Federal income tax.

Summary

There are three major forms of business organization. A proprietorship exists if an individual or family does business in its own name and receives all the benefits and risks of its business. A partnership occurs when two or more persons join forces in a venture and share the benefits and risks of the venture; the partnership, like the proprietorship, can be organized very informally.

A corporation is a formally organized institution which can be owned by several, or even millions, of people. A corporation is a separate legal entity, and individuals who own the corporation do not participate directly in the ownership of the corporation's assets; instead they own claims against these assets which are called shares of stock.

The corporation has the advantage of limited liability. It may confer tax advantages, although this is not necessarily true. This form of organization is almost essential for large-scale business ventures that require the use of the money of many owners.

The stockholder in the corporation owns a share of the corporation. He thus owns a proportionate share of the corporation's earnings and is entitled to a proportionate share of any dividends paid by the corporation. He is also entitled to a proportionate vote in electing the directors who control the corporation's business.

Stocks are normally bought and sold through a securities firm that charges a commission for its buying and selling services. The money benefits individuals expect to receive from stockholding are in the form of dividends payments and rises in the prices of stock. (Benefits may also be lost if the price of the stock falls.)

Two possible strategies are suggested for stock market participation. The first, the dart method, is based on the assumption that a stock market participant is not likely to know much more about the value of a particular stock than other participants, and therefore can justify simply selecting stocks at random. The second strategy involves an attempt to know more than other market participants and with this extra information to buy stocks which are currently undervalued or sell stocks which are currently overvalued. There is no clear evidence, at least for most investors, that the second method will yield results superior to the first.

Stock may be purchased "on the margin"; borrowing for stock purchases, in general, is not distinguishable from other borrowing that the individual may wish to undertake.

Short selling of stock is a technique for speculating on the downward movement of the stock's price.

Stocks of most major corporations are sold on stock exchanges; however, other markets for securities also exist. The over-the-counter market is a term that describes many of the opportunities for carrying on stock transactions outside the stock exchanges.

SUGGESTED READINGS

Sources of current information about stocks are discussed within the chapter.

Two informal and very readable books about the securities market are Adam Smith, *The Money Game* (New York: Random House, Inc., 1968) and Martin Mayer, *Wall Street: Men and Money* (New York: Collier Books, rev. ed. 1966).

A widely used university textbook on investments, which is based on the extra information strategy, is Benjamin Graham, David L. Dodd, and Sidney Cottle, *Security Analysis*, 4th ed. (New York: McGraw-Hill, Inc., 1962).

Two popular business law texts are *Business Law: Principles and Cases*, Uniform Commercial Code Edition by Harold F. Lusk (Homewood, Ill.: Richard D. Irwin, Inc., rev. ed. 1970) and *Elements of Business Law* by Maurice Albert Unger (Englewood Cliffs, N.J.: Prentice-Hall, 1968).

Two major studies of stock market performance, representative of the studies on which the statements above average stock performance made in the chapters were based, are Brigham and Pappas, "Rates of Return on Common Stock" (*The Journal of Business*, July 1969) and Fisher and Lorie, "Rates of Return on Investments in Common Stocks" (*The Journal of Business*, January 1964).

QUESTIONS

1. How does one start a single proprietorship?
2. What are the legal dangers of partnership?
3. Why are all large businesses organized in the form of corporations?
4. Why can it be said that the corporate form of business organization may convey either a tax advantage or tax disadvantage, depending on the situation?
5. What is a dividend? Do corporations guarantee to pay dividends? What are possible reasons for a corporation not paying a dividend in a particular year?
6. Who owns a corporation? How is the corporation controlled?
7. What services does a securities firm perform?
8. What is the possible advantage and disadvantage in buying securities "at the market"?
9. Translate the following stock market quotation.

High	Low	Stocks	Sales in 100s	Open	High	Low	Close	Net Change
60	33	Ajax	40	33	34	29	30	−5

10. How are stock prices determined?
11. How does one select common stock by the dart method? What is the advantage of this method?
12. How does one select common stock by the extra information method? What factors would influence an individual's choice between the dart and extra information methods?
13. What is book value? Why is book value often different from a stock's market value?
14. What is a margin purchase?
15. Translate the following: On today's over-the-counter market XYZ Corporation stock was quoted at Bid 24, Ask 27.
16. What is a prospectus?

PROBLEMS

1. Joe and Bill form a partnership to operate a store. Each partner pays in $5000 toward the purchase of their partnership's initial assets. Shortly after the partnership has begun business, Bill, without consulting Joe, contracts with one of the partnership's customers to supply that customer with $100,000 worth of merchandise. Later it develops that Bill has made a serious error and that this merchandise will actually cost the partnership $200,000. After this enormous goof Bill and Joe split up their partnership; all that remains of their venture after all assets have been sold is a $90,000 liability. (A $100,000 loss on the contract is offset by $10,000 recovered from sale of assets.)
   (a) What is the most money either partner could lose in this venture?
   (b) Under what circumstances would a partner lose this maximum amount?
   (c) Under what circumstances could a partner lose lesser amounts?
2. Consider a situation exactly the same as Problem 1 except that the business was organized as a corporation. What is the most that Joe could now lose by having participated in the unfortunate venture?
3. An individual bought a stock in 1960 at a price of $40 per share. During the decade from 1960 through 1969, the stock paid dividends of $2 per share. The stock was sold in late 1969 at $75. The stockholder's marginal rate is 30%. Find his after-tax rate of return on the stock.
4. X considers buying stock at a price of $40. He expects that next year's dividends will be $1 and that the stock will rise in price at a rate of 5% per year. His marginal tax rate is 20%. What is his estimated after-tax dividend rate and his estimated after-tax rate of return?
5. Y Corporation shows the following balance sheet:

Assets	$1,000,000	Liabilities	$300,000
		Net Worth	$700,000

   Y Corporation has 10,000 shares of stock outstanding.
   (a) What is the book value of the stock per share?
   (b) What would be the book value per share if the stock was split four for one?

chapter seven

Other claims

Corporate bonds

Another type of claim which is sometimes included in collections of personal assets is the corporation bond. Just as a common stock represents a fraction of a corporation's net worth, a bond represents a fraction of a type of corporate liability. In order to borrow from a wide number of individuals and businesses, corporations do some of their borrowing in the form of bond issues. For example, a corporation may wish to borrow $1 million for 20 years. To do this it may offer a $1 million bond issue to the public. If a family wishes to lend the corporation $1000, it buys a $1000 bond. It now becomes a participant in the $1 million bond issue and is entitled to the rights of a corporation bondholder.

The rights of bondholders

When a corporation issues bonds, it makes two basic promises to its bondholders. It promises to pay interest to them for the use of their money and it promises to repay a specified or *face* amount of the bond (principal) at a specified date. Thus, if the 20-year bonds in our example paid interest at a rate of 6% per year, the owner of the bond would have two rights: the right to interest of $60 a year for 20 years and the right to a $1000 payment at the end of the 20-year period.

Bonds are liabilities, and a corporation is subject to severe treatment if it fails to discharge promises it made in connection with its liabilities. In general, if the corporation fails to meet its promises on bonds or other liabilities, all of the assets of the corporation may be seized by the liability-holders and sold to satisfy the promises. The individual bondholder does not even have to involve himself personally in the enforcement of the promises, since bond issues normally provide that a large banking company or other institution will act on behalf of individual bondholders.

Sometimes, of course, even though a corporation's assets are seized and sold, the proceeds from the sale are insufficient to discharge all of the corporation's promises. When corporate promises are not discharged, the bond issue is said to be in default. The possibility of default must be considered when bonds are bought. Corporations earn credit ratings just as individuals do. These credit ratings are discussed in a following section, but now we should note that in buying a bond the prospective bondholder ought to expect a higher rate of return on a bond from a corporation with a poor credit rating than from a corporation with a good rating.

Return on bonds

At first glance it might appear that the return on a bond can be easily identified. If a corporation issues a 6% bond, will this 6% constitute the rate of return for the bondholder? The major reason for a negative answer to this question lies in the existence of a secondary market in bonds. Bondholders can easily sell bonds they have purchased and, as with stock, the typical purchaser of a bond is likely to buy a "secondhand" bond rather than a newly issued one. When bonds are sold second hand (after the time of original issue), they may not always sell for the same price at which they were originally issued (usually the face value of the bond, approximately).

There are two reasons why bond prices change. One is a change in the credit rating of the company that has issued the bonds. Let us consider an example. Delta Company issues a $1000, 6%, 20-year bond in 1961. Between 1961 and 1971 the company encounters misfortunes and its credit rating drops because there is a prospect that its bonds may be defaulted. Investors are still willing to buy bonds with lower credit ratings, but, as mentioned earlier, it is normal for investors to expect a higher rate of return on a bond with a low credit rating. Let us suppose that the credit rating of Delta bonds has changed to the point where they are now comparable in credit rating to newly issued bonds that are providing a rate of return (in bonds this return is usually called the *yield*) of 10%. If an individual holding the 6% Delta bond wants to sell it, he will not find any buyers for it as long as it yields 6% because of the availability of new 10% bonds. However, if he is willing to sell it for a lower price, the actual yield on the bond will be greater and his bond may be salable.

Recalling the methods of Chapter 3, let us now find the price that will cause the Delta bonds to yield a return of 10%. In 1971 the 20-year Delta bond has only ten years left before its promised repayment date (maturity). Thus the remaining part of the Delta bond's promises consists of the payment of 6% interest which is $60 per year for the remaining ten years and a payment of $1000 at the end of ten years. We can find the present value of these promises by discounting at 10%. The present value of the ten-year $60 annuity is about $370 and the present value of a future $1000 in ten years is about $390. Thus the present value of the Delta bond, discounted at 10%, is $370 + $390, or about $760. Unless the $1000 price of Delta bonds drops to about $760 we can expect that there will be more offers to sell these bonds than offers to buy them. This oversupply will continue to exert downward pressure on price until the Delta bonds do sell for about $760. At that price their yield will be comparable to the 10% yield on a newly issued bond of similar credit risk.

A second and more common reason for a change in bond prices is due to a change in the general level of interest rates. Even borrowers with virtually perfect credit ratings find that sometimes it is quite easy for them to borrow money and they are able to offer only low interest rates on their bond issues. At other times money is much more difficult to obtain (most of us have heard the expression "tight money" used to describe these periods) and a higher interest rate must be offered. If a change takes place in the general level of interest rates, the price of secondhand bonds is affected.

Let us recast the example of the 6%, 20-year Delta bond. The bond was issued in 1961; now suppose that in 1971 the Delta Company's credit record remains the same as at the time of issue, but because money is not as tight in 1971 as in 1961, similar companies issuing new bonds now need to offer only a 4% interest rate. In this case, individuals wishing to sell old 6% bonds will find that they have very attractive merchandise to offer. To determine the selling price of one of the old bonds, its present value can be found using a 4% interest rate. The promises of the bond remain the same: $60 per year for the remaining ten years and $1000 at the end of 10 years. Present value of these promises, using a 4% discount rate, is approximately $1160. Thus the Delta bonds could be expected to sell for substantially more than their face value or original price.

Bond price quotations

The prices of bonds, like stocks, can often be obtained on newspaper financial pages. Bond prices, however, are quoted in a different manner. Bond price quotations are in percentages rather than in dollar amounts. If a bond is quoted at a price of 90, this means that the bond is selling at 90% of its face value; therefore a $1000 face value bond would sell for $900 and a $10,000 face value bond would sell for $9000. Short descriptions of bond issues are also often employed. The 7% bonds of the Jones Corporation, maturing in 1982, would be simply called the Jones 7s of 82.

Identifying rate of return on bonds

If a family contemplates purchase of an individual bond, it can identify rate of return in either of two ways. The difference will lie only in the assumption about the time that it will be holding the bond. If the family expects to hold the bond until maturity, it first identifies the bond's promises in money terms. Suppose the bond is a Global Corporation 5 of 85 in a $1000 face value and the family is considering buying the bond during 1970. It identifies the Global bond's promises as being for the payment of $50 per year interest for 15 years and for the payment of $1000 at the end of 15 years. Suppose the Global bond's price is 90 and there will also be a 1% commission involved in the transactions. Thus total cost of the $1000 bond will be about $910.

Income taxes, assuming a 20% ordinary tax rate, reduce the estimated annual interest to an after-tax $40. When the bond is repaid at maturity, capital gains tax of 10% will be due on the difference between price paid, $910, and the maturity value, $1000. This difference is $90 and hence the capital gain tax is $9; deduction of this tax from the maturity value leaves an after-tax $991 expected at maturity. Thus the problem of finding yield sets up as follows.

Interest	*Principal*
$A = \$40$	$F = \$991$
$n = 15$	$n = 15$

$$P = \$910$$
$$r = \text{unknown}$$

An experimental application of $r = 5\%$ produces $P = \$893$ and a trial of $r = 4\%$ results in $P = \$994$. By interpolating the family may conclude that the Global bond's yield, when bought at a cost of $910, will be about 4.8% after tax.

A Global bond may be bought with the assumption that it will not be held to maturity. In this case, the family may simply want to use the return until maturity, as identified above, as an approximation of the return during the period in which the bond will be held. However, if the family considering the Global bond purchase uses an extra information strategy, it might want to make a more refined calculation. In this case it would want to estimate (subject to the same difficulties as estimating a future stock price) the price that will prevail at the time when the family expects to sell the Global bond. If, for example, the family anticipated that the bond would be sold in two years at a price of 95, it would identify returns on the bonds as $50 interest for two years and $950 at the end of two years. However, if the bond is to be sold rather than held to maturity, a commission will have to be paid for selling the bond. If this commission is $10, the same as the commission for buying the bonds, the net amount to be received from the bond at the end of two years will be $950 — $10, or $940.

Assuming the same level of taxes as the preceding example, the family will reduce interest payments to an after-tax $40 per year. It will also recognize that it is expecting a $30 capital gain ($940 — $910). This will reduce the amount it receives when the bond is sold by $3, leaving $937 after tax, expected when the bond is sold. Thus the problem of finding a yield can be set up as follows.

Interest	*Principal*
$A = \$40$	$F = \$937$
$n = 2$	$n = 2$

$$P = \$910$$
$$r = \text{unknown}$$

Solving experimentally, r is now expected to be about 6% after tax.

The market for bonds

Bonds, too, are normally available through securities firms. This is true both for corporate bonds and the government bonds that we discuss in the next section. The bonds of major corporations are usually traded through exchanges in the same manner as stocks, and other bonds, including government bonds, are handled on an over-the-counter basis. Usually security firms also provide the primary market for bonds, although some government bonds are marketed in other ways. (The sale of U.S. Government Savings Bonds through post offices and banks is an example of a different marketing arrangement.)

Government bonds

Bonds are also issued by the U.S. Government, state and local governments, and the governments of many foreign countries. These bonds are basically the same type of instrument as those issued by corporations. They contain promises to pay interest and promises of repayment at a specified maturity date (except for savings bonds on which interest may be accumulated and paid at the maturity also). Bonds issued by the U.S. Government are not subject to default. Since they are payable in United States dollars, the U.S. Government can print additional dollars if necessary rather than default the bonds. With other types of government bonds, it is desirable to obtain a credit rating since there may be a chance of default on some of these.

With the exception of special savings bonds, government bonds are very similar to corporation bonds. Savings bonds, such as the popular Series "E" bonds issued by the U.S. Government, differ not only in the fact that they may not make regular interest payments and instead pay a lump sum at maturity, but also because these bonds cannot normally be sold in a secondary market. If one wishes to convert a savings bond into cash, he does so by turning it in to the issuing government and receiving a redemption value for it that will be specified on the bond; the redemption will vary with the date at which the bond is turned in.

Price quotations are published on government bonds that can be sold in secondary markets (these are called negotiable bonds). These bonds are subject to price fluctuation in the same way that corporate bonds are. Even negotiable U.S. Government bonds fluctuate in price, not because of credit rating change but because of the second reason given for price fluctuation, changes in the general level of interest rates.

Yields on negotiable government bonds can be calculated in the same way as those on corporate bonds. In the case of savings bonds, if disposal of the bonds is contemplated before maturity, the redemption value on the date at which one expects to turn the bond in would be used in determining the rate of return on the bonds. For example, if a U.S. bond were to be purchased at \$75 and if it were to be redeemed in four years for \$85, one would just consider tax treatment. Usually all returns on a U.S. Government savings bond are taxable as ordinary income (another special tax rule); therefore, in this instance, if the holder paid 20% marginal tax, the tax on the \$10 gain would reduce the proceeds to \$83. The yield identification would now set up as

$$\begin{aligned} F &= \$83 \\ P &= \$75 \\ n &= 4 \\ r &= \text{unknown} \end{aligned}$$

and would reveal that yield would be about 2⅓%.

Some government bonds have the added advantage that they are exempt from various income taxes. For example, interest received on a state bond is not subject to Federal income tax, though it may still be subject to state tax. Because of the attractiveness of this tax feature, tax exempt bonds tend to command high prices and thus offer lower before-tax yield. The lower income investor can usually secure a better after-tax return by buying bonds which are not tax exempt and which yield a much higher before-tax return, but the high income investor may find tax exempt bonds to his advantage. To illustrate this point, consider another example. Suppose that two bonds are available, a tax exempt bond yielding 5% and a nonexempt bond yielding 8% before tax. If an individual is in a 25% marginal tax bracket, the after-tax return on the nonexempt bond is 6%, which is better than on the exempt bond. On the other hand, if the individual is in a 50% marginal tax bracket, the nonexempt bond returns an after-tax return of 4% which is inferior to the tax exempt bond's 5% return.

Notes and bills

So far we have been using the term bonds to indicate all government and corporate liabilities that are sold to the public. Sometimes in financial literature the use of the word bonds is restricted to issues of these liabilities which mature at least several years from the date of issue. Shorter lived instruments are issued by both governments and corporations. These instruments are often distinguished with names such as notes, bills, or commercial paper. Beyond this difference in name they do not differ from bonds except in length of life and can be analyzed in exactly the same way. In fact, they do not even differ in length of life with bonds that are being sold second hand at a time very close to their maturity date.

Credit ratings on bonds

Two companies specialize in the providing of a particularly useful form of information for the prospective bond purchaser: the credit rating on bond issues. These credit reports, Moody's and Standard and Poor's, are too high priced for most individual investors but are available at the offices of security firms or in larger libraries.

Bonds summarized

Bonds, like stocks, have the advantage of being readily bought and sold. The return on bonds is normally easier to predict than that on stocks, but predictions have to be made subject to the possibility of default on some bonds. Predictions of bond returns may be difficult when the sale of the bonds before maturity is contemplated. Bond interest is taxable at ordinary income tax rates, but bonds bought at low prices may yield part of their return in the form of price appreciation which will be subject to capital gain tax treatment. Tax exempt bonds offer opportunities for high income investors.

Preferred stock and convertible bonds

Midway between bonds and common stocks lie two compromise assets which offer some of the features of both. Preferred stock, despite its name, may actually be more similar to debt than to common stock. A share of preferred stock might have the following characteristics.

1. A promise that no common stock dividends would be paid in any year unless a 5% dividend is paid on the face value (often called par value) of the preferred stock.
2. A promise that no common stock dividends would be paid in any year, unless dividends of 5% were paid to preferred stockholders for each of past years in which the company had paid no dividends to either preferred or common stockholders. (A feature of this type is called a cumulative provision.)
3. A promise that if the corporation's business is discontinued, the corporation must return the par value of their shares to preferred stockholders before any money can be withdrawn by common stockholders (preference in asset distribution).

Preferred shares occur in many variations, but most of them have the disadvantage that although dividends are declared preferentially, these dividends, and hence the price of the shares, do not have as much chance of increasing as do those of common stocks. Since only a few large corporations have issued preferred stock recently, it is not likely that many families will be acquiring this type of asset.

A more popular variety of "compromise" asset is the convertible bond. The purchase of such a bond conveys to its owner the right to exchange the bond for common stock of the issuing corporation on the basis of a specified formula. For example, if Carbon Company's stock is selling at 50, a Carbon $1000 convertible bond might offer, along with the usual bond promises, the opportunity for the holder to exchange (convert) the bond for ten shares of common stock. Thus, if before the bond's maturity, Carbon common stock increased in price to over 100, the convertible bondholder would have the opportunity to share in the company's success. On the other bond, if the stock did not go to 100, the bondholder would still obtain his promised $1000 face value.

Convertibles look like an ideal asset, combining the safety of a bond with the appreciation possibilities of stock, until one remembers how markets operate. If a security has desirable features and if these features are widely known, either the original issuer will compensate for the bond's convertibility by dropping the interest rate or else the secondhand price of the bond will rise and dim the bond's attractiveness. Thus convertible bonds do not necessarily have special merit; a dart theory market participant would have no reason for avoiding them, but an "extra information" participant would only choose a convertible if he felt he knew something about the value of the conversion opportunity that was not widely known by other market participants.

Diversification

One possible device for simplifying the management of assets is the use of specialization. This policy seems very applicable to the extra information approach to stock and bond market activity in which obviously one will be able to acquire extra information only by intensively examining some stocks and bonds. Specialization also seems advantageous to the dart approach because brokerage commission costs will be lowered if only one or a few stocks and bonds are bought in larger quantities, since commissions on any one security are subject to a "volume discount."

The difficulty with specialization arises in the fact that this approach places many eggs in one basket. If, for example, a stockholder is holding only one issue of stock and the corporation that issued this stock encounters misfortunes, the effect on the wealth of the stockholder can be severe. On the other hand, if he held a variety of stocks, losses on some stocks would probably be offset by fortunate occurrences in others. This approach, called *diversification* (buying a collection of stocks rather than just one), will usually result in more stable performance. The stability works both ways; a diversified approach will usually yield not only fewer serious losses but also fewer spectacular gains, since good luck in one company is likely to be offset by bad luck in another when a large number of stocks are being held.

In a later chapter we inquire into whether or not an individual is likely to desire diversification for purposes of stabilizing the return on his stocks and bonds. We note that diversification has two difficulties for the individual investor; this approach requires higher commissions and it also has a danger of spreading the efforts of a searcher for extra information too thin.

Mutual funds

There are ways for an individual to obtain diversification without high commission costs and costly search behavior. Like other opportunities offered in the market place this chance for diversification is not offered without cost. It is an opportunity, however, that is becoming popular with individuals who desire to participate in the stock market. The most popular of these diversifying arrangements, which usually, although not necessarily, concentrate on stocks, is the *mutual fund.*

When an individual participates in stocks or bonds through the mutual fund, he participates indirectly. The mutual fund can be thought of as a special type of corporation which holds as assets a collection of stocks and sometimes bonds. The mutual fund usually has no liabilities, although there are some exceptions, and the net worth of the mutual funds is divided up into shares of ownership. These shares are sold to the public and thus the purchaser of the share becomes a fractional participant in the collection of securities held by the mutual fund. These shares participate in the price increases and decreases in the mutual fund's collection of securities and in any dividends or interest that is paid on the securities. Since the mutual fund is large enough to buy many securities on a large scale, it is not subject to the problem of diversification becoming expensive because of brokerage commissions. Furthermore, because mutual funds own stock in very large quantities, they can afford to have a large research staff who attempts to obtain extra information about a wide variety of stocks.

The services provided by the mutual fund are not free. All mutual funds charge a management fee to provide themselves with a profit and cover the cost of managing the collection of securities they hold. Some mutual funds charge an additional fee to an individual when he initially puts money into the mutual fund; this fee, called a loading charge, is supposed to cover the cost of advertising the fund and paying for the sales organizations which encourage individuals to use the fund. Some funds, which do little advertising and hence which must be sought by the investor, do not levy a loading charge; these are called no-load funds.

Many academic studies have been done in an attempt to find whether or not participation in mutual funds has been worth the cost. These studies are not conclusive, but they seem to indicate that any superiority in the selection of stocks and bonds accomplished by the mutual fund is likely to be offset by the management fees and loading charges of the fund.

The individual needs to note, even if he decides to participate in the market through mutual funds, that he must still make the same strategy choice as before. Either he must select his mutual fund by the dart method or by seeking out the extra information needed to help form a preference for one mutual fund as opposed to others. Since some mutual funds have performed in a very spectacular manner, there may be fruitful possibilities for the individual who wants to employ the extra information approach in a search for funds.

Even if they do not offer extra yields, mutual funds do offer diversification which may be useful to many individuals. Furthermore, it may be psychologically more pleasing for the investor who does not want to undertake extensive searches for extra information to make a once-and-for-all dart-type choice of a mutual fund than to regularly employ the dart approach in selecting individual stocks and bonds.

Other Diversifying Arrangements

Other institutions similar to mutual funds are also available to the investor and in general have the same advantages and disadvantages. Banks are developing services called commingled trusts which perform mutual fund-type services for some investors. Insurance companies are rapidly moving to provide this type of service also. There are also some corporations, called closed-end investment companies, which do the same thing. Finally, note that some corporations hold a very wide collection of assets of different types (the so-called conglomerate corporations) and purchase of the stock of corporations of this type may provide some diversification to the investor. (However, all the assets in the conglomerate, no matter how diverse, are at least partially under a single management; therefore the assets are not diversified against possible flaws in this management.)

Mortgages

Another possibility that may be attractive to a few households is the holding of real estate mortgages, which are a special type of loan extended to the owners of real estate and which contain promises very similar to those in a bond: promises to pay interest over a period of time and to pay a face amount at the end of a period. To enforce these promises, the mortgage is legally attached to a house or other piece of real estate and gives the mortgage holder the right to seize the real estate in the event that the promises are not fulfilled. (In the event that the real estate does not have sufficient value to fulfill the promises made, the mortgage holder has other rights as well. A prospective mortgage holder would be well-advised to consult a lawyer if he envisions any possibility of default on a mortgage.)

We will not dwell at length on the identification of the rate of return on mortgages, but there is one point that should be made. Sometimes when an individual is selling a house or another piece of property, he can obtain a better price if he is willing to provide some financing for the buyer. Suppose X is selling a house to Y for $30,000. Y can borrow two-thirds of the purchase price, $20,000, from a bank. X will receive this $20,000 (borrowed by Y) and requires an additional $10,000. Suppose Y has only $5000 available for a *down payment*, the amount of the sale price that is paid in cash.

To make up the remaining $5000 on the purchase price of the house,

Y offers a $5000 second mortgage. The term *second mortgage* means that this mortgage takes second place to the first mortgage, which in this case is held by the bank. If default occurs, the bank is entitled to have the promises made to it fulfilled first; then any remaining proceeds from the seizure of the house are available to the holder of the second mortgage.

Suppose also that, if the house is not sold to Y, the only other available offer is from Z, who offers $28,000, financed with a $20,000 bank loan and an $8000 down payment. We can now examine the choice confronting A.

X's alternatives can be described as:

Sell to Y	Sell to Z
Cash $25,000	Cash $28,000
Second mortgage $5000	

Thus, if X sells to Y, he gives up $3000 in cash to receive a $5000 second mortgage. Suppose the second mortgage pays off over ten years with 6% interest in equal monthly installments of about $60 a month. Now X can set this decision up in the form of a solution for r.

$P = \$3000$, cash forgone now
$A = \$700$, approximate *annual* mortgage payments
$n = 10$
$r =$ unknown

By finding r we may identify the second mortgage's return as approximately 20% before tax. Since part of this gain is in the form of interest payments and part is in the form of a higher price for the house, not all of this return will be subject to ordinary income tax. However, we do not attempt to precisely identify the after-tax rate of return.

One can see that there is sometimes greater benefit to mortgages than is at first obvious. One of the disadvantages of mortgages is that they are often not very easy to sell. If one acquires a mortgage and thinks he will not hold it to maturity, he ought to consider his prospects for selling it and try to anticipate any discount he may experience when disposing of his mortgage. There is no reason why mortgages cannot be a useful addition to an individual's collection of assets if they yield satisfactory returns, but an individual acquiring a mortgage ought to carefully consider the absence of an orderly secondary market in which secondhand mortgages can be sold.

Summary

Bonds are liabilities; a bond issue is a loan divided up among a large number of participants called bondholders.

A bond is a contract that promises to pay an interest rate during the life of the bond issue and also promises to return the face amount of the bond to the bondholder at the maturity date of the bond issue. In general the market value of the bond is determined by discounting the promised dollar amount of interest to be paid each year on the bond and also discounting the maturity value or face value of the bond. The sum of these present values is the approximate market value.

The return that a bond provides for a bondholder depends not only on the promises made in the bond contract (the interest rate and the maturity value) but also on the price at which the bondholder buys the bond. If the bond is purchased at a discount, part of the return from the bond will normally be subject to capital gains tax rather than ordinary income tax.

Prices of bonds may fluctuate if there is a change in the general level of interest rates or if the credit rating of a particular company changes. Credit ratings are available on all major bond issues.

Governments as well as corporations issue bonds. These do not differ materially from corporation bonds except that bonds issued by the U.S. Government may be regarded as having a perfect credit rating.

Preferred stock and convertible bonds are securities that attempt to offer some of the advantages of both stocks and bonds. Both securities purport to offer their holder more protection than the stock of the issuing company but more opportunity to share in the company's good fortune than a bond of the company.

Stockholders who wish to hold common stock but who do not wish to expose themselves to large risks may use the policy of diversification, in which they buy the securities of a large number of companies in the hope that losses experienced in some companies may be offset by extraordinary gains experienced in others. One commonly used method of diversification is through purchasing shares in a mutual fund.

Mortgages are another claim which may be available to the individual investor. There are occasions where it might be quite advantageous to the seller of a house to offer some supplemental financing, such as a second mortgage, to the prospective purchaser.

SUGGESTED READINGS

The investment text, Graham, Dodd, and Cottle referred to in Chapter 6, also discusses bonds in considerable detail.

QUESTIONS

1. What is the basic difference between a bond and a common stock?
2. Why do you think a corporation would issue bonds instead of just borrowing money from a bank?
3. Carefully explain how the long-term bond of a very reliable company can be subject to substantial price fluctuations.
4. What is meant by the description of a bond issue, 4s of 88?

5. How does a convertible bond differ from an ordinary bond?
6. Suppose you have $1000 which you wish to invest in the stock market. What are the pros and cons of investing through a mutual fund as opposed to buying stock directly?
7. Can you think of any reason why the type of stock that an individual might wish to pick would be related to the timing and riskiness of the earnings that he expects from his job?

PROBLEMS

1. Suppose that in 1972 a new ten-year government bond yields 7%. What would you expect the price to be for an old government bond which is part of an issue described as 5s of 82?
2. Suppose in 1972 you could buy a bond described as a 6 of 92 at a price of 80. What would be your yield on this bond before tax? after tax?
3. A 5% X Corporation bond is convertible into 20 shares of X common stock. At the time the bond was issued, X stock was selling for $30 per share. At present X stock is priced at $80 per share. What would you expect to be the approximate price of the X convertible bond?
4. You are given the following information about the average price of the stock of three companies during each of three years.

	Year 1	*Year 2*	*Year 3*
Company A	40	70	50
Company B	80	50	60
Company C	25	35	20

(a) Suppose that you purchase $3000 worth of stock from Company A in year 1. How many shares would you have been able to buy? What would the shares be worth in year 2? in year 3?
(b) Now do the same thing for a $3000 investment in Company B and also for a $3000 investment in Company C.
(c) Now suppose that instead of buying $3000 worth of any one stock you would instead in year 1 purchase $1000 worth each of A, B, and C stocks. How many shares of each would you have purchased? What would be the total value of these stocks in year 2? in year 3?
(d) From your answers can you make any general statement about the effect of diversification on the risk of stock price fluctuation?

chapter eight

Physical capital

In this chapter three principal types of physical capital will be discussed: housing, household appliances and equipment, and automobiles. These assets differ from claims in that, except when they are acquired for rental to others, they yield their returns in the form of services. However, attempts can be made to place money values on the benefits that are conferred by the assets. These money values can then be compared with the cost of acquiring the asset by calculating a rate of return. Using the rates of return on physical assets, these assets can be subjected to comparisons among themselves and with nonphysical assets.

Other types of physical assets are excluded from consideration. Sometimes individuals buy business property directly rather than participating in business through the purchase of securities. Rates of return can also be identified on these direct purchases of business assets. However, since only a small portion of individuals are likely to acquire business assets, we do not provide an additional analysis of this type of asset here. By this same line of reasoning, we also omit such personal investments as land, and commodities that are bought and sold in organized commodity markets.

In the first paragraph a distinction was made between physical assets acquired to provide services and physical assets acquired for rental to others. Most households are likely to be much more concerned with service-yielding assets. Therefore the term physical capital will be used to denote only service-yielding assets unless a specific exception is made. (This eliminates the need for many "except for" expressions later.)

Comparison with other assets

It has been noted that physical assets acquired by individuals usually yield their return in the form of services. Even though a rate of return can be identified on these services, there is one possible danger in making a comparison between this rate of return and the return on assets that yield their benefits in money. Services provided by an asset in a future time period must usually be used up during that time period or they will be lost. Money acquired in a future time period, however, can be reinvested for use in time periods still further into the future.

Consider an example. A household saves $2000 in a year and considers two possible uses for the $2000: common stocks yielding an after-tax return of 7% and home appliances which are estimated to yield services valued by the household so highly that the rate of return on these assets will be 20% after tax. At first glance the appliances appear to be the obvious choice; however, acquisition of the appliances implies that the $2000 will be used up over the life of the appliances. If there is a possibility that the household may find itself short of funds in future time periods (if, for example, a member reaches retirement age or encounters some other income decline), the decision might be reconsidered. If the stocks with a more moderate return were purchased, this return could have been withheld from use during the near future and reinvested for availability at a time of anticipated need.

Despite this problem there are major advantages to making rate of return comparisons between physical assets and other types of assets. Often the household will want to choose physical assets if they are higher yielding than claims or human capital. Furthermore, the household will certainly want to reject assets if their yield in services is less than the rate of return on other assets. Otherwise a family would be committing itself to a policy of buying assets that provided benefits with a money value less than the amount of money that could be obtained on alternative assets. The family would be engaging in self-contradictory behavior if it first asserted that the benefits conferred from some article of household equipment were worth $100 a year and then selected household equipment in preference to a claim that would yield, say, $110 a year in after-tax cash.

To summarize, we are always justified in comparing the rate of return on physical assets with other assets and rejecting the physical asset if its rate of return is less than the alternatives. On the other hand, the higher rate of return on the service-yielding physical asset may not by itself be sufficient cause for choosing that asset over the nonphysical one.

"Default" on physical assets

When the purchase of bonds was discussed, we considered the possibility that the promises made by issuing companies might not always be fulfilled. The individual considering physical assets should also recognize that some of the expectations from these assets may not materialize. The purchaser of a dishwasher might subsequently discover that she really liked to do dishes the old way and hence does not receive as much benefit from her new appliance as she thought. A home purchased with the intention of a lifetime of use may, after a few years, become undesirable and also fall in resale price because of the noise from a relocated airport. Some products may not live up to advertising claims or their "novelty may wear off." An individual should try to be as realistic as possible in assessing the future benefits he expects to receive from service-producing physical assets. Then he should recognize that some of his carefully formed estimates may still prove wrong.

Home ownership

It is frequently said that housing is a primary want, a bare necessity that a household requires for survival. This assertion, however, has little relevance for personal decision making. Only a very minimal standard of housing is essential for survival. Individuals normally acquire housing in a far greater quantity and quality than this bare minimum. Marginal housing expenditures for the typical family are probably subject to free choice as much as other expenditures made by the family. Furthermore, although some housing may be essential, home ownership is not as long as rental housing is available. Thus we can proceed on the assumption that home purchase is an ordinary asset acquisition decision which is appropriately compared with other asset alternatives.

Identification of gross benefits

The most obvious advantage in home ownership is rent saving. The first step in identifying the benefits of acquiring a house is to identify the rental value. If the family is already renting the house, this identification is quite obvious. If, on the other hand, the house has not been rented, as in the case of the newly constructed home or a house being bought second hand from another owner-occupier, a more difficult estimation problem exists. This estimate should be formulated on the basis of what the family would be willing to pay rather than the amount that could be charged for the house. This difference can be illustrated in an example.

A family considers the purchase of a particular house and finds no house of exactly the same type being offered for rent, but it does find a slightly smaller one renting for $200 per month. The family consults with various people who are familiar with the local housing market and receives the opinion that the house it is considering, because it is larger and has extra features, would probably rent for about $250 a month. However, the family feels that the larger house would be worth only about $30 more per month to it than the $200 a month house. Therefore the rental value to the family is $230 per month. If the house does not represent a satisfactory asset acquisition prospect with calculations based on $230 per month benefit, the family will be better off actually renting a $200-a-month house.

Since the house represents a major investment, the house evaluation process is worth considerable effort. Considerable care should be taken in determining the house's rental value. When comparing the house with rental possibilities available, not only should factors such as size, appearance, condition, and convenience be taken into consideration but also location. An inconveniently located house may subject the family to substantial amounts of extra automobile costs and loss of leisure or income opportunities because of time spent in commuting.

In addition to rental value of the house, the family may also wish to include an estimate of the benefit conferred by pride of ownership. Closely related to that is the matter of security of tenure. One of the advantages of owning a house instead of renting is that the family does not have to be concerned about being evicted. There is always a chance when a house is rented that the owner might decide to live in it himself, rent it to a favorite nephew, or convert it to some other purpose. Security of tenure would not be worth much to a family that was only planning to live in a house for a short time. Nor would it be worth much if satisfactory rental housing was available under a long-term lease (a contract assuring the right of occupancy for a long period of time). However, in many cases the family will want to consider security of tenure.

There is no easy general method to determine the money value of the "extra benefits" for a particular family. The family will have to ask itself, "What would we be willing to pay for these extra benefits," and no one but the family can answer this. Some families may feel that, for example, if the rental value of a house is $230 per month, the satisfaction and security of living in their own house are worth an additional $40 per month. This difference can then be considered in determining gross benefits; in this case, gross benefits would amount to $270 per month ($230 rent saved + $40 extra benefit = $270).

Net benefits

With ownership go responsibilities of a financial nature. In determining the net benefits obtained from home ownership, costs that are associated with ownership but not with rentership need to be deducted from gross benefits. Real estate taxes are one major cost item for the owner. These taxes are usually very substantial and the prospective home purchaser should identify their amount carefully. Only taxes on the house and lot (real estate) should be deducted, however, because other property taxes such as those on furniture would have to be paid even if the house were rented. An owner of a house must also pay many maintenance expenses that are not borne by a renter. Many houses need to be painted on the outside periodically. Interior surfaces and floor coverings usually require fairly regular expense. Plumbers and electricians need to be called occasionally.

Other potential repair and maintenance expenses may also be disclosed by carefully examining a used house. Additionally, houses are exposed to possible damage from fire, flood, windstorms, and other causes. The owner and not the renter bears the loss when these calamaties occur. Therefore the cost of insuring against such misfortunes should be deducted from the rental value.

Following through with the previous example, in which gross benefits were $270, we may consider some of the cost of ownership and reach a net benefit figure in the following manner.

Gross yearly benefits ($270 × 12)		$3240
Ownership costs (yearly estimated)		
Real estate taxes	$500	
Painting	200	
Repairs	100	
Insurance	100	
Total yearly costs		900
Net yearly benefits		$2340

Home financing

The means of financing other assets has been deferred until Chapter 14, which deals with the question of when and how much to borrow. A home, however, is such a large purchase by the standards of most households that borrowing for this acquisition is almost taken for granted. Because the buying and financing of a home are so often parts of, in effect, a single transaction, it would be rather artificial to try to divorce these components in this text.

Therefore, in the case of housing, we will go one step further in the identification of net benefits and consider "net benefits after first mortgage payments." We will thus think of the home purchase as consisting of the present spending of a down payment plus any other money the family must spend on the house at the time of purchase. This total amount of spending is discussed in detail in the following section.

In considering mortgage payments we will presume the existence of only one mortgage. As we noted in Chapter 7 second mortgages are sometimes given in lieu of part of the down payment. However, this borrowing arrangement is less common than the first mortgage. Since a family may often borrow part of its down payment under other arrangements than a second mortgage, we leave the question of financing the down payment until we consider the general problem of borrowing.

Nearly all first mortgage home loans are repaid in equal monthly payments over a rather long period. Twenty to thirty-year mortgages are common; some even run for longer periods. For simplicity in our calculations we multiply the required monthly payment by 12 and work with annual payments.

Some mortgage payments not only provide for the repayment of a loan, with interest, but also for property taxes on the house. Such payments are described as IPT payments (interest, principal, and taxes). The examples we use are based on payments that do not cover property taxes; if one was making IPT payments, he would not need to deduct property taxes when he calculated his net benefits from home ownership.

It first appears that we can simply subtract yearly mortgage payments from yearly net benefits to obtain net benefits after first mortgage payments. Mortgage payments, however, also may result in tax savings, since the portion of the payment that is designated as interest *may* be deductible. Therefore, even though we now follow the simple approach just mentioned, we want to return to this question later when we give more detailed attention to borrowing.

To return to the previous example of net benefit determination, these benefits had been identified as \$2340 per year. Now, suppose the home is financed with a first mortgage that requires payment of \$130 per month (the approximate payment on a 30-year 7% mortgage of \$20,000). Yearly first mortgage payments (FMP) are \$130 × 12, or \$1560. Accordingly,

Net benefits	\$2340
FMP	1560
Net benefit after FMP	\$ 780

Initial cost of the house

To identify the rate of return on a house, the net benefits after FMP must be compared with the cash outlay required when a house is bought. Obviously, one will want to include the down payment as part of the initial cost of acquiring the house. Additionally, he will want to ascertain whether there are any "closing costs" that must be paid at the time of purchase. Such costs include the costs of transferring ownership, the payment of any fees to real estate firms (although these are normally paid by the seller), and payment of any back taxes (although these, too, are normally paid by the seller). Any initial payments associated with securing financing for the house should be counted so that all cash requirements are included. Initial remodeling expense should also be included in the initial cost figure; in this case, benefit identification should be based on the rental value of a remodeled house rather than on the house's present condition.

Additional items might be required for a family that had previously lived in an apartment or a furnished house. Although a garbage can, a pipe wrench, a ladder, a rake, or a lawn sprinkler each seem almost negligibly small, the sum of such "small" purchases is usually not negligible. "Odd jobs," such as painting "a room or two" or hiring some help in initial cleaning, can add to this total of miscellaneous items. Particular care needs to be taken in estimating the initial cost of a newly constructed house. Even a completed home in a housing development may require landscaping, driveway paving, or other potential initial costs. If one is having a house built, accurate cost estimation is both difficult and highly important. Even house construction under contracts that specify the total price in advance may not offer complete assurance that construction cost will not exceed a specific amount, since the family commonly sees possible modifications as construction progresses, and the cost of these modifications adds to the price. Of course, the difficulties are magnified if the owner undertakes construction on the basis of an estimated cost of construction, rather than a contract for construction containing a fixed price.

Moving to a different home often requires the purchase of different and more furniture and draperies. Of course, additional furniture would probably also have to be purchased if the family moved into a rented home; therefore the acquisition of furniture could be logically separated from the home ownership decision. Still, the two decisions are interrelated, for when the family moves into a newly purchased house, furniture acquisition may be nearly essential at a time when household financial resources are already strained by the home purchase. Although related furniture will not be added on to the cost used in determining the rate of return on a house, the family should recognize this additional potential need for cash. We return to the topic of furniture decisions later in this chapter.

To continue our example, the purchasers of a house priced at $25,000, which was to be financed with a $20,000 mortgage, might make the following estimates of their initial outlay.

House Cost

Down payment		$5000
"Closing costs"		
Initial financing charge	$200	
Legal fees	75	
Total "closing costs"		275
Repairs and remodeling		
Painting	$300	
Check furnace	20	
Miscellaneous repairs	100	
Total repairs and remodeling		420
Landscaping		400
Miscellaneous purchases		150
Total House Cost		$6245

The family will have to face the issue of providing this $6245 plus other extra spending required, such as furniture purchases or moving expense. If the family has sold another house, proceeds from that sale may defray at least part of these cash needs. The remainder will have to come from tapping other household assets, such as accumulated cash, bonds, or stocks or from borrowing. These problems, however, will be considered later; at present we want to consider whether the house is a *desirable* asset. To do that we proceed to an identification of its rate of return.

Identifying the full benefits

Before net benefits are compared with the initial cost of acquiring a house, tax aspects should be noted. In general the benefits conferred by home purchase are exempt from income tax. As opposed to assets that yield benefits in money that may be subject to taxation, a family-occupied house yields benefits in services that do not have to be reported as income. Therefore, net benefits after mortgage payments may be regarded as after-tax benefits.

The duration of benefits also needs to be considered. A family may view its prospective house as a permanent residence or it may anticipate living in the house only for a definite time period. The nonpermanent view would be taken by a family that expected to make a future move to another area or one that anticipated a move to a house of different size or quality. Furthermore, even the family who plans to remain permanently will be able to anticipate a change in the level of its net benefits after FMP, for eventually the mortgage will be paid off.

This analysis can be kept simple by assuming that the family who takes the permanent view will receive two separate benefits. They will obtain a flow of net benefits after FMP over the life of the mortgage. They will also have a paid-for house at the end of the mortgage's life. To arrive at this second value, an estimate of the house's market value will have to be made at the time the mortgage is repaid.

The nonpermanent purchaser's analysis will differ only slightly. He will have to estimate the benefits he will receive during the period he expects to live in the house and the amount of cash he will receive from the house when he sells it. This amount of cash, in turn, will be determined by the expected selling price less deductions for selling costs and for the remaining amount of the mortgage. Thus, in both cases, a future market value must be estimated. If adequate provision is made for the maintenance of a house, it may be subject to little physical deterioration as time passes.

Increases in the cost of constructing new housing and increasing scarcity of land on which to place it have exerted some upward pressure on values of older homes. Therefore it may usually be safe to assume that the future market value of a house will be about the same as its current price. Specific circumstances, however, may need to be considered; if, for example, a household anticipates a future move because of a possible deterioration of the neighborhood, a resale price estimate that is lower than the initial cost, perhaps by a substantial amount, would be in order.

Once a market value estimate has been made, we can identify the full set of benefits for the permanent resident. In our earlier example, we had estimated net benefits after FMP of $780 per year. If the original $25,000 price of the house is used as the estimated market value at the time the mortgage will be discharged, the full statement of benefits is

Net benefits after FMP: $780 per year for 30 years
Market value at end of 30 years: $25,000

If the family planned to move after five years, the net benefits after FMP would run only for five years. If $25,000 was still used at the estimated market price, an expected cash amount to be received at the end of five years might be determined as follows.

Estimated market price		$25,000
Deductions		
Selling expense (6% of market price)	$ 1,500	
Mortgage remaining	17,800	
Mortgage charge	180	
Total deductions		19,480
Net cash from sale		$ 5,520

A brief word of explanation is in order on the deductions. The 6% selling expense represents a typical selling commission that might be charged by a real estate firm. The $17,800 mortgage remaining could normally be obtained by consulting the lender. If not, it could be estimated by finding the future value of $20,000 (the original amount of the mortgage) with $n = 5$ and $r = 7\%$, and subtracting from this the future value of the mortgage payments, where $A = \$1560$ (from our example), $r = 7\%$ and $n = 5$.

The mortgage charge, approximately 1% of the outstanding mortgage, denotes a possible charge for either repaying the mortgage before maturity or transferring it to the home's new owner. On some mortgages there might be no charge for prepayment or transfer; on others the charge might be considerably higher. The proposed mortgage should be examined for this feature.

No provision for capital gains tax on the sale was made, since the selling price is the same as the purchase price. Normally, even if "profit" was made on the sale of a home, this would not be taxable if the family bought another home within a year. (This is a special benefit for homeowners provided under current income tax laws.)

Calculating rate of return

We can now calculate the rate of return in our example both for a permanent resident, X, and for Y, who plans to move in five years. For X the important facts are

$$\begin{aligned}
P &= \text{present cash outlay} = \$6245 \\
A &= \text{net benefits after FMP} = \$780 \\
F &= \text{estimated future value} = \$25{,}000 \\
n &= \text{years until mortgage is paid} = 30 \\
r &= \text{unknown}
\end{aligned}$$

The experimental search for r is illustrated as

	Approximate values of P, where $n = 30$	
	$r = 12\%$	$r = 14\%$
$A = \$780$	\$6200	\$5500
$F = \$25{,}000$	800	500
	\$7000	\$6000

Since P was actually \$6245, it is apparent that the house offers an after-tax return of slightly less than 14%, if it is bought by X.

One may observe that the present value of the estimated market value F is very small. This should give comfort to someone who was worried about the accuracy of estimates that are possible for a market value 30 years in the future. In our example, if the future market value had been set 50% lower or 50% higher than \$25,000, our answer would have been virtually unaffected.

The calculation made by Y follows the same form; his problem is based on

$$\begin{aligned} P &= \$6245 \\ A &= \$780 \\ F &= \text{net cash from sale} = \$5520 \\ n &= 5 \\ r &= \text{unknown} \end{aligned}$$

The search for r is again illustrated:

	Approximate values of P, where $n = 5$	
	$r = 8\%$	$r = 10\%$
$A = \$780$	\$3000	\$3000
$F = \$5520$	3700	3400
	\$6700	\$6400

In this case, r is apparently slightly over 10% or considerably lower than in X's case. This result should not be surprising. There are extra costs, such as selling expenses and mortgage charges, associated with selling a home, and when these extra items are associated with the use of a home for only a few years, they pull down the home's rate of return. This effect probably explains why persons who expect to live in an area for only a year or two often prefer to rent a home rather than buy one.

Exceptional cases

Our example has been based on families who planned to finance a \$25,000 home with a \$5000 down payment (20% of the price) and a \$20,000 first mortgage (80% of the price). Although this may be a fairly typical arrangement, some families may be able to finance a larger amount, say 90% or more with a first mortgage, and some others may pay cash for the entire amount of the purchase. Our analysis needs to be altered slightly for both cases.

If an individual makes virtually no down payment (say, under $1000), the approach we have set forth should be used with considerable caution. Even a very small net benefit after FMP may make the rate of return very high on such a small investment. In this instance it may be useful to also look at the dollar amount of the net benefit after FMP. For example, a house may be bought for $500 down payment; net benefits after FMP of $100 per year are expected. Although $100 per year may provide an attractive-looking return on a $500 cash outlay, the family may decide that, for such a small dollar amount of benefit (less than $10 per month), they would still prefer to rent an avoid worrying about issues such as, What if we change our mind and decide to move? What if taxes go up more than we expect?

In the case of the family that pays all cash and plans to move within a few years, the same method can be used as for family Y in our example. No mortgage payments would be deducted from net benefits, the down payment would equal the price of the house, and no mortgage repayment outlays would have to be deducted in identifying the cash the family would receive when it sold the house.

If, however, the cash buyer plans to live in the house permanently, we cannot estimate the value of the house at the end of the life of the mortgage since there is no mortgage. Therefore it may be reasonable to estimate the value of the house at the end of 20 or 30 years and to base calculations on one of these time periods.

Advantages and disadvantages of home ownership

We have previously noted that the borrowing costs for home ownership may be partially offset by a tax advantage; this will be discussed in detail in Chapter 14. This tax advantage is available on borrowing for all purposes, and is not unique to home ownership.

However, there is a distinctive income tax advantage associated with the ownership of a home and other physical assets, which is already implicit in the calculations described in previous sections. These assets yield nonmoney benefits which are not subject to income tax. Even rent saving falls into this nontaxable category. This probably explains why most families concentrate a large portion of their wealth in physical assets, and why home ownership can be attractive to a family even though the same family may not regard the purchasing of buildings for rental to others (which yields taxable money benefits) as desirable.

On the other hand, there are two disadvantages of ownership. One of these is the cost and uncertainty of resale, as we previously noted. If the family is planning to be in one location only a fairly short time, it may find that the difficulty and the cost of buying and then reselling a house are sufficiently great to make the house an unattractive investment. Another disadvantage of home ownership may arise from the fact that houses are usually available only in a minimum size. An individual, for example, who wishes to occupy only a one bedroom house with no lawn, would probably find that houses of this type were not available in acceptable locations and that they could not be built because of zoning restrictions. Such an individual would probably be content with renting a small apartment. If he buys a large house, the rental value to him may be only the rental value of that small apartment. This may be inadequate to provide an acceptable return on the house investment.

Condominiums and cooperatives

Two forms of ownership comprise attempts to overcome the disadvantages of home ownership mentioned in the previous section. Condominium is the legal term for an apartment building in which individual apartments are sold to occupiers of the apartments. Ownership of a condominium has the same tax advantage as ownership of a home. Since condominiums are available in smaller sizes than houses, an individual needing only apartment-size accommodations may find that a condominium represents an acceptable investment in housing even though a house would not.

Another ownership form quite similar to the condominium is a cooperatively owned building. In this instance each apartment occupant buys a fraction of the entire building rather than his own particular apartment. This arrangement has the same tax advantage as condominium ownership; that is, it confers tax advantage comparable to home ownership. These ownership arrangements are rather new in practice and may not be available in all areas; however, where they are available, they represent an asset possibility that should be considered, especially by families who would otherwise rent an apartment.

Purchasing rental housing

In addition to its home a family may consider the possibility of acquiring buildings for rent. In this alternative asset the differences between the landlord's position and the owner-occupier's position should be emphasized. When the building is being rented out, it confers benefits in the form of rent (rather than a nonmoney rental value) which must be reduced to an after-tax value in determining gross benefits. Security of tenure does not apply to the landlord, and it is unlikely that there is more pride of ownership associated with the owning of rental buildings than there is with other investment alternatives, such as common stocks. Additionally, maintenance expense is likely to be higher for the landlord than the owner-occupier because the landlord is not likely to be willing or able to make repairs during his leisure time. After these adjustments are made, the analysis on housing for rent is similar to the previous discussion on buying a home for occupancy.

Second homes

It is becoming increasingly popular for families to acquire vacation homes. Such an acquisition ought to be analyzed along the same lines as the home ownership decision discussed previously. The rental value of a second home to its owner is sometimes limited by the amount of time that can be spent at the second home. If an individual can only use his second home for, say, one month out of the year, his purchase could probably only be justified if the owner were willing to pay a very high rent for that particular home or if a very high premium could be attached to pride of ownership and security of tenure.

Furniture, appliances, and other household equipment

The analysis of these smaller items appears to be less important than a house because less money is being spent when one of these items is purchased. However, since a family's total expenditure on these items can amount to many thousands of dollars in only a few years' time, collectively, the analysis of spending on these items may be quite important. What is required for these smaller items is a simplified type of analysis. One does not want to ignore the analysis of furniture and equipment, but at the same time it would seem irrational to give the same degree of thought to the purchase of a $100 lawn mower as to a $25,000 house. (Even though it seems irrational it is still done in some cases.)

The returns on these assets are varied. Appliances may yield benefits principally in labor saving. Furniture can provide comfort and beauty. Recreational equipment affords family fun, although some of this equipment, such as boats, is available for rent; hence the asset might be more appropriately regarded as rent saving rather than fun producing, since the fun could be obtained without the asset.

A direct identification of rate of return with methods followed previously is possible on these assets. In a labor-saving appliance, such as a dishwasher, a fairly direct rate of return identification may be undertaken. Some academic studies have been done along these lines and they seem to indicate the potential for quite high rates of return, often over 10%. Even here some care must be taken; if the extra time is to be used for leisure, what value does the family place on additional leisure for the housewife? If the time released is to be for a part-time job, what wage (after taxes) is actually available?

The implicit rent approach

As noted before, a simplified method for decisions about smaller household assets would be useful. The method proposed here deviates from the previous rate of return asset selection method, although it still bears quite close relationship to that general policy. Suppose an individual could identify some rate of return as being readily available on a particular type of asset. For example, the individual feels that he could make 7% after tax by buying common stocks. He can then say that wealth will be used inefficiently if household assets are acquired with rates of return of less than 7% after tax. (Since household assets normally yield returns in the form of services, they usually do not require any tax adjustment.)

He could justify comparing common stocks and household assets by saying that both these purchases are marked by some uncertainty. Although one is not sure just what actual benefits he will get from buying a stock, neither is he sure about the actual amount of benefit he may receive from many household purchases. (Will the deep-freeze actually be kept full? Will we get tired of the boat after a season and decide to sell it—possibly at a large loss? Will the new reclining chair seem hopelessly out of style after a year or two?) Thus one might say that if, "on the average," he expects 7% on stock, he should also have the right to expect that much return on household assets.

After an alternative return, such as the 7% on stock, has been identified, this can be used to estimate the opportunity cost of owning any household asset. To proceed with this approach it is necessary to estimate the cost of buying and installing the asset, the annual maintenance costs (repairs, utilities, personal property taxes), and the length of life of the asset. It will then be possible to estimate the total annual cost of owning the asset, including the opportunity cost of giving up money-yielding alternative assets. Unless the family purchasing the asset thinks the services from the asset will be worth these annual costs (implicit rents), the asset should not be acquired.

Consider an example. Purchase of a color television is contemplated for $600. The life of the set is estimated at ten years and maintenance costs at $50 per year. This household feels that it can buy other assets that will yield 6% after tax if it does not buy the television set with the $600.

This can now be turned into an annuity problem along the lines discussed in Chapter 3. We would like to know how much money the family could receive each year for ten years if $600 were invested at 6%. This is the annual amount the family will have to give up if it decides to buy the television set instead of another asset, and this amount plus the maintenance cost will give it a guideline for the purchase of the television set. To set up the annuity problem,

$$P = \$600$$
$$r = 10 \text{ years}$$
$$A = \text{unknown}$$

Solving, $A =$ approximately \$80.

The total annual cost of owning the asset therefore becomes

Annuity foregone by not investing \$600 but using it for television	\$80
Maintenance cost	50
Total cost per year	\$130

If the family would be willing to *pay* \$130 per year, or about \$21 per month, to rent a set of this type, ownership should be seriously considered. For reasons discussed previously this acceptance may still not *necessarily* be desirable, since the television yields nonmoney benefits.

In another example, if the family calculated the implicit rent on a set of new living room furniture as \$40 per month, it might be able to dismiss this purchase possibility on the grounds that these benefits were just not worth that much to the family when compared to other items which could be bought for \$40 per month. In other words, we can require that household assets pass an implicit rent "test." If a family would not be willing to rent an asset for its implicit rent (the amount of money the family could expect to get per year or per month by investing the cost of the asset in claims), the asset should not be purchased. We reconsider the question of the buying assets which *pass* an implicit rent test, but which may concentrate nonmoney benefits in periods too near the time of purchase, when the lifetime financial plan is examined in Chapters 15 and 16.

Car purchases

Car purchases represent major household asset acquisition decisions. Not only is the purchase price fairly high but the purchase is one that is often repeated frequently. Again, the benefits derived from the ownership of a car are very difficult to identify. Because of the recurring nature of car purchases, it is probably useful to think about a policy for car acquisition rather than a single decision about buying a particular car.

Some families buy cars on a "time payment plan" and pay for them in monthly installments. Others elect to pay cash. We leave this issue of how the car is to be financed until Chapter 14. Now we concentrate on the question: "What type of car purchase policy is desirable?" rather than "How should this policy be financed?" Some families may just choose the highest price car that they can arrange to finance, but any buyer who wishes to analyze the car purchase decision is more likely to be concerned with the first question before he tries to answer the second.

One approach toward car purchase policy choice is to identify an implicit car rental with various plans for car ownership and attempt to select one policy on this basis. Suppose the prospective car purchaser considers a number of policies.

1. Buy a medium-priced new car and trade for a similar car every two years.
2. Buy a medium-priced new car and trade for a similar car every four years.
3. Buy a new compact car and trade every year.
4. Buy a new compact car and trade every four years.
5. Buy a three-year-old car and trade every three years.

To compare these policies, a number of estimates will be required.

A. The original car price required at the time the policy begins. (Not the "sticker" price, but the actual price that the buyer thinks he will have to pay, including a realistic assessment of the value of his trade-in.)

B. The trade-in money difference that will be required each time the car is replaced.

C. Annual maintenance cost, which will include license fees, collision insurance, property taxes, repairs, tire replacement, gasoline and oil, and other maintenance expenditures. Let us assume that these estimates have been made for the alternative policies and are those that are summarized in Table 8.1.

Note that the expense estimates differ on the basis of car size and on

TABLE 8.1

Policy	Initial price	Years between trade-ins	Estimated trade-in difference	Oil and gas on 10,000 miles	License, taxes, collision insurance	Tires, repairs, etc.	Total annual mainte-nance
1	$4000	2	$1500	$300	$300	$200	$800
2	$4000	4	$2500	$300	$280	$300	$880
3	$3000	1	$ 700	$200	$250	$100	$550
4	$3000	4	$2000	$200	$220	$200	$620
5	$1500	3	$1000	$250	$180	$300	$730

the length of time that cars are kept. Larger cars may be expected to require larger expenditures than smaller cars. Older cars are likely to need more repairs, but they should have lower costs for license, taxes, and collision insurance. (The cost of maintaining automobile liability insurance is not included in the calculation. This does not normally vary from car to car, and many individuals would want to carry insurance of this type even if they did not own a car, as long as they planned to operate one occasionally. Car insurance is discussed in more detail in Chapter 14.)

Another estimate is necessary to complete the appraisal of the various policies. Suppose that the prospective car purchaser thinks a 7% return is available on alternative assets such as common stock. Also, let us assume that policy 5 is the lowest cost transportation alternative he is willing to consider.

Varying initial expenditures are required under the different policies. Policy 1 requires that $4000 be used immediately, whereas policy 5 requires an initial outlay of only $1500. Since the use of money on a car means that the money cannot be used elsewhere, we will, as in the case of the household asset decisions, try to identify an annual cost for the money that is "tied up" by each of the different car policies. We call this cost the car's capital cost. When this is found, it can be added to the annual maintenance cost on each policy to determine each policy's implicit annual rent for the use of a car. To identify capital cost, it is first necessary to consider two subcategories of capital costs.

In policy 1, $4000 must first be committed to physical asset purchase. This asset then drops in value to $2500 at the end of two years. ($2500 is the difference between the value of a new car and the $1500 difference required to trade for a new car, when the original car is two years old.) Looking at the physical capital employed under policy 1 in another way, we can divide the original asset value into two components: $2500 that will remain at the end of the two year trade-in period and each following trade-in period and $1500 that will be used up in a trade-in period and have to be replaced every two years. Let us call these components *continuing capital* and *depreciating capital.*

The capital cost on continuing capital is simply the alternatively available (opportunity cost) rate of return (here, 7%) multiplied by the amount of continuing capital. In policy 1, this is $2500 × 7%, or $225 per year. That is the amount that $2500 could earn annually if it were not permanently used for providing a car.

Capital cost on the depreciating capital is the amount of annual payment that would be available to the prospective car buyer if $1500 were invested elsewhere and "used up" in two years. Depreciating capital cost can thus be identified as

$$P = \$1500$$
$$n = 2$$
$$r = 7\%$$
$$A = \text{unknown}$$

Solving, $A = \$830$ per year.

These two annual capital costs total $1055. Adding them to the $800 annual maintenance expense of policy 1 yields a total cost of $1855 per year for car ownership under policy 1. Table 8.2 summarizes this calculation and those for other policies. Total cost in this table is determined by adding total annual capital cost, assembled in Table 8.2, with total annual maintenance expense from Table 8.1.

TABLE 8.2

Policy	Continuing investment	Annual cost at 7%	Depre-ciating capital	Annual cost	Total annual capital cost	Implicit annual rent (Total capital cost and total maintenance cost from Table 8.1)
1	$2500	$175	$1500	$830	$1005	$1805
2	$1500	$105	$2500	$735	$ 840	$1720
3	$2300	$160	$ 700	$770	$ 930	$1480
4	$1000	$ 70	$2000	$590	$ 660	$1280
5	$ 500	$ 35	$1000	$345	$ 380	$1110

The prospective car purchaser can now observe that, according to his estimates, he can vary his car expense from a little less than $100 a month to over $150 per month depending on the policy that he elects. Choice between policies is obviously susceptible to marginal analysis in which the buyer decides whether or not each successive step up in car investment is worth the cost of undertaking it.

Another approach

Although most families would not consider being without a first car, a second car (or a third or a fourth) is usually a much more optional matter. An annual cost associated with various second car policies can be calculated along the lines just illustrated. However, it is usually very desirable in the case of the second car to not only inquire whether its services are worth the amount of its implicit rent but also whether alternative transportation is available at a lower cost. Sometimes a second car may be replaced by the use of taxis, buses, and rental cars on occasions when a second car is required without sacrificing much convenience and with a substantial reduction in annual cost.

Especially with the second car, consideration should also be given to facilities for car storage. If extra space is deemed necessary, the annual ownership cost of the extra space (garage) ought to be added in determining its full cost. However, before the garage is undertaken some thought might be given to the propriety of the garage as an investment; will it confer enough benefits to constitute an acceptable investment or would it be better to leave the second car outside?

Summary

Physical assets can be compared with other assets by the identification of an internal rate of return. However, a superior internal rate of return on a physical asset may not necessarily mean that the asset should be preferred over claims.

As in the case of other assets there is risk associated with the purchase of physical assets.

For most families the home is the most important physical asset purchased. Because homes are not normally bought with all cash, our analysis is based on the assumption that a first mortgage is used to finance a home purchase. To find rate of return on a house, a family first needs to identify the amount and timing of gross benefits they will receive from home ownership. The principal benefit will be rent saving. Ownership costs, including items such as taxes, repairs, and insurance, and first mortgage payments, are subtracted from gross benefits to obtain net benefits after first mortgage payments. These net benefits can then be used, along with the initial cash outlay required for the house, to obtain internal rate of return.

One major advantage of home ownership is that rent savings are benefits which are not subject to income tax. Two major disadvantages are the possible difficulty of resale if the family plans to live in the house only for a short time and the fact that a family or individual who requires only a small amount of space cannot usually find a suitable house that will provide accommodations of this size.

Condominiums and cooperatives may be attractive to some families because they can combine the size of an apartment with the tax advantages of home ownership.

To simplify analysis on smaller assets, an implicit rent approach is suggested. This approach attempts to identify for the family what the annual cost of owning a particular asset is each year. Once this cost is known it should be easier for the family to decide whether or not the benefits conferred by this asset are worth that cost.

This implicit rent approach is also applied to car purchase decisions. One can think of various car purchase policies and by applying the implicit rent approach he can compare the relative cost of the policies and then decide whether the relative benefits of the various policies are worth their cost differences.

SUGGESTED READINGS

For facts about a wide variety of physical assets, *Consumer Reports* is an excellent source. Another source, which often includes problems associated with home ownership, is the magazine, *Changing Times*.

Banks and other financial institutions make available various publications discussing the problems of deciding whether or not to buy a house and the associated problems of obtaining financing.

The Federal Housing Administration provides a variety of literature. A list of this literature can be obtained by writing the Office of Public Information, Federal Housing Administration, Washington, 25, D.C.

QUESTIONS

1. Why is a superior rate of return not always enough to justify the choice of a physical asset over a claim?
2. Try to recall some examples of "default" that you have experienced on physical assets. What ways can you suggest for coping with the possibility of "default" on future physical asset purchases?
3. Why are most house purchase decisions not in the "bare necessity" category even though, in most of the United States, shelter is probably necessary for survival?
4. What reasons can you advance for regarding security of tenure as being a benefit on which a family might place a substantial money value?
5. In your own case what value if any would you place on the "pride of ownership" that may go with owning your own home? What cost would you place on the necessity of doing extra household chores often associated with home ownership, such as lawn mowing or making minor repairs?
6. Why do you think that most individuals who buy houses borrow a substantial amount of the purchase price rather than wait until they have saved the cash necessary to purchase the house? (Consider the shifting of consumption over a period of time when you compose your answer.)
7. Try to find out whether the money value of your family's house or one like it has increased or decreased over the past five years. If possible, also obtain the information for an even longer period.
8. Explain the tax advantage offered by condominiums and cooperatives as compared to renting.
9. Is the implicit rent approach a more correct method of evaluating physical asset prospects than the internal rate of return method? If it is not more correct, what is the advantage of the implicit rent method?
10. Why has the analysis in this chapter been based on the assumption that a house would be financed by a mortgage but that financing would not be considered in analyzing a car purchase?

11. If you have the cash necessary to buy a car, why is it necessary to take capital costs into account in determining the implicit annual rent on the car?

PROBLEMS

1. You estimate gross annual benefits of $300 per month from home ownership. You also estimate ownership costs of $100 per month and mortgage payments of $150 per month. You can buy the house at a total cost of $5000, including down payment and other costs that will be incurred at the time of purchase. The mortgage pays off at the end of 20 years. You expect to live in the house for 30 years; at the end of this period you expect that the house will be worth $25,000. Calculate rate of return on this proposed house investment. Is this a before-tax or after-tax rate of return?
2. You can rent an apartment for $250 per month or you can obtain housing almost identical to the apartment by purchasing a condominium. You can purchase a condominium with no down payment and with monthly payments of $300 a month. These monthly payments include a service charge that provides you with all the maintenance services that you would normally expect to receive if you rented an apartment. Compose an example to illustrate why a family might be willing to pay $300 per month for the condominium in preference to paying $250 a month for a similar apartment.
3. You can buy a washer and dryer, installed, for $500. You expect that operating and repair costs on this equipment will be $80 per year. You expect that the equipment will last for eight years, and you feel that you could make a 7% after-tax return on claim purchases.
   (a) Calculate the implicit annual rent for the washer and dryer.
   (b) Specifically, how would you use this implicit figure to help determine whether or not you should buy the equipment?

chapter nine

Human capital and a review of asset policy

The topic of human capital relates principally to investments in education and training. Only in recent years has it become common to regard obtaining skills as a form of asset acquisition. This development has come about for at least two reasons. First, current levels of educational cost are now extremely high compared to earlier periods in history, and thus attention has been focused on analysis of the fruitfulness of educational expenditures. It is apparent that these expenses are not exclusively consumption, but represent the accumulation of a stock of wealth that is capable of conferring benefits in future time periods.

A second reason for the recent emphasis on human capital has been the failure of earlier systems of economic resource measurement to explain the path of economic development in various countries. Even though a country's total stock of physical assets (such as industrial plants, railroads, and housing) and its population were both growing moderately, the country might be rapidly increasing its standard of living. Broadening of the definition of capital to include human as well as physical capital form has substantially increased the ability of economists to explain why economic growth occurs.

Total analysis versus personal analysis

Human capital investments can influence the amount and timing of personal consumption. When an individual decides to give up current income or leisure and use his time to improve his skills, he gives up the opportunity for present consumption. In return he usually expects a future payoff in the form of higher income or other benefits which allow him to increase his future level of consumption. In this chapter we consider the cost to the individual of acquiring human capital and the benefits that will be gained as a result of this acquisition. As in the case of other assets, a comparison between benefits and costs can be made in the form of a rate of return identification.

To avoid confusion one needs to distinguish between the personal viewpoint toward human capital decisions and another attitude which often appears in written discussions of the topic. Writers, particularly those concerned with national economic policy, attempt to assess the total benefits and costs associated with investment in human capital rather than those that affect the individual who is undertaking the education. For example, nearly all colleges and other educational institutions are heavily supported by tax money and other outside sources, such as donations. Because of this support, an individual who goes to college usually pays only part of the total costs associated with providing his education. The individual deciding whether to undertake education needs to consider only those costs that he personally must bear. Thus his personal calculation of rate of return will differ from one based on total cost (sometimes called *total social cost*).

Similarly, the total social benefits from an education may differ from those which are received by an individual. For example, if an education results in an individual's becoming more productive, and hence capable of earning more, part of these earnings will be received by the individual as after-tax earnings and part will be drawn off by the government in the form of taxes. Thus the government or other citizens become a beneficiary as well as the individual. As another example, social scientists may observe that investments in human capital have some desirable (or undesirable) effects on the crime rate, with the result that the lives of other citizens are affected by an individual's participation in education. Again, an individual's decision should be based on benefits to be obtained personally. To conclude, it is very likely that personal return from education will differ from total social return.

Personal educational costs

Discussion in this section is confined to the costs of college education. Although primary and secondary education also represent the development of human capital, the undertaking of this education, because of compulsory school attendance laws and the pressure of current employment requirements and social usage, is usually not a matter of choice. Of course, the method of analysis developed here for the college education decision could be applied to the individual who is considering "dropping out" of an earlier educational phase.

The initial cost of acquiring human capital differs from physical capital and claims because opportunity costs are normally greater than direct money costs. The major opportunity costs are the earnings that the individual must give up at the time that he is undertaking the education. To identify these the individual needs to estimate the amount he would be able to earn, after tax, if he did not go to college and deduct from this the amount he expects to earn, after tax, during the years that he is going to college.

For example, Andrew Apt might estimate that if he takes a job after he leaves high school, he can earn $5000 a year after taxes. He also might estimate that summer and part-time work during his college period would yield $1500 a year, after tax. He thus estimates a $3500 annual opportunity cost.

Beyond opportunity costs there are some extra money costs of education. Colleges often provide students with information not only about tuition and fees but also about estimated other costs, such as those for books and field trips. When one uses the cost estimates, however, he should exclude items such as estimated expense for room and board in his cost calculation, since this expense is required even if the individual does not go to college. Suppose Andrew Apt estimates that his cost for tuition, fees, and other college-related expenses will be $1000 a year. Added to his $3500 opportunity cost, this makes his total cost per year an estimated $4500. There are two adjustments that should be performed before this figure is accepted as final.

The first adjustment arises from other expense differences that may occur because of attendance in college, beyond consideration of tuition and so forth. There is some chance that other expenses may be lower if college is attended. For example, since housing accomodations in college may be partly subsidized, this expense might lower. Because large numbers of college students are living on fairly limited budgets, an individual may find it rather easy to reduce living expenditures while going to college; he may wish to regard this absence of pressure for society-conforming expenditures as a cost difference that should be recognized. Suppose Andrew Apt's living expenses can be painlessly reduced by $50 per month because he attends college instead of working at his former job. The deduction of this $600 per year could result in a revision of his estimated annual cost from $4500 down to $3900.

The second adjustment is solely an individual question. Some persons may enjoy undertaking skill-building activities, such as college attendance, and others may not. Thus the money costs of human capital formation may not tell the whole story. By attempting to place a money value on the pleasure or pain of the educational process itself, a more conclusive measure of cost is obtained. However, only the person directly involved can decide that "I would pay $100 per month just for the fun of attending classes and learning new things" or "I would pay $100 per month for the pleasure of working at a regular job instead of studying." In our example we assume that Andrew Apt does not expect to obtain any extra enjoyment or loss of enjoyment from the process of going to college.

Usually the decision to go to college is made with the intention that more than one year of college will be undertaken. If Andrew Apt plans to attend college for four years, the cost of all four years should be considered in the decision to attend; thus he should express his cost of attending college as $3900 a year for four years.

Benefits from education

The most obvious personal benefit from education is enhancement of earning power. Unfortunately, there is often an element of exaggeration in estimates of the extra earning power of educated people. Sometimes the earnings of those who have attended college are compared with those who have not. One must not conclude on the basis that college graduates earn more than those who have not attended college that college will improve earning power.

Consider an example. A is an intelligent, energetic high school student from a prosperous, middle class family. B receives low grades in school and comes from a "deprived" economic and cultural background. A goes to college and prospers afterwards; B does not go to college and does not prosper.

One must probably conclude that A might have prospered without going to college. Certainly it would not be appropriate to tell B that by going to college he could earn the same income as A. In more general terms, the persons who *enter* college are probably better equipped by their abilities and cultural background to occupy high paying jobs. Therefore the fact that college graduates earn more does not *prove* that going to college provides increased incomes.

A carefully formulated estimate of increased earnings attributable to college must attempt to compare persons who attended college to persons with equal ability and background who did not attend. The individual, assessing the benefits of going to or remaining in college, must ask himself, "Will *I* be able to earn more with more education?"

Beyond increased income an individual may wish to consider other benefits that result from attending college. A person may feel that he is a better parent because he has attended college or he may feel that college will impart to him some extra social acceptability. An assessment of the personal benefits from college would have to include a money estimate of these items as well as the amount of after-tax income added by college attendance.

The timing of benefits will also have to be considered. It has been asserted that college graduates do not gain very much increase in pay during their first years out of college, but because of the entry that the college education gives them into managerial and professional positions, they are able to obtain substantial income benefits later in their careers. For example, Andrew Apt might want to make an estimate of his extra income from college in the following form.

AVERAGE EARNINGS FOR DIFFERENT TIME PERIODS

1975 (expected date of graduation)–1984		
Earnings if college is attended	$10,000	
Earnings if college is not attended	9,000	
Extra earnings from college	$ 1,000	
Tax on extra earnings (marginal rate 20%)[a]	—200	
Extra earnings after tax		$ 800
1985–1994		
Earnings if college is attended	$14,000	
Earnings if college is not attended	11,000	
Extra earnings from college	$ 3,000	
Tax on extra earnings (marginal rate 25%)[a]	—750	
Extra earnings after tax		$2,250
1995–2014 (calculations not shown)		
Extra earnings after tax		$3,000
2015–2024 (semiretirement)		
Extra earnings after tax		$1,000

[a] Marginal tax rate is estimated to increase as income rises.

The benefits from college may extend beyond an estimated retirement age. This would be possible if jobs available to the college graduate carried better retirement opportunities than those jobs available to the noncollege graduate.

The after-tax value of any other fringe benefits should also be included in examining the difference in earnings power obtainable by the college graduate. In the above example the estimation of benefits would not be complete until Andrew had considered adding an additional amount to express the money value he places on the nonmoney benefits, such as social standing, which he feels he will attain from college attendance. In order to keep our example simple, assume Andrew places no value on this extra category.

Identification of rate of return

This section contains a rather laborious computation. Unfortunately, there is no easier way of identifying rate of return on a personal investment in human capital. Although some comments are made later about academic studies that have attempted to find the rate of return on human capital investments, these studies are not likely to be directly applicable to the reader's personal situation. Thus emphasis must be placed on the *method* by which rate of return can be determined for each individual case. To aid in the personal calculation, some data on earnings in various occupations and from various levels of education are provided in the appendix at the end of this chapter.

Because the cost of a college education is spread out over a number of time periods and the level of benefits received is likely to vary in different time periods, the identification of rate of return on human capital is a laborious one. Since it is a search for r, a trial-and-error method must be used. In Andrew's situation costs were \$3700 per year for four years. His estimated costs and benefits are shown in Table 9.1.

To find r, he must experiment with different discount rates until he finds one that will cause the present value of costs to equal the present value of benefits.

This problem can be approached in two stages. First, for each of the five series of annual money amounts in Table 9.1, a present value can be found as of the beginning of the particular time period. For example, one would find the present value of the benefits from 2015 to 2024 to be, in 2015, the present value of $A = 1000$, $n = 10$, $r = 10\%$. This P is \$1000

TABLE 9.1

Costs	Per year amounts
1971–1974	\$3700
Benefits	
1975–1984	800
1985–1994	2250
1995–2014	3000
2015–2024	1000

TABLE 9.2

	A	n	P ($r = 10\%$)	in year ($r = 10\%$)
Costs	$3,700	4	$11,700	1971
Benefits	800	10	4,900	1975
	2,250	10	13,800	1985
	3,000	20	25,500	1995
	1,000	10	6,100	2015

$\times$ 6.145, or about $6100. Continuing to use an experimental r of 10% we can identify present values for all benefits and costs in Table 9.1. These are shown in Table 9.2.

Table 9.2 gives present values for various time periods—1971, 1975, 1985, 1995 and 2015. To compare these values, a second stage of analysis is necessary. If, for example, Andrew expects to receive a flow of benefits during semiretirement that will be worth a present value of $6100 in year 2015, we can next ask, "What is the present value of this $6100 in 1971?" To find this, we regard the $6100 as a future value to be received in 2015, or 44 years from 1971, and solve for P where F = $6100, n = 44, r = 10%. P = $6100 $\times$ about .015, or roughly $100. Similarly, other present values in 1971 can be identified as shown in Table 9.3.

From this we can observe that the rate of return on Andrew's proposed college education is under 10%. (Only if his benefits had a present value of $11,700 would his human capital yield 10%.)

To proceed with the search for r, set r experimentally at a lower value, say 9%. The results of this calculation are shown in Table 9.4. At 9% the present value of benefits and costs are quite close to equal. Thus Andrew's human capital is expected to return a little less than 9%, after tax.

Many academic studies have attempted to identify the rate of return on past investment in human capital. These estimates have varied enormously,

TABLE 9.3

	P ($r = 10\%$)	in year ($r = 10\%$)	n	P in 1971
Costs	$11,700	1971	0	$11,700
Benefits	4,900	1975	4	3,300
	13,800	1985	14	3,600
	25,500	1995	24	2,600
	6,100	2015	44	100
Total benefits (1971 present value)				$9,600

TABLE 9.4

	r = 9%			
	P	in year	n	P in 1971
Costs	$11,900	1971	0	$11,900
Benefits	5,100	1975	4	3,600
	14,400	1985	14	4,300
	27,300	1995	24	3,500
	6,400	2015	44	200
Total benefits (1971 present value)				$11,600

but in general suggest that human capital has compared favorably to other assets, such as common stock, in its rate of return. However, one must be very careful when reading any rates of return cited on human capital. For his own decision purposes he must make sure the return cited is the personal rate of return rather than the total social return. He should also look to see whether the author of the estimate has attempted to measure the impact of college education on people with similar ability and background. He would want to observe whether the estimate gave any recognition to the pleasure or displeasure derived from attending college and the nonmoney benefits which college might confer. (Most studies would not include these last items since they depend on personal tastes, but consideration of these by some individuals might substantially change the attractiveness of a human capital investment.)

Marginal Analysis

Human capital investments can be subjected to marginal analysis if one proposed course of study or choice of college appears to require different costs or to confer different benefits than another. A higher cost alternative can be compared with a lower cost one by analyzing the marginal benefits of the step upward in cost. One could also, at any point in a college career, apply marginal analysis and identify the additional costs and benefits to be derived from finishing an existing program or undertaking a new one. Since uncompleted college programs probably do not convey very much advantage to the student (although this certainly would not be true in all cases), it is possible that identification of marginal rate of return undertaken during the middle of a college program might indicate that finishing college was a good investment. This could be true even if the same person, had he identified rate of return when he started his college career, might not have gone.

This rather curious result is possible because if an individual is, say halfway through a two-year program and if an incompleted program in worthless, then the individual's choice, at the end of one year, is (a) go one more year and gain all benefits or (b) quit the program and lose all benefits. Therefore the individual's marginal benefit from staying another year turns out to be all of the benefits from the whole program.

"Default" Possibilities

Like other assets the benefits conferred upon the individual undertaking a college education are not predictable. No individual can foretell precisely how he is going to respond to college or to his employment afterwards; therefore he cannot be certain of the amount of benefits that will be obtained. Although not very much has been written on the topic, it is possible that an individual could not only identify different rates of return on different courses of study, such as law or education, but also identify different degrees of safety in different human capital investment opportunities. A guess would be that education, because of its shorter course of study, the secure jobs available to teachers, and the student's greater familiarity with the life of the teacher than with the life of the lawyer, would provide the safer undertaking. Like other safe investments it might also afford a lower return, although this is only a speculation.

Technical schools and night classes

Technical schools can be analyzed in the same way as a college education. At least one academic study has suggested that the post-high school technical education may have a higher return than a college education. This does not imply that many persons now going to college would be better off transferring to technical schools; not everyone would be suited for or wish to undertake the jobs for which technical schools train. These jobs would certainly restrict the earning power of many present college students. However, the return on technical schools does suggest that some individuals can profitably undertake these courses of study and the concept of human capital should not be limited to the college situation.

Similarly, enrollment in night classes might provide a rewarding field toward human capital investment. These classes might be undertaken at a low cost if the student enjoyed the class and did not mind using his existing leisure in this way. In this case no opportunity cost would have to be included in the rate of return calculation and, thus even a fairly low level of benefits might provide an acceptable investment return.

Job selection as a form of human capital acquisition

An individual may also undertake human capital investment by selecting a job that he thinks provides educational advantage, even though this job does not pay as well as some existing opportunities. For example, an individual might be able to earn more as an unskilled laborer than he could if he entered an apprenticeship program for a skilled trade. However, the after-tax income foregone by entering the trade (some of this might be offset because the apprenticeship was more stimulating work) could well yield an acceptable rate of return because of future increases in earning power and job satisfaction.

One note of caution is in order. Sometimes a prospective employer will ask an individual to accept lower pay because of the learning opportunities in his job. One can think of this as an investment opportunity, but a careful attempt should be made to see whether the benefits promised actually exist. Sometimes, especially in jobs such as management training, firms who can hire employees very cheaply are tempted to use them for routine tasks. At the same time, firms who pay more for their employees feel an incentive to subject them to more intensive training so that they can more quickly fit into skilled jobs where they are productive enough to justify their higher salaries.

Preventive medicine as a human capital investment

Education is not the only form of self-improvement that an individual can undertake. Much has been written about the total social returns available on health expenditures. It should also be noted that some health expenditures can be regarded as the procurement of an asset by an individual. Often the cost of preventative medical expenditures, such as thorough check-ups and innoculations, even when the time required to undergo them is given an opportunity cost value, are of almost negligible cost. Yet the undertaking of these costs may lead to large future benefits in the form of possible longer life, increased productivity and hence earning power, and freedom from discomfort.

Human capital reconsidered

Some people still do not think of the undertaking of education or other forms of self-improvement as an asset acquisition. Yet we have seen that costs incurred for such purposes may yield increased future consumption opportunities. Thus they conform to our definition of assets. Accordingly it is appropriate for us to consider human capital undertakings in comparison with other investment opportunities, since individuals might increase their well-being by switching from the accumulation of physical assets or claims to the acquisition of human capital. On the other side of the coin, some individuals might benefit themselves more by giving up some education and investing instead in other forms of assets.

The general asset selection problem

We have now considered the general problem of making selections from various asset alternatives and examined the three classes of these alternatives in some detail. The method of analysis we have suggested has been the ranking of claims, human capital, and houses by marginal rate of return. When return identification was too difficult, as in the case of smaller physical assets, the use of a marginal return available elsewhere to calculate implicit rent was suggested. When examining these methods, we admitted that the estimates involved would sometimes be rather crude and that other considerations as well as rate of return could be important in personal asset choice. Nevertheless, without this attempt at a systematic comparison of asset opportunities, one would almost certainly be left with a cruder process for his asset selection decisions. Before considering the direction that the analysis is going to take during the remainder of this text, two other general issues on asset selection can now be usefully introduced: inflation and the effect of asset choices on borrowing opportunities.

Inflation

Inflation, used in the sense in which it means rising prices, has become a household word. Price rises are not necessarily harmful to a particular family, but they may be. The difficulties (and there may also be benefits) that arise from inflation are attributable to the fact that some prices rise more rapidly than others. For example, if the price of the items purchased by a family rises by 5% in one year but the family income also rises by 5% in that year, then the family may not be harmed by the inflation. Since the family income itself is based on price (the price of the husband's labor, for example), it is not unreasonable to suppose that many incomes will keep pace with rising prices of goods and services purchased.

Some types of income are much more rigid than other types during inflationary periods and may cause their recipient to be injured by the inflation. To analyze the effects of inflation we need a measurement for change in the prices of items bought by families. The most widely used measure of price change is the Consumer Price Index. A price index is a percentage comparison between prices in various periods. Its construction consists of comparing prices in one period, called a base period, and prices in other periods expressed as a percentage of base period prices. For example, if 1970 is selected as a base period and the average price of goods bought by families has increased by 20% by 1975, the 1975 price index would be 120 (prices in 1975 are 120% of what they were in the base period, 1970).

Suppose an individual starts to draw a $6000 per year retirement pension in 1970. By 1975, because the price of goods has risen, the purchasing power of the pension has declined. Since prices have risen to 120% of their 1970 level, or 6/5 of the base level, dollars received in 1975 will buy only 5/6 as many goods as they would in 1970. We can, if we wish, say that the 1975 dollar is worth 5/6 or 83% as much as the 1970 dollar. The pensioner's $6000 in 1975 will buy the same amount of goods as only $5000 would in 1970.

The importance of protection against inflation needs to be recognized in the asset selection process. If the amount of dollar benefits from some assets rise during periods of inflation and thus protect their recipient against rising prices of goods he has to buy, this characteristic should be given recognition when comparing these assets with others whose return is rigid during inflationary periods.

The erosion of money's buying power by inflation appears to be substantial. In the 25-year period from 1945 through 1969, the Consumer Price Index (CPI) approximately doubled, with an annual compound increase of nearly 3% through the period. In the shorter period from 1960 through 1969, the inflation rate was lower, at about 2%. In a longer period from 1920 through 1969 (which includes the Great Depression), CPI increases were at the annual rate of a little over 1%.

One can also note that the inflation rate has not been stable. Within the 50-year period mentioned, the annual rates have been over 10% and almost down to —10% (price decline) in individual years. In allowing for inflation on asset purchases, one needs to formulate an expected rate; with this erratic history any such formulation contains a substantial element of guesswork. The difficulty is compounded even further by the fact that the CPI is itself subject to some controversy among statisticians and economists and has been alleged by some reputable economists to exaggerate the amount of inflation.

In general, physical capital that yields benefits in the form of services is likely to offer inflation protection. If prices in general are rising, the prices of items such as housing and appliances will probably also rise. Therefore the dollar value of benefits received by the owners of houses and appliances will probably also rise and keep pace with the inflation. Since human capital investments yield much of their benefit in the form of increased income and many incomes rise during inflationary periods (unless they are rigidly specified in some contract, such as a pension agreement), there is also reason to suppose that the benefits from human capital will be inflation protected.

A further note on benefit estimation

There is apt to be some confusion in the relationship between expected inflation and the formulation of asset estimates. To illustrate this problem in estimation, an example will be helpful. In 1970 a college graduate is considering going on for a master's degree. To help him make his decision he assembles the following statistics about the salaries of other people who (a) hold master's degrees in the same field of study and (b) have only bachelor's degrees in that field.

Year in which degree was granted	Salaries of holders of bachelor's degrees	Salaries of holders of master's degrees
1969	$ 8,000	$ 9,000
1960	11,000	13,000
1950	13,000	16,000

He is satisfied that these figures are appropriate measures of the difference in his own earnings ability, with and without his master's degree. On the basis of this information, he reaches the following preliminary conclusion about the effect of a master's degree on salary.

Years out of college	Salary difference
Just out	$1000
10 years	2000
20 years	3000

He then asks himself the following two questions.

1. These are salary differences that prevail now; when I have worked 10 or 20 years, will the difference due to a master's degree be greater?
2. If the answer to question 1 is Yes, will that difference just be due to inflation and hence just be in the form of extra money, without extra purchasing power?

In answer to the first question, we note that in general salaries have been rising, even on an after-tax basis. Over the 20-year period in the example, they have increased by about 5% per year in the United States. At the same time, however, two other factors have been present. There has been inflation, which we take up when we answer question 2, and there has been substantial investment in human capital.

To the extent that human capital increases have been responsible for salary changes, the historical rate of salary increase would not provide much hope for the individual in our example. Average salary changes in the past would have been caused by people undertaking investments just like his; and he could thus not look for any *extra* income increases beyond his already projected earnings difference.

On the other hand, if human capital changes were not solely responsible for past salary increases, he might then have reason to believe that as an investor in human capital, he could expect the salary difference he had projected, plus some share in general growth as well. Thus the answer to question 1 is not yet clear.

To question 2 we can first say that we have had inflation in the past and there is no reason to expect that we shall not have it in the future. In the past 20 years, when salaries were rising about 5% a year, inflation at an annual rate of about 2% was occurring. Thus "real" salaries, after considering the declining purchasing power of money, were only rising at about 3%. If an individual is to expect any future increase in real salary, the history of the past 20 years suggests that it will only be about 3% at most.

Now, to return again to question 1, experts are not sure of the full relationship between human capital investment and salary increases. Certainly though, some of the 3% "real" increase would have been caused by human capital investment. Maybe the individual is justified in predicting a 1 or 2% annual increase in "real" benefits to be derived from human capital investment, but 3% would definitely be too large. At the least it seems reasonable to assume that there will be some "real" increase above the inflation rate and therefore benefits on human capital, estimated on the basis of current salary levels, as in our example, are likely at least to be adequately inflation protected.

Inflation and claims

Although we have assumed that investments in physical and human capital are inflation protected, this assumption cannot be extended to all claims. Interest and principal payments on bonds and mortgages in particular, which are rigidly fixed in dollar amount, offer no direct protection against inflation. To compensate for this inadequacy, one should deduct the expected inflation rate (on the basis of history 1% to 3% might be a reasonable guess) from the after-tax yield on bonds or mortgages. The deduction is made from the after-tax yield because any loss in purchasing power from inflation is not a tax-deductible expense. Thus, for a person in a 30% marginal tax bracket who expects 2% annual inflation, a bond yielding 7% before tax would yield 5% after tax adjustment and 3% after inflation adjustment. We will refer to this 3% as an after-tax, inflation-adjusted rate.

Common stocks differ from bonds in that they are shares in the net worth of corporations and consequently, if the corporations keep pace with inflation, the stocks will too. The principal danger in the relation of stock purchase decisions to inflation probably lies in a potential double-counting error. We can recall from Chapter 6 that the yield on a stock could be estimated either with the simple approach of adding the current dividend rate to the growth rate or making specific projections of dividends and prices. If these estimates of growth rates and projections of dividend and price changes are (a) in money amounts and (b) based on the assumption of future inflation, then the yield calculated on the stock will be a money yield that is not inflation adjusted. Because projections are likely to be based on experience in a past and therefore inflationary period, there is a good chance that stocks' rates of return may be based on inflationary expectations. To both calculate this type of yield and then to assert that the stock will keep up with future inflation, too, is to count the stock's protection against inflation twice—once in formulating the yield estimate and again in stating that the yield is safe from inflation.

For example, one might observe that a stock was currently paying a $4 dividend and that from 1960 to 1970 the price of this stock had risen from $50 per share to $100 per share, a compound annual rate of price increase of 7%. Thus he might at first think of this stock as affording a $4 dividend return and a 7% price increase during 1970. His marginal tax rate is 30%. To obtain an after-tax rate of return, he may calculate

Dividend	$4.00	
Tax on dividend at 30%	−1.20	
After-tax dividend	$2.80	
After-tax dividend rate ($2.80 on $100 current price)		2.8%
Before-tax rate of price increase	7%	
Reduction of rate of price increase by tax at 15%	−1.05%	
After-tax growth rate		5.95%
After-tax rate of return on stock		8.75%

He may believe that the dividend will rise to keep pace with any current inflation, but, if there has been inflation between 1960 and 1970, he cannot expect that his stock price rise will be 7% (5.95% after tax) net of inflation. Since the inflation rate from 1960 to 1970 was about 2%, he could therefore say that, after tax, the *real* rate of increase in the value of his stock had been 5.95% − 2%, or 3.95%. Thus his return on the stock would be a dividend rate of 2.8% plus 3.95% *real* rise in share value, or a total return of 6.75% as an inflation-protected, tax-adjusted rate of return.

In general, the *real* after-tax return on a stock ought to be regarded as the after-tax rate of return (dividends and price increase) minus the inflation rate that is expected to occur in the future.

The reader may recall that in Chapter 6 we noted that various scientific studies of common stock performance suggested that, on the average, stocks had provided an after-tax return of 7%. Although inflation problems were not discussed in Chapter 6, we may now note that this return was determined *after* adjustment for inflation. We can therefore amend the previous statement to note that stocks have provided a 7% real after-tax return on the average. It therefore may be reasonable, at least for those who use a dart strategy, to assume that common stocks are likely to provide an inflation-protected, after-tax 7% return in the future.

Returns: inflation protected or inflation adjusted

One may note a distinction in word usage in these sections on inflation. We have referred to the returns on human and physical capital and stocks as *inflation protected*, and the return bonds and mortgages as *inflation adjusted*. The difference lies in the fact that inflation rates have been, and will probably continue to be, rather erratic. When we refer to an inflation-protected asset, we are denoting an asset whose dollar net benefits can probably keep up with the inflation rate, whatever it happens to be, and whose real net benefits are therefore unaffected by inflation. For example, returns on human capital are regarded as inflation protected because money wages and salaries are expected to rise during inflationary periods.

On the other hand, assets subject to inflation adjustment have dollar net benefits that are fixed, and do not keep up with inflation. Therefore the real net benefits from these assets decline during inflation. The best we can do in evaluating the prospects for these assets is to deduct an estimated inflation rate, and convert their after-tax rate of return to an inflation-adjusted one. For example, benefits from bonds are not inflation protected, and hence must be inflation adjusted, to compensate for an expected rate of inflation.

More general comments on inflation

To consider the effect of expected inflation on asset adjustment, let us look at another example. An individual is considering three investments: human capital with an estimated after-tax return of 8%, bonds with an estimated after-tax return of 7%, and a house with an estimated after-tax return of 5%, before any inflation adjustment is undertaken. If one assumes that a 3% inflation rate is expected, the estimated after-tax return on bonds is reduced to 4% and they move from second place to third place in the investment alternatives.

A note of caution is in order. Bonds and other assets that yield fixed money returns are not necessarily undesirable during inflationary periods. If the inflation is widely expected, many individuals sell, or avoid buying, fixed return assets; hence their prices fall and their yield rises. Therefore some of these claims may be acceptable asset purchases during periods when inflation is expected because their rate of return before inflation adjustment is high enough to compensate for the expected inflation rate.

We should also observe that there are no assets that are entirely inflation protected. During inflation, prices rise at different rates and there is always a chance that the returns on some particular type of asset will be left behind. However, the fact that inflation is difficult to predict ought not to deter the individual from recognizing that some inflation seems to be a fact of life in the United States or to keep him from penalizing those assets which, by their very nature, offer no chance of keeping pace with inflation.

Remaining issues relating to assets

Assets are accumulated by saving (increases in net worth) or borrowing. Thus one needs to ask not only what kinds of assets should be held, but whether it is worthwhile to either save or borrow for purposes of building assets.

These questions are intimately connected with the timing of consumption desired by particular families. If a family wants to increase future consumption at the expense of present consumption, it should save. If it wants the services of some assets, such as a house, but does not want to give up present consumption to the extent required for a house purchase, it should borrow for the asset accumulation.

Before we can answer in detail the question of how much saving and borrowing a family should undertake, we need to consider the family's desires for a lifetime pattern of consumption. Thus it is advantageous to leave the detailed answers to the questions, "How much should be saved and how much should be borrowed?" (or what amount of total assets should be held) until Chapter 15 and 16, which deal with lifetime economic plans.

The remainder of the book

We want to build toward the development of a lifetime financial plan for an individual, not with the intention that the individual ought to bind his actions to this plan for life, but that the development of a plan will enable him to more effectively examine the consequences of some of the decisions that he is making now. In the development of a plan one thing that we need to consider is the provision that an individual makes for various misfortunes and uncertain events that may occur in the future. To introduce this topic Chapter 10 deals with the issue of risk and one method of providing for it. Chapter 11 recognizes that some protection against risk and some future financial benefits are provided by government, employers, and others, and attempts to relate these facts to the development of a comprehensive economic plan. Chapters 12 and 13 then consider insurance, a major way in which individuals protect themselves against financial misfortune and attempt to provide themselves with future benefits.

After we have considered these issues, we return to the question of how assets are financed by considering borrowing policy. Then, within the context of a lifetime financial plan, we return to basic issues such as the appropriate amount of saving and borrowing, and the possibility of "managing" the availability of consumption during different periods of an expected lifetime.

Summary

When earning power is used for self-improvement, human capital is formed. Money expenditures such as tuition may also be required in formation of human capital. However, the opportunity cost of giving up earning power that could have been used to earn money income is likely to be the most important cost of human capital for the individual.

When one reads information about the rate of return on human capital, he needs to distinguish between the social benefits and costs of human capital and the benefits and costs that affect the individual. For an individual decision about whether or not to undertake the acquisition of human capital, the appropriate rate of return is that obtained by comparing after-tax costs, including opportunity costs, with after-tax future benefits. As in other assets there is risk in human capital.

Inflation, or rising prices, appears to be a fact of life in the United States. The most widely used indicator of inflation is the Consumer Price Index; the history of the past several decades suggests that prices may rise at a rate of 2% per year. (This is a highly uncertain prediction; but it appears superior to ignoring the problem and thus implicitly predicting no inflation.)

When one projects the benefits that he will obtain from human capital, he should base these projections on current earnings levels, after tax. Although future *money* incomes will almost certainly be greater than the projected amount, these projections may still be quite accurate in terms of *real* income.

Wages and salaries cannot be expected to rise much faster than inflation, but there is good reason to believe that most wages and salaries will keep up to the rate of inflation; thus we may regard most job income as inflation protected.

Returns on common stock and physical assets may also be regarded as inflation protected, but returns in the form of fixed dollar amounts, such as those on bonds, require inflation adjustment. A person buying a bond needs to subtract the inflation rate from the bonds' after-tax rate of return before comparing the bond to inflation-protected asset possibilities.

SUGGESTED READINGS

The topic of human capital is now discussed in most elementary economic textbooks. One widely used text of this type is *Economics*, 8th ed., by Paul Samuelson (New York: McGraw-Hill, Inc., 1970). Two widely cited academic discussions of human capital are Gary S. Becker, *Human Capital: A Theoretical and Empirical Analysis* (New York: Columbia University Press National Bureau of Economic Research, 1964) and T. W. Schultz, "Investments in Human Capital," *American Economic Review*, 1961.

The topic of inflation is also discussed in the book by Samuelson just cited, as well as in current magazine and newspaper articles. The magazine, *Changing Times*, has frequent discussions of the problem.

QUESTIONS

1. What value would you place on the stock of human capital that you currently hold? (Do not attempt to evaluate the elementary and high school training you have received.) How did you determine the original cost of the human capital that you had acquired?
2. Do you think that human capital depreciates? Justify your answer.
3. Do you feel that you have derived any nonmoney benefits from past investments in human capital? What money value would you place on these benefits?
4. Discuss the problems of identifying the rate of return on human capital by comparing the earnings of those who have acquired the human capital to those who have not.
5. How can preventative medicine be regarded as human capital?
6. Define inflation and explain the statement, "During inflation, the value of money falls."
7. What is the Consumer Price Index? What has been the historical behavior of this index?
8. Why do we use current earnings information in projecting the benefits that will be received from human capital investments?
9. What effect does inflation have on the recipient of a fixed income, such as a bondholder or a person receiving a fixed pension?
10. What are inflation-adjusted and inflation-protected returns?
11. Look at the data in the appendix of this chapter. Suppose you thought that you were personally capable of earning the projected incomes of an industrial buyer without going to college or those of an engineer if you went to college. What factors would determine your choice?

PROBLEMS

1. By going to college for another year, X thinks he can earn $500 more, after tax, for each of the following 40 years. If he did not go to college, X could earn take-home pay of $6000. He estimates that his cost for tuition

and books during the year of college will be $800 and that he well be able to save about $1000 per year on his housing cost by living in the university-subsidized housing while he attends college. Estimate rate of return on the proposed human capital investment.

2. Joe Brown starts work at a job where he earns take-home pay of $7000 per year. By the end of ten years his take-home pay is increased to $12,000 per year. At the time he began work the consumer price index was 140; after ten years this index has advanced to 165. By what proportion had Joe's real take-home pay increased during the ten years?
3. In 1972 X buys a bond for a price of 90, in a bond series described as 6s of 80. His marginal tax bracket is 30% and he expects 2% annual inflation. What after-tax, inflation-adjusted rate of return does he expect on the bond?

Appendix

To aid in projecting benefits from human capital, two sets of information are provided in this section. The first (Table 9A.1) is estimated "take-home" pay after taxes and other deductions from a number of jobs. Pay is given for various levels. The junior level of pay would be that approximate pay which could be expected during the first several years of the job. The middle range of pay would apply to persons who were moderately successful in the job after their first several years. Senior levels of pay would be available only to persons who proved to be more than moderately capable in their job, and usually only after 10 or 15, or more, years on the job.

TABLE 9A.1

SAMPLE JOBS AND THEIR ESTIMATED AVERAGE TAKE-HOME PAY, 1971

	Accountant	Attorney	Office management	Industrial buying	Draftsman
Junior	$ 7,500	$ 9,000	$ 9,000	$ 7,000	$5,000
Middle	8,500	13,000	12,000	8,000	7,000
Senior	12,000	23,000	14,000	11,000	8,500

	Personnel management	Chemist	Engineer	Engineering technician
Junior	$ 9,000	$ 8,000	$ 9,000	$5,500
Middle	11,000	13,000	13,000	6,500
Senior	17,000	21,000	16,000	9,000

SOURCE: Bureau of Labor Statistics data for 1968, adjusted upward by estimated three year income increase of 15% and downward for estimated income and social security taxes, state income taxes, and other payroll deductions. Tax calculations assume a family of four and standard deduction.

A second set of information (Table 9A.2) is provided about average income differences by educational categories. This table should be used with caution for two reasons. As noted earlier in this chapter, the association of higher incomes with higher education does not prove that education necessarily causes higher incomes. Also the incomes included here are total incomes, after deductions, and therefore may include interest and other nonsalary earnings.

TABLE 9A.2
ESTIMATED AVERAGE TAKE-HOME PAY BY EDUCATIONAL LEVEL, 1971

Level of education	Estimated take-home pay
Less than 8 years elementary school	$ 5,000
8 years elementary school	6,500
1–3 years high school	8,000
4 years high school	9,000
1–3 years college	10,000
4 years college	12,000

SOURCE: U.S. Bureau of Census data, projected by same method as data in Table 9A.1.

chapter ten

Risk and liquid assets

A complete financial plan should consider the earning power of a family (or single person) over its expected lifetime and the lifetime needs and desires of the family for consumption (including possibly, gifts to others and the formation of an estate—a special type of gift). An individual might begin planning with a very simple set of estimates along the lines given in Table 10.1. These estimates have been prepared on the assumption that the planner is 30 years old and expects to live to 75.

If the family assumes that savings can be invested at 5%, it can, by the methods discussed in Chapter 3, verify that its consumption desires can be met. To review, the future value of the savings in the first decade can be found as

$$\begin{aligned} A &= \$1000 \\ n &= 10 \\ r &= 5\% \\ F &= \text{unknown} \end{aligned}$$

This value is about $12,600. During the second

TABLE 10.1

	Age of wage earner			
	31–40	41–50	51–60	(Retirement) 61–75
Estimated annual after-tax earnings from employment	$8,000	$ 9,500	$10,000	None
Estimated annual consumption expenditures	7,000	10,000[a]	7,000	$4,000
Estimated annual savings	1,000	—500	3,000	—4,000
Years from present	1–10	11–20	21–30	31–45

[a] Children in college.

decade, when children are in college, dissaving of $500 per year is desired. The present value of this $500 stream at the beginning of year 11, $3900, can be deducted from the value of compounded savings at the end of year 10, $12,600, leaving a balance of $8700. This balance (*not* needed for college), can be compounded to $14,000 at the end of the second decade. During the third decade, not only does the $14,000 continue to grow but another $3000 annuity compounds. The combined future values of these amounts is $60,000, the amount available when retirement begins. The value (at the beginning of year 31) of the anticipated retirement needs ($A = 4000$, $n = 15$) is about $42,000; therefore not only are retirement needs provided for, but $18,000 is available to start building an estate. By age 75 this amount will have grown to $38,000, the amount of the expected estate.

If the estate is not large enough or if the family's income was less or its consumption desires more, ways of amending the plan would have to be considered. The family might try to increase earnings by giving up leisure or reduce its spending plans for some time periods.

Let us now take another look at the very simple financial plan illustrated and subject it to some questions. What will happen to the family if the husband becomes disabled at age 35 and thus has his earnings interrupted? What will happen if serious inflation occurs and this inflation is of such a nature that the cost of education for the children rises much more rapidly than the family's income does? What will happen if the estimated rate of return on savings does not materialize? In each of these cases we can envision the plan going awry with the result that the family's consumption desires are thwarted during the latter part of its life.

We can identify two major causes of disruption of a financial plan. First, benefits may not materialize as expected. A wage earner may be disabled or die unexpectedly and leave a family without a paycheck. In addition to this potential loss of income from work, other expected benefits from human capital may fail to materialize if the husband is not as successful in his career as he originally expected.

Second, consumption requirements may be higher than anticipated. Serious illness or accident may result in large medical and hospital expenses. An family member may accidentally injure someone and be subjected to a costly law suit and damage settlement. Or one may simply live longer than expected, and thus be required to meet prolonged consumption requirements.

There are a number of actions that an individual can take to cope with these potential interruptions in the financial plan which we will call *risk*. One of these actions, discussed in later chapters, is the purchase of insurance policies. The second, usually available only to individuals who are quite young, is the consideration of security of earnings in the selection of a career. Attempts can also be made to select assets that offer safe returns. A special case of asset selection, analyzed later in this chapter, is the maintenance of liquid assets, such as cash, which are used as reserves to provide a buffer against unexpected income interruptions or increased consumption requirements.

In each of these cases we see that protection against risks is not available without cost. Insurance policies require premiums. Safe jobs and safe assets may yield lower incomes and benefits than more venturesome ones (since more individuals are competing for safe jobs and investment opportunities). The accumulation of liquid assets may result in the holding of assets that yield almost no rate of return or even, in some cases, a negative return.

Risk control

Before considering the incurring of costs for risk control, it is first useful to examine the idea of risk in more detail. Consider one example of a risky situation. Suppose an individual has estimated that in a given year he will earn $10,000 from a job. If we were to question him about how he had formed his estimate, he might tell us that he thought that $10,000 was more likely to occur than other possible incomes, but that he could foresee the possibility of his income being more or less than $10,000. He might tell us that he thought his income could go as low as $8000 or as high as $12,000.

With this information we can now view the individual's income estimate as containing two dimensions. One of these, $10,000, is the income that best describes his general expectation; we may call this a *mean expected* amount. The other dimension, which we may describe as "plus or minus $2000," is the amount by which he thinks his income could possibly vary from his mean expected estimate. This range of possible variation around the mean expected estimate is the dimension usually called risk.

For example, the individual might also consider another job with a mean expected income of $12,000 per year but with possibilities for income as high as $20,000 or as low as $5000. In this case, the risk dimension could be described as "+$6000 or —$7000." Perhaps this second job is selling cars, from which income may vary because of the amount of sales commissions earned, whereas the first job is an office job in which the uncertainty in the individual's estimate is based only on the question in his mind about how rapidly he would be promoted. One can observe that each job is superior in one dimension: the salesman's mean expected income is higher, but the office job is freer from risk. Thus the salesman, in formulating a financial plan, could perhaps plan for more consumption, but at the same time he would be exposed to a greater chance that his planned consumption would be interrupted, leaving him worse off than the office employee.

The problem in risk control will always be one of this nature. An individual will often have the opportunity of reducing risk in his flow of lifetime consumption, but the risk reduction will be at the cost of lowering mean expected consumption. We return to a more intense discussion of coping with risks in following chapters; in the remainder of this chapter, we consider one possible device for risk control—the accumulation of liquid assets.

Liquid assets

The assets classified as liquid assets include cash and special types of claims that can be very safely and conveniently converted into cash. Liquid assets are themselves relatively free from risk although we shall see that none of them are completely risk-free. Liquid assets, in addition to cash, include bank deposits, accounts in saving and loan associations and credit unions, and certain types of short-lived and safe securities.

There are two principal reasons for holding liquid assets. First, some of these assets are accumulated as a matter of convenience. For example, an individual who receives his paycheck and finds some of it remaining after bills are paid may not wish to spend the balance immediately on consumption or on the types of assets discussed in the previous chapters. Instead he may hold this remaining balance in cash or in a bank deposit with the intention of using it later for consumption or for the purchase of other assets. In other words, individuals hold some cash and deposits because it is inconvenient to use all money at the time it is received.

Second, an important use for liquid assets is for the maintenance of reserves as a protection against risk. The receipt of income may be delayed or some unexpected expense may occur. To cover situations of this type, in which consumption or asset purchase plans would otherwise have to be interrupted, it is often convenient to have a stock of liquid assets which can be drawn upon to meet unusual cash requirements. This stock can then be restored in later periods.

Cash forecasting

In an attempt to determine the amount of liquid assets that it is desirable to hold, a very simple form of estimating cash requirements can be used. This type of cash estimate, or cash budget, is a special type of financial plan that is useful for examining the immediate future. Potential cash shortages that may occur within a short period, such as a few months hence, are especially difficult to cope with since major alterations of an individual's economic planning often take time to make. If persistent cash shortages are expected for a long period of time, an individual can adjust by selling assets, by arranging borrowing, or by reducing consumption. For example, a curtailment of consumption by $20 a month may do a lot for an individual's long-term problems, but will not help very much in coping with cash shortages within a month or two.

An example of a cash budget is shown in Table 10.2. This budget is prepared for each month of a forthcoming year. It is simply a listing of all the money that a family expects to take in and to pay out regardless of purpose during the year. Note that interest collected by the family is included among the receipts, as is an amount ($1050) which will be obtained when a bond owned by the family matures. Similarly, note that the cash payments include items such as an appliance purchase and loan repayments as well as spending for items to be consumed during the year.

Money coming in is added together and called total inflows. The sum of money paid out is called total outflows. The row below total inflows, which is called net inflows, is determined by subtracting total outflows from total inflows. During months when outflows exceed inflows, net inflows are negative. For example, since March inflows are $700 and outflows are $1250, March net inflows are designated as − $550 to show a cash deficiency, or net outflow.

The bottom line of Table 10.2, which is called cumulative inflow, tells what the relationship between the family's inflows and outflows has been up to and including each particular month. To find cumulative inflow, one adds the net inflows for all previous months to the particular month. For January, since there are no previous months in 1971, cumulative inflow is the same as net inflow, $310. In February, January's net inflow of $310 is added to February's net inflow of $170 to provide a cumulative inflow of $480. By the end of February, the family expects to accumulate total net inflows of $480.

In March, net inflows are shown as – $550. Since the family expected to accumulate $480 by the end of February and to have a net outflow of $550 that month, a cumulative net outflow of – $70 is indicated to note an expected cash deficiency.

By April, things look better and the family expects to be ahead of their beginning-of-the-year position by $1130. However, somehow the family will have to cope with the shortage which will occur *before* April.

One guideline suggested in preparing such a budget is to delay the estimation of cash receipts for one month. If William Coke's pay in Table 10.2 was to have increased from $700 to $750 in June, the impact of the pay increase is not recorded until July. The reason for this is that pay and other receipts may arrive at the end of the month or sometime during the month, but later than cash must be paid out. Thus the pay increase to $750 is regarded as first usable in July, not in June.

The cash budget in Table 10.2 shows, as we have noted, that a $70 cumulative outflow will occur in March. This deficiency need not be serious. If the family starts the year with some money in the bank (over $70), it could draw on this previously accumulated cash to meet the current deficiency. If a cash reserve was not available at the beginning of the period, the family would have to cover the deficiency by another method, such as borrowing, postponement of the air conditioner purchase, or arranging delayed payment on the dental bills.

Each of these alternatives has some disadvantages. Postponement of the air conditioner purchase may cause the family to miss a "preseason discount" which it had been planning on. Arranging a loan will probably involve a little inconvenience and will necessitate the payment of interest. Delaying payment of the dental bill will also involve the trouble of making special arrangements or, if nothing else, may be a blow to the pride of a family which likes to meet its bills promptly.

In addition to forecasting known cash requirements, a cash budget may also cause its preparer to reflect the consequences of unpredictable cash requirements. What would be the consequences if the dental bill were $200 higher than the estimated? Or if major car repairs were required during the year? The cash budget will probably suggest two courses of action to its preparer. One of these will be to attempt to either increase expected cash inflows (this is not often possible within a short time period, but part-time employment for the wife and moonlighting are possibilities) or curtail expected outflows through restriction of consumption or asset purchases. We can jointly classify these measures as an attempt to increase the mean expected net inflow of cash to the individual.

A second course of action that ought to be suggested by examining the

TABLE 10.2
WILLIAM COKE'S CASH BUDGET, 1971

	Jan.	Feb.	Mar.	Apr.	May	Jun.	Jul.	Aug.	Sep.	Oct.	Nov.	Dec.
Cash to be received												
Salary	$700	$700	$700	$700	$700	$700	$750	$750	$750	$750	$750	$750
Interest	60						60					
Maturing of bond				1050								
Total inflows	760	700	700	1750	700	700	810	750	750	750	750	750
Cash to be paid out												
Food and other regular expenses	450	450	450	450	450	450	450	450	450	450	450	450
Planned purchase of air conditioner			300									
Income tax payment				100								
Painting house						600						
Loan repayments								730				320
Estimated dental bill			500									
Vacation										400		
Insurance premiums		80			135			80				
Total outflows	450	530	1250	550	585	1050	450	1260	450	850	450	770
Net inflows	310	170	−550	1200	115	−350	360	(510)	300	(100)	300	(20)
Cumulative inflow	310	480	−70	1130	1245	895	1255	745	1045	945	1245	1225

cash budget is the desirability of a buffer against risk in net cash inflows. Although this may not be an easy step, a rearrangement of the family's collection of assets to include some liquid assets would seem desirable. If William Coke owned $1000 in bank deposits and other liquid assets at the beginning of the period, he might be saved considerable worry and inconvenience.

Temporary larger buildups of liquid assets

Liquid assets are very useful as a buffer against net cash outflows because they reduce the chance of possible cost and inconvenience from running short of cash. They also have another important value as a temporary asset to be held for meeting predicted future cash requirements, even when that requirement is expected a year or more in the future. To examine this second use, it is helpful to return briefly to a consideration of some other assets that might be used for temporary investment.

Neither most physical capital, which yields nonmoney services, nor human capital, which cannot be sold after a short period of time, are very useful devices for holding $5000 that has already been saved for the purpose of making part of a house down payment two years hence. Claims appear much more desirable because they can be selected either to mature in two years or they can be sold at the end of two years. The question arises, is there a difference between selecting claims that will mature and claims to be resold?

Common stocks or bonds with maturity dates far into the future could be used for temporary investment. However, both of these investments may be subject to substantial price fluctuations. Over a long period of time these "ups and downs" may average out to a fairly predictable return, especially if some diversification is practiced. In a short period, though, there is not a sufficient time for "ups and downs" to average. Thus one's short period yield expectation on a common stock might be described as a mean expected 7% plus or minus 20%, whereas a long period expectation on the same stock might be a 7% plus or minus 3%.

Because safe claims maturing in a short period (liquid assets) possess this extra degree of safety beyond their freedom from significant default possibilities, they may be preferable for temporary holding even though their mean expected return is less than that on stocks or long-term bonds bought for resale. Particularly when assets are being used to store wealth for an important purpose, such as home purchase, and when fluctuation in the price of the temporarily held asset may cause possible disruption to the family's plans, the family would probably be wise to think about using liquid assets even though their yields may not appear as attractive as other asset alternatives. Again, this is a case of buying freedom from risk, an advantage that is usually obtainable only at some cost. In this case, that cost is in the form of accepting a lower rate of return.

Bank Deposits

Bank deposits are so closely interchangeable with cash that we normally do not distinguish between the two. The most widely used bank deposit is the checking account, or demand deposit. When an individual deposits money at a bank, he is given credit for this amount on the bank's records. These amounts on deposit are a particular form of liabilities of that bank. They are called demand deposits because they are actually payable when demanded. A checking account thus differs from the claims we have discussed previously, such as bonds, in that the maturity date may occur immediately at the whim of the claim's holder. Banks that offer checking accounts are often called commercial banks.

A check written by the owner of a checking account is an order to the bank requiring the discharge of part or all of the bank's liability to him. The bank's promise to meet its obligations is especially trustworthy because nearly all banks that offer checking services hold insurance with an agency of the Federal Government (the Federal Deposit Insurance Corporation) which guarantees that payment will be made. (This insurance currently extends only up to checking account balances of $20,000, although a family may hold several accounts, each of which is insured. This amount, however, is in excess of checking account balances normally held by all but a few wealthy individuals or families.)

Under present banking laws banks that offer checking accounts are not allowed to pay interest on the deposits. They often levy a small service charge on personal checking accounts that usually depends on the number of checks written and the size of the deposit being maintained. This policy is based on the fact that it costs the bank money to handle each check. However, if the deposit balance maintained is large enough, the interest that the bank is able to earn by reinvesting part of the money deposited will be enough to offset all or part of the handling costs of the account. Banks typically offer the depositor some choice in the way his service charges will be determined; therefore the checking account holder should make sure that he is choosing the method that will set his service charges at the lowest level.

A simplified example of a bank balance sheet (Table 10.3) may serve to illustrate the nature of the role fulfilled by banks. Note that the bank holds many interest-bearing assets (bonds and loans) which produce most of its income and that it buys these assets principally with depositor's

TABLE 10.3

BANK BALANCE SHEET, DECEMBER 31, 19—

Cash and reserves	$ 1,000,000	Demand deposits	$ 4,500,000
Other liquid assets	1,000,000	Time deposits	4,000,000
Bonds	2,000,000	Other liabilities	500,000
Loans	5,500,000	Net worth	1,000,000
Buildings and other property	500,000		
	$10,000,000		$10,000,000

money. A bank's net worth is usually quite small when compared with its liabilities. Any major reduction in the value of the bank's assets through defaults on loans held by the bank would be sufficient to reduce the value of the bank's net worth to zero. Because of this, banks, as we see in Chapter 14, are very cautious about the quality of loans that they make.

In addition to the demand deposits which are listed among the bank's liabilities, another large category also appears—time deposits. The popular name for these deposits is savings accounts. Savings accounts differ from demand deposits in several important ways. In the first place, they are not legally payable "on demand." For example, when a savings account is opened, the agreement between the depositor and the bank may specify that 90-day notice of withdrawals is required. This means that the bank is not legally bound to discharge its obligation to the depositor until 90 days after the depositor has requested his money. The agreements between bank and depositor vary on time deposits; often an individual bank will offer more than one type of time deposit. In no case, however, is the bank *legally* obligated to pay money immediately upon request to the holder of a time deposit.

A distinction should be made between legality and practical usage. Banks will usually allow time depositors to withdraw their money any time they wish. However, the depositor should be forewarned that this is a privilege extended by the bank rather than his contractual right.

Because of their different legal nature, time deposits are not subject to checking privileges. The normal method of withdrawing funds from a savings account is to go to the bank in person, although the bank may respond to a mailed request for a withdrawal. Thus time deposits are not as convenient a source of cash as checking deposits.

Another difference, an advantage for the holder of time deposits, lies in the fact that these deposits typically pay interest. (Often money must left on deposit for a minimum length of time, such as 90 days, before interest will be paid.) The bank is able to pay interest on time deposits both because banking laws permit this and because time deposits are not nearly as costly as checking accounts for the bank to administer. When interest is paid, it is subject to ordinary income taxes; therefore the interest rate on a deposit needs to be converted to an after-tax amount.

Credit Unions

Credit unions bear considerable similarity to banks in the services they provide, but they differ in several important respects. One of these is that they are owned by their members. Thus the right-hand side of the credit union balance sheet will not contain deposit liabilities but will have a very large net worth section. This net worth section will be divided into shares in the organization, but these shares are different from corporation common stock.

The credit union's form of organization is that of a cooperative rather than a corporation. Its shares are owned by persons who use its services; in fact, as we shall see, share ownership constitutes a type of service offered by this organization. Additionally, if a shareholder wishes to vote for directors or other matters at the annual meeting of the organization, he does not, as in the corporation, have voting power proportionate to the number of shares he holds, but instead has one vote as a member of the organization, irrespective of his shareholdings.

The liquid assets available at a credit union are shares in the net worth of the organization. These shares bear much similarity to time deposits. If an individual wishes to place money in a credit union, he does not buy a particular number of shares; instead cash paid to the organization is recorded in a share account. Money placed in a share account can normally be withdrawn on demand, but, as in the case of the time deposit, this is a privilege extended by the organization and not a legal right of the shareholder. Instead of paying interest, a share in the credit union pays dividends. Payment of dividends differs legally from the payment of interest in that there is no legal obligation for this payment, although credit unions normally regard themselves as morally obligated to pay dividends.

Credit union accounts are not protected by government insurance as are bank deposits. One advantage of a credit union account is that this account is sometimes more convenient for an individual to use, since credit union facilities are often located at or near places of employment. Also, some individuals may derive an idealogical satisfaction from participating in a cooperative venture. Since credit unions do not offer checking accounts, it is very common for credit union shareholders to also maintain bank demand deposits.

Savings and Loan Associations

Savings and loan associations also offer share accounts, which are liquid assets that are close substitutes for bank time deposits. These accounts, like share accounts of credit unions, are technically not liabilities but an ownership share. The associated "interest" paid on the account is legally a dividend rather than interest. (Unlike credit unions, the savings and loan associations are not organized as cooperatives and often issue common stock.) Like bank deposits, savings and loan accounts are federally insured up to $20,000 (Federal Savings and Loan Corporation), therefore these assets have a very high degree of safety. Aside from the possible idealogical preference for credit unions, the choice between time deposits, credit union accounts, and savings and loan accounts is likely to be made on the basis of their relative convenience of location, quality of service offered by particular local institutions, and amount of interest and dividends being offered under local circumstances. (Some large savings and loan associations have also been very actively soliciting deposits by mail.)

Other Liquid Assets

Although the types of liquid assets that we have mentioned are the most important variety employed by individuals, several types of banks, which do not offer checking account services, do offer time deposit facilities. For individuals who wish to hold larger amounts of liquid assets, short-term securities may also be employed. Normally these securities are only available in $1000 amounts or larger; there are a variety of these short-term securities that are both very safe and quite convenient. These include the short-term obligations of both governments and some large corporations.

It should also be noted that banks are now attempting to eliminate some of the disadvantage of running out of cash by providing what is called an automatic overdraft privilege. For a charge, the bank will agree that the individual can write checks in excess of the balance he is maintaining in his checking account. Such a privilege may reduce an individual's reliance on the ownership of liquid assets; however, this is discussed in Chapter 14 under the topic of borrowing.

Return, or cost, on liquid assets

The return on liquid assets can be identified by conventional means. As noted before, the returns on liquid assets are subject to income taxes. Since the returns on these assets are in fixed dollar amounts, they are not inflation protected and an estimated inflation rate should be deducted also. For example, if a savings and loan account yields a dividend of 5% annually and if its owner is in a 20% marginal tax bracket, the after-tax return will be 4%. If a 2% inflation rate is expected, subtraction of this rate leaves an inflation-adjusted rate of return of 2% on the savings and loan account. In the case of demand deposit, on which no interest is paid, the rate of return will be negative by the amount of expected inflation rate (and any service charges).

These assets are not usually bought primarily for rate of return, although this feature may have some influence on the type of liquid asset selected and the quantity of these assets held. One useful approach to the problem of holding liquid assets is to revert to the concept of implicit rent introduced in connection with household assets. For example, suppose that an individual feels that he can readily get an inflation-protected, after-tax rate of return of 3% on some other safe investment, such as a bond. Suppose he considers the possibility of keeping an extra $1000 in a checking account with an inflation-adjusted rate of — 2%. The full cost of maintaining the checking account is then the giving up of the 3% elsewhere plus the 2% annual loss on the checking account, or 5%. Thus he can identify an implicit rent of $50 annually on the marginal $1000 of checking account balance.

Benefits versus costs

The benefits conferred by liquid assets offer convenience in the form of accessibility and protection from risk in that the availability of funds from these assets is almost certain and the rate of return is fairly predictable. (Some risk is introduced by an inability to predict the inflation rate precisely.)

The individual can now use marginal analysis to decide whether liquid assets should be employed. Suppose he considers a $300 average checking account as a bare essential, and then considers adding $200 to the amount he regularly tries to keep in his account. Suppose the implicit rent on this is $10 per year. The individual may very well decide that it is worthwhile for him to keep this extra amount, since the trouble of procuring only one short-term loan, the failure to take advantage of only one bargain that was available to someone with cash on hand, or the opportunity to pay only one expected bill on time might each be worth more than $10. Because of the interest yielded by time deposits, credit union accounts, and savings and loan accounts, the implicit rent that must be reckoned on these liquid assets is substantially less. Thus an individual who desires the protection of some liquid assets could elect to keep only a small checking account balance and to keep some extra cushion against unexpected cash outflow in the form of these other interest-bearing liquid assets.

Summary

In planning a family needs to consider risk. Expected income may fail to materialize, and consumption requirements may be greater than expected; a planner must consider how he can cope with these possible adversities.

There are a variety of methods for risk control. The method considered in this chapter is the accumulation of liquid assets. Liquid assets are cash or those assets that could be almost immediately converted into cash without a major chance of loss. The holding of liquid assets provides a buffer against many small, everyday risks.

Cash forecasts try to anticipate the cash requirement of a future period. These are simple financial statements projecting the amount of cash that will be received during each month, or other time interval, and the amount of cash that will be paid out. The difference each month between these amounts will be the projected net cash inflow which may be either positive (a surplus) or negative (a deficit).

Preparation of a cash budget can help to indicate a family's need for liquid assets and may also signal to the family that its liquid asset holdings will be temporarily inadequate unless the family changes some of its spending plans.

In addition to providing reserves for emergencies, liquid assets can often be advantageously held in preparation for a large purchase of some other type of asset.

Some important types of liquid assets are commercial bank demand deposits (checking accounts) and time deposits (savings accounts), and accounts with savings and loan associations and credit unions. Bank accounts are liabilities of the bank and are federally insured. Savings and loan accounts are also federally insured.

The rate of return on liquid assets is low and may even be negative. By comparing the return on a liquid asset to an alternative asset possibility, such as common stock, one can identify an implicit rent associated with holding the asset. One can then try to decide whether the marginal benefit from holding liquid assets justifies their cost (the marginal implicit rent).

SUGGESTED READINGS

Most financial institutions provide free material describing their operations. District Federal Reserve Banks also provide some elementary descriptions of the banking system upon request.

Standard accounting textbooks normally discuss cash budgets. These descriptions are included in the accounting textbooks cited in Chapter 2.

Elementary economic books, such as Samuelson (cited in Chapter 9), describe the role of money and the banking system in the economy. There are also a number of textbooks which deal solely with the topic of money and banking; one example is Eli Shapiro, Ezra Solomon, and William L. White, *Money and Banking*, 5th ed. (New York: Holt, Rinehart and Winston, Inc., 1968).

QUESTIONS

1. See if you can recall from your own experiences some instances when expected income has failed to materialize or when unexpected consumption requirements have developed.
2. Juan feels that his income next year could be anywhere between $12,000 and $18,000. Approximate his mean expected income and indicate the range of possible variation?
3. Try to think of an original example in which risk would be an important factor in the choice of jobs.
4. Which of the following would you classify as liquid assets? (Why or why not?)

(a) $200 owed you by a friend who has promised to pay you this amount within a month.
(b) The money in your pocket.
(c) A credit union account.
(d) A U.S. Government bond of a series described as 7s of 84.
(e) A Series E Government bond.
(f) Your car.

5. Prepare a cash budget for yourself for next week.
6. Explain why a common stock or long-term bond might be regarded as a safer asset if held for a long period of time than if held with the understanding that it must be sold only a few months after purchase.
7. Why do demand deposits (checking accounts) appear in the liability section of the bank's balance sheet?
8. Both credit union accounts and bank deposits are usually very safe assets. Can you explain why the bank deposit is the safer of the two?
9. What is the return currently available on bank time deposits in your locality? on savings and loan association accounts? on credit union accounts?
10. With a marginal income tax rate of 25% and an expected inflation rate of 2%, what are the after-tax, inflation-adjusted returns on the liquid assets mentioned in Question 9?
11. Assuming that 7% is available on common stock investment, what is the implicit rent of holding $1000 for a year in each of the liquid assets noted in the above questions? Do you think the benefits of holding the $1000 in liquid assets justify this cost in your situation? How about the marginal benefits of an extra $1000? of a third $1000?

PROBLEMS

1. During March, the McGill family expects to repay a personal loan; this payment will require $1040. During April, the family expects to pay $300 in income taxes. In addition the family expects to pay $600 per month for food and other regular expenditures.

   The McGill family earns $750 per month take-home pay. In addition it expects to receive a $200 dividend during February on some stocks that it owns and a $100 check for bond interest in April.

   (a) Compose a cash budget for the McGill family for the months from January through June.
   (b) Indicate the amount of cash the McGills would need to have on January 1 to avoid running out of money during this six-month period. Can you suggest any reasons why they should have a larger amount on hand if possible?
   (c) Suppose that the McGill family has no cash on hand on January 1 and that it prepares a cash budget at that time. What course of action would you recommend for it?

2. R normally maintains a $1000 checking account. Service charges on this account average $2 per month. His marginal personal tax rate is 20%, he

expects an inflation rate of 2%, and he can earn 7% (after tax, inflation adjusted) on common stock.

(a) What is the implicit rent of the checking account?

(b) As an alternative R considers transferring $500 from his checking account to a 5% savings account. With a smaller checking account balance, however, service charges on this account will increase by 50¢ per month. How much would this $500 transfer lower the implicit rent on his liquid assets? Do you think the lost marginal benefits would be greater or less than this cost reduction?

chapter eleven

Involuntary benefit programs

In developing a financial plan one needs to consider a number of benefits which are received by the individual without planning. Some of these are conferred by government, others by employers. The distinguishing feature of the benefits described in this chapter is that they are not selected by the family as are the flows of benefits from assets, except in that the family chooses to live in the state or country that confers the government benefits or to accept a job that confers the job-connected benefits.

To the extent that these benefits will be received in some time periods or in some situations, they help to meet some of the family's consumption needs under those circumstances and relieve the family from providing for these requirements from other sources. It is especially appropriate to consider these benefits before considering further aspects of risk control through insurance, for some involuntary benefits are designed to cope with elements of personal financial risk.

Social security

Nearly all Americans are now eligible for participation in the benefits accorded by the U.S. Government's Social Security Act. However, the extent of participation in these benefits varies, so that the individual will have to consider his own circumstances in formulating his estimates of the social security benefits he will receive.

There are four major types of benefits conferred by social security: old age pensions, disability payments, payments to survivors, and Medicare. The first three are quite closely related because they provide specified cash amounts under certain circumstances. The amounts paid often have some direct relationship to the amount of social security taxes that have been paid by the family. Payments under the Medicare program, on the other hand, are related to the amount of medical expenses incurred and are extended equally to all persons who have paid social security taxes.

Benefits under the social security plan are limited to individuals who have paid some social security taxes, their spouses, and in some cases their "survivors." However, since nearly all American families pay social security taxes, nearly all families will be eligible for some social security benefits.

Old Age Benefits

When an individual reaches "retirement age" and is covered by the social security program, he receives monthly payments for the remainder of his life. At the time when a spouse reaches retirement age she also is eligible for monthly payments; these may be based on taxes that she has paid into the social security program, but even if she has not paid taxes, she is eligible for some benefits because of her spouse's tax payments.

The original retirement age specified in the social security program was 65, but recently potential beneficiaries of the program have been given the option of retiring earlier, at age 62. If an individual or his wife wishes to begin receiving payments before age 65, however, these payments are at a reduced rate. Of course, an individual may also wish to wait until he reaches an age greater than 65 before he retires and starts receiving payments, but if he does so his payments are not increased. If an individual is still working at age 70, he becomes eligible for social security payments commencing at that time, without retiring, at the same level as those given to an individual retiring at age 65.

When an individual considers social security old age payments in a financial plan, he needs to recognize that these payments are not subject to income taxes. Social security payments appear to be reasonably well protected against inflation. Congress, which votes the amount of payments made under the social security program, has normally recognized the increased burdens placed on retired people by rising prices and adjusted old age payments upward accordingly.

An individual can easily ascertain the amount of social security payments that will be made under different circumstances by contacting his local office of the Social Security Administration. At the time that this book was being written, these payments were made according to the schedule in Table 11.1.

TABLE 11.1[a]

RETIREMENT BENEFITS AVAILABLE TO WORKER

Average covered earnings during base period	Retirement benefit at age 65 (monthly)	Retirement benefit at age 62 (monthly)
$5400	$189.80	$151.90
4200	161.50	129.20
3000	132.30	105.90
1800	101.70	81.40
minimum	64.00	51.20

[a] Data in effect in March 1971.

The wife of a surviving worker is eligible to receive benefits at one-half of the level for the worker. (If both husband and wife have worked, they may both draw worker benefits; however, a wife may elect to receive wife benefits if these are greater than her worker benefits.) Fully disabled workers are eligible for the same schedule of benefits as those currently retiring at age 65. Because these amounts change frequently and also because there are special circumstances not fully covered by the table, it is desirable when planning to obtain the information from the Social Security Administration.

Disability and Survivor Benefits

If an individual is disabled by injury or illness he may begin collecting social security payments before he reaches the specified retirement age. For purposes of payment determination, the individual who is disabled is given the same benefits as someone in his income bracket who is retiring at age 65. These payments continue all of his life if he remains disabled.

If an individual who has paid taxes into the social security program dies, his spouse and children are eligible to receive benefits. The amount of the benefit is determined by the number of children under the age of 18 and, as well, by whether the individual is survived by a spouse. These payments to the surviving family may be substantially greater than disability or retirement payments. In March 1971 the following schedule was in effect.

Widow Benefits If a widow retires at age 65, she is eligible to benefits at a level equal to 82½% of those benefits a worker could draw, retiring at age 65. The worker income level is based on the earnings history of her deceased husband.

Family Benefits If the surviving family includes one or more children under 18, the family receives a monthly income equal to 1½ times the age 65 worker retirement benefit. These benefits continue until all children have reached 18. (They continue longer if one child over 18 is disabled.)

Student Benefits Surviving children who are age 18 or over, and who are enrolled in school, are entitled to receive half the age 65 worker retirement benefit until they reach the age of 22.

Lump Sum Survivor Payment This small payment (maximum $255) is also available to survivors.

Medicare

The Social Security Administration also offers very comprehensive benefits to persons over 65 who require hospital and medical services. Not all of this program is strictly involuntary, although even the voluntary part approximates an involuntary benefit program. Social Security Medicare currently provides for the payment of hospital expenses for the first 90 days of an individual's hospitalization. Any 60-day period in which an individual does not use hospital or nursing home facilities results in another renewal of the 90 days hospitalization. Present coverage also allows a 60-day "lifetime reserve"; this allows the individual 60 days hospitalization coverage beyond the 90-day periods discussed before, but these 60 days can only be used once and are not renewable.

Virtually all hospital expenses are paid under this plan during the periods when an individual is eligible for the coverage. A small initial contribution to cost is required, but this amount may be regarded as negligible when an individual is developing a financial plan.

In addition to the hospitalization coverage, nursing home care is also provided under the Medicare program for the individuals who have recently been hospitalized. This program pays for the first 20 days of care and all but $5 of daily expenses for a following 80-day period in the nursing home. Visits to homes by nurses and other health workers (but not doctors) are also provided for a year after an individual has been in a hospital or nursing home.

The Medicare program allows persons over 65 to participate in a medical insurance program that pays for the services of doctors and some other health services. A charge is made for this protection, but because this program is also subsidized from taxes, the charge is kept at quite a low level (currently $4 per month). Thus participation in the program is made so attractive that it may be practically regarded as an involuntary benefit program. For nearly everyone the money saved by not entering the program would be far too small to justify giving up the potential benefits that would be lost by withdrawing.

Two notes of caution are in order to the individual studying Medicare. First, this chapter's coverage has been quite brief and has not touched on many technicalities relating to this program. An individual would also find it desirable to discuss this coverage at an office of the Social Security Administration.

Additionally, it should be noted that although the social security program covers most potential health expenses for persons over 65, there are still some possible expenses, such as very long hospitalizations, and drugs for persons not hospitalized, that are not covered. Therefore, when medical insurance is discussed in the next chapter, the possibility of providing supplementary protection is suggested to cover these omissions in the Medicare benefits.

Veterans benefits programs

Veterans may be eligible for additional government benefits beyond those conferred by social security. Extensive benefits are provided to those veterans who were fully or partially disabled during their military service. Any veteran may be eligible for some types of benefits, although the chances of being a beneficiary are much higher if the veteran experienced wartime service. Benefits which may be available to a veteran are hospitalization, old age pension, and disability and survivor payments. Again, if one is a veteran and is developing a financial plan, contact with an office of the Veterans Administration or a local Veteran's Service Officer would be useful. We do not attempt to detail the benefits available to veterans here, since the eligibility for these benefits is often a rather complex question.

Unemployment compensation

One of the serious risks confronting an individual in his financial planning is the possibility of interruption of his income. Many individuals are provided some protection from the loss of a job by working in positions in which they are covered by unemployment compensation programs. Although partially financed by the Federal Government, these programs are controlled by individual states and differ from state to state. Basically the programs provide that an individual who has lost his job through no fault of his own and who is seeking another job, will receive a specified money payment each week. Payments, like many of those under social security, are related to an individual's previous earnings;

therefore those who have held low income jobs before being unemployed may receive only rather limited benefits.

Because unemployment payments may be quite low in comparison to previous salary and also because the duration in which these payments can be received is limited, the possibility of receiving unemployment compensation payments will probably not play a large part in the formulation of most financial plans. However, for an individual who works in an industry which is subject to periodic layoffs, or is seasonal in nature, the payments may be very consequential.

Other public assistance programs

Most individuals who formulate a financial plan would like to develop the plan in such a way that they are protected from serious impoverishment at any time in their lives. However, there is always some chance that a series of unpredicted events may disrupt the plan. One of the advantages of living in the United States or in most relatively prosperous countries is that government policy limits the degree of impoverishment that needs to be borne by an individual. In the United States an individual normally no longer needs to fear that he will be deprived of bare necessities. In the event that an individual encounters unfortunate financial straits, various programs of public assistance will usually provide for basic food, shelter, and clothing requirements.

It is not likely that many readers of this book will explicitly consider the possibility of receiving "relief" in their own planning. Nevertheless, this possibility may affect the financial planning undertaken by most individuals in modern countries. People can now take a few more chances in the jobs they select or in the assets they accumulate, when they realize, if only subconsciously, that there are some limits on privation if their plans do not succeed.

Job-connected involuntary benefits

In addition to considering various government-provided benefits, an individual should also look at those benefits that arise from his employment situation. Many jobs provide pensions for employees and various types of protection against personal misfortune. Employers also have certain legal responsibilities to their employees under the workmen's compensation doctrine. Additionally, unions may provide some benefits to their members

Pension Plans

In discussing pension plans, some distinctive vocabulary is usually employed. To avoid confusion, this section begins with a short glossary of these terms.

EMPLOYEE CONTRIBUTION A payment made by an employee to provide for future pension payments.

CONTRIBUTORY PLANS Pension plans in which employee contributions are required.

NONCONTRIBUTORY PLANS Pension plans in which employee contributions are not required. Cost of providing pensions, in this case, is born entirely by employer.

PENSION FUND A collection of assets, such as bonds and stocks, which has been purchased for the purpose of providing for future pensions.

FUNDED PLAN A pension plan in which pension payments are made out of a pension fund. Payments from such a plan may be dependent on the returns earned by the fund's assets. Most contributory plans are funded.

NONFUNDED PLAN A plan in which no fund is established. Pension payments are made directly by the employer.

PENSION FUND TRUSTEE A separate organization, often a bank or insurance company, which holds the assets of a pension fund to make sure that these assets are used only to provide pension payments.

Pension funds may be either contributory or noncontributory. In either case, they are almost always either actually or practically involuntary. Usually the employee does not have a choice about whether he participates in his company's pension plan. Even if he does have a choice, nonparticipation will probably be impractical, for the future benefits will normally be based not only on the employee's contributions but also on participation of the employer. Withdrawal from the fund will mean loss of benefits provided by the employer as well as those provided by the employee's contributions.

Pension plans may take a wide variety of forms. As noted in the glossary above, they may be funded or nonfunded. In a funded plan, the employer makes contributions to the fund during the period in which he is employing an individual. At the time of the individual's retirement, these contributions and their accumulated interest are then available for providing a pension for the employee.

Noncontributory plans are often nonfunded. The employer may simply agree to make pension payments to employees at the time of their retirement. When an employee retires, the payments are made by the employer in the same way that he would meet other current expenses, instead of their being paid out of a fund. In a stable, reliable company a nonfunded plan may provide a very secure and predictable pension arrangement since the pension payments are liabilities of the company. However, a funded plan is often more desirable from the employee's viewpoint. This fund is normally separated from the other business of the company and hence may offer protection even though the company itself should be unable to meet its regular liabilities. Often pension funds are completely separate from company affairs and under the full control of a trustee who is not connected with the company.

Contributory funds are usually funded and often have another feature as well. The investment accumulated in the pension fund may belong, at least partly, to the participating employee even before retirement. This feature is very important to the employee who decides to change jobs, for he then retains the right to receive a pension upon retirement out of the proceeds from that part of the fund that belonged to him. A fund with this feature is said to be vested, or portable. In a contributory plan the employee's contribution is normally vested, and sometimes the contributions made by the employer are, too. Funded noncontributory plans may also be vested.

Vesting is an important feature to be considered in relating a pension plan to an overall financial plan. If part or all of the plan is vested, the employee can depend on some pension from the plan even though he changes jobs. Since the pension will be based on the amount of payments that have been made to the fund and their accumulated interest, the length of time the individual has participated in the plan will determine the amount of the pension fund that is vested with him. An individual who contemplated changing jobs would want to distinguish between that level of expected pension payment that would result from the part of the pension fund already vested in him and that part that he would not receive unless his new employer offers a similar pension plan.

In planning one needs to consider the income taxes that will be levied on pensions when they are received. In general, pension payments are taxable, but the individual might wish to inquire whether his own particular plan is likely to be taxed at less than full income tax rates. One tax advantage exists in most pension plans for the reason that the recipient of a pension often has a lower taxable income during his retirement years and thus will pay lower marginal rates on proceeds from pensions than he will on income received during his working years.

Pensions and Inflation

Expected money amounts of pension benefits may have varying degrees of inflation protection. The protection may arise from several sources. Nonfunded benefits may be adjusted upward by the employer in response to changing economic conditions. (If prices have risen, higher pension benefits are needed to attract new employees. These benefits may be extended to existing or past employees also.)

A funded plan may be subject to two types of inflation protection. Payments into the fund are usually related directly to the income being earned by the employee. If inflation occurs before retirement, payments into the fund, whether by employee contribution or by the employer, will usually rise and thus increase the money amount of the assets available to provide pension payments.

The second type of inflation protection for pension funds lies in the nature of the assets that comprise the fund. If these assets consist of items such as common stocks, the benefits available from the fund may be inflation protected. Even if the fund consists mostly of bonds, it may provide some compensation for inflation because of the fact that interest rates on bonds usually rise during periods when inflation is more serious.

If expected pension benefits are only partly inflation protected or completely unprotected, they should be subject to some inflation adjustment for planning purposes. A formal adjustment process would consist of finding the present value of each year's expected money pension payments at the time of planning, using the expected inflation rate as r. When the pension is partially protected, some compromise between full adjustment and no adjustment could be used or, more informally, one could simply be conservative in estimating the dollar amounts of the pension.

For an example of a formal adjustment, consider the following situation. Carl is 50 now and expects to retire at age 65. He expects that he will receive a \$200 per month (\$2400 per year) pension and sees little chance that this pension will rise if inflation prevails. He foresees inflation at 2% per year. To find the inflation-adjusted amount of pension payments, he would need to take each year individually and solve for P where $F =$ \$2400, $r = 2\%$, $n =$ years between present time and year pension payment will be received, and $P =$ unknown.

His first year's pension will be received about 15 years from now; therefore using that value he can solve with the following results. If $F =$ \$2400, $r = 2\%$, and $n = 15$, then $P =$ about \$1800, or \$150 per month. His second year's pension payment will have an inflation-adjusted value based on $n = 16$, and so forth.

The importance of this adjustment can be illustrated. Suppose Carl also expects to receive about \$100 per month in social security payments. He expects that these are fully inflation protected, as discussed earlier in this chapter. He also expects that if *current* prices were to continue, he would like to spend about \$400 per month during his retirement years.

He can now calculate:

Spending needs at age 65		\$400
Involuntary benefits at age 65		
Pension	\$150	
Social security	100	
Total		250
Deficiency		\$150

Carl now knows that he must plan to build up assets which will provide an inflation-protected or inflation-adjusted return of \$150 per month when he is age 65. (Slightly more each year in years past age 65, as inflation eats away more of his pension.)

His planning may still not be perfect. Inflation may eat away his pension faster than expected (perhaps 3% per year instead of 2%). Carl's social security payments may not fully keep pace with inflation, nor may some of the returns on his assets. However, he has still made an attempt to allow for inflation, and this seems like a superior approach to just ignoring the problem. Perhaps an analysis like this will warn Carl that he must either save more now or else plan to retire later, or spend less during retirement; without this advance planning, Carl might be very disappointed when his retirement period arrived.

Payments under a Pension Plan

Once an individual reaches retirement age, the pension payments are normally made for life rather than for a definite period of years. This protects the individual from the possibility that he may be subjected to extraordinary consumption expenses because of the fact that he lives much longer than normal. At the same time, of course, if an individual dies a short time after he starts receiving his pension, he will receive very few payments from it. In this case his needs for consumption were for only a short period. Plans differ in their provision for the needs of surviving spouses.

To determine the amount of payments to be made to a beneficiary, pension funds make use of mean expected estimates of the lives of pension recipients. Suppose that Bill begins contributing to a pension plan at age 35 and expects to continue on the same job until he is 65. Suppose that the payments that he and his employers make are expected to total $500 per year, and that an expected rate of return of 4% is used in pension fund calculations. Since the future value of a $500 annuity for 30 years is $28,000, we may predict that Bill's share of the pension fund will be about this amount when he retires. A *mortality table*, which shows "life expectancies" for people of various ages, indicates that Bill is likely to live for ten years after retirement. The approximate calculation performed to determine his annual pension will then be

$P =$ \$28,000, amount available in fund at retirement
$n =$ 10 years, expected period during which pension will be paid
$r =$ 4%, earnings rate on pension fund assets
$A =$ unknown

Solving, we obtain an estimated annual payment of about $3500; Bill's pension will be about $300 per month.

If Bill's pension fund was invested at least partly in common stocks, and if the interest rate on any bonds and other assets that provide fixed-money incomes had been inflation adjusted or very conservatively estimated, Bill might regard this $300 per month as reasonably well inflation protected.

If inflation occurs, his pension may be greater than $300, because the common stocks in the fund have gone up in value or because bonds bought by the fund have paid high interest rates. However, the increased amount of money will probably be offset by rising prices of things Bill buys, so that his *real* income may still be only about $300.

The Form of the Pension Payment

Some funded pensions pay fixed annual payments, which are determined at the time of retirement. Increasingly, pension plans are changing to a device called a variable annuity in which, even after retirement, the pension payments actually made to the retired individual may fluctuate. The payment received by the individual will be determined by the returns on the pension fund's assets during his retirement period. Such a plan is called a *variable annuity* and is designed to afford greater inflation protection than a *fixed annuity* plan.

Workmen's Compensation

Accidents on the job can cause both interruption of income and possible increased consumption expenses because of the care needed by an injured person. In almost all cases in which these accidents occur, except when the employee has intentionally injured himself, the employer is responsible for helping to ease the financial difficulties caused by the accident. The employer in turn will normally cover this responsibility by taking out insurance which will make payments to injured employees. Responsibility under workmen's compensation extends to survivors of the employee also. Benefits payable under workmen's compensation need to be considered in the development of the financial plan. It should be noted, however, that these benefits offer no protection when the employee is injured under off-the-job circumstances.

Other Employee Benefits

If the individual is not already familiar with other benefits provided in connection with his job, it is important for him to obtain this familiarity before he develops a financial plan. This can normally be done by contacting the personnel office of his employer and, in some cases, a union representative. Extra employer-provided benefits may include payments in connection with other disabilities and illnesses not covered by workmen's compensation. Unions may provide benefits under union-sponsored insurance and pension programs, as well as possible financial protection for workers unemployed or on strike.

Integration of involuntary programs into a personal economic plan

Involuntary benefit programs are likely to offer an individual some protection against income interruption and extraordinary expenses. These programs ordinarily offer no protection against disruption of benefits from assets held by the individual (excluding human capital); thus the individual himself must provide for the consequences of a precipitous decline in his favorite common stock or a fire in his house. To supplement the benefits offered by involuntary programs and to provide other protection, most individuals will want to consider the purchase of insurance. However, both in the development of an insurance program and in the formulation of a more comprehensive economic plan, it is essential to consider the usually substantial amounts of available involuntary benefits.

Summary

Some economic planning has already been done on behalf of the individual; involuntary benefits have been arranged for him. It is important to understand these involuntary benefits, since otherwise one might unnecessarily plan to provide himself with benefits which duplicate those of the involuntary programs.

Virtually all Americans participate in involuntary benefits under the social security program. These benefits include old age pensions, disability payments, payments to survivors, and Medicare.

Veterans may be eligible for additional benefits through various veterans' programs. Unemployment compensation and other public assistance programs may help individuals who fall into periods of serious economic difficulty.

In addition to these government programs, there are many job-connected involuntary benefits including a variety of pension plans.

Past experience seems to indicate that social security benefits are protected against inflation. Other involuntary benefits are also often protected, but there are instances in which these benefits are not inflation protected. Variable annuities provide one device for explicitly building inflation protection into a benefits program.

SUGGESTED READINGS

Descriptions and current information about social security programs can, as noted in the chapter, be obtained from the Social Security Administration.

A rather detailed text on private pension programs is *Fundamentals of Private Pensions*, 2d ed. by Dan M. McGill (Homewood, Ill.: Richard D. Irwin, Inc., 1964).

QUESTIONS

1. Why are the benefit programs described in this chapter referred to as "involuntary"?
2. What are the four major types of benefits provided by social security? How do the benefits paid under Medicare differ in their determination from the other social security benefits?
3. Why do you think social security old age benefit payments are exempt from Federal income tax?
4. If one looks at the history of the adoption of the Medicare program, he finds that this adoption was extremely controversial. What arguments do you think were raised for and against the program?
5. How would you incorporate your knowledge of social security benefits and possibly veterans' benefits into the formation of a financial plan?
6. Why do you think contributory pension plans are always funded?
7. What reason would an employer have for not offering his employees a vested plan? What reason would he have in favor of offering this type of plan?
8. Would you say that the social security old age benefit program was a funded pension plan? Is it contributory? Is it vested?
9. Why may social security payments be regarded as inflation protected?
10. What is a mortality table? Can you think of other uses for a mortality table besides those connected with pensions?
11. How would workmen's compensation benefits influence the development of a financial plan?

PROBLEMS

1. Max plans to begin work as a teacher upon graduation from college. He expects a starting salary of $9000 per year. He is married and has one child. He expects to use the standard deduction in income tax calculation. At the school where he will be employed, 5% of his gross income will be deducted for involuntary contributory pension and insurance programs. In addition, of course, his social security contributions will be deducted from his income. Referring to the material on income taxes in Chapter 4 and assuming social security tax contributions of 4% on incomes up to $9000 (all of Max's income), estimate Max's annual take-home pay.
2. In addition to his social security benefits, Albert expects to receive a pension of $300 per month commencing 30 years from the present. He expects that he will be receiving the pension payments for 20 years after his retirement. He regards these pension benefits as inadequately inflation protected and wishes to allow for 2% inflation. What is his inflation-adjusted monthly pension payment during the first year of his pension? during the twentieth year?

chapter twelve

Life insurance and annuities

Risk concerns the individual and the family because hardships or disruption of plans can result from unpredicted consumption requirements or the interruption of earnings. Life insurance is directed at an important potential source of disruption in family earnings, the death of a member of that family. Annuities, which are frequently sold by life insurance companies, provide for the possible extra consumption requirements of a longer-than-expected life.

General principles of insurance

To consider the protection afforded by these two types of insurance and the other types examined in Chapter 13, we need to analyze some of the characteristics common to all insurance protection. In spite of the fact that betting is ordinarily associated with the undertaking of risk instead of the avoiding of risk, there is a very close relationship between insurance policies and bets.

Consider a simple betting situation. A and B each bet a dollar on the flip of a coin. From either point of view the betting decision looks like this: In exchange for venturing \$1, the bet presents an opportunity to receive back either nothing or \$2. Unless the coin is badly balanced, there are equal chances that it will come up either heads or tails; thus each bettor views himself as having an equal chance of either losing his dollar or winning an additional one. Alternatively, each bet could be described as having a mean expected return of \$1 with a plus \$1 or minus \$1 range of possible variation from the mean expected return. (The mean expected return is an average of possible returns; of course, the \$1 return itself will never occur in this particular situation.) When entering the betting arrangement, each bettor exchanges \$1 which he already has for a mean expected \$1 return accompanied by considerable risk. Thus the simple bet exposes the bettor to additional risk, without any mean expected gain (mean expected return — cost of participation) or loss.

Why would an individual enter into such a bet? Many people probably bet because of the fun of taking a little risk as long as the consequences of the risk taking are not very great. (Although many people bet, very few people make large bets.) Now consider a second type of bet in which participation is harder to explain. Suppose that the bet between the individuals in the example above is arranged in a gambling casino in which the casino acts as a broker in bringing interested gamblers together. To cover expenses and make a profit, the casino charges a 10% commission on bets that it arranges.

Now the opportunity offered each bettor is the surrender of \$1 in exchange for equal chances of getting either nothing back if the bet loses or \$1.80 (\$2 less the 10% commission) in the event that the bet succeeds. The betting situation can now be described as the surrender of \$1 to obtain a mean expected return of \$.90 (the average of zero and \$1.80). Because of the mean expected loss of \$.10, many people would not make bets of this second type, except in "fun" amounts that would not significantly affect the participant's total financial picture.

The second situation, in which the mean expected return is less than the amount of the bet, may be called an adverse gamble. In addition to possibly affording fun, bets may make sense in a special situation even when they are adverse gambles. Consider a very simple example. A restaurant owner has observed that, when his local football team wins an afternoon home game, he has an unusually large dinner business and can expect to make \$100 extra profit above a normal day's business. However, if the team loses, fans cancel plans for eating out and the restaurant can expect that the day's profit will be \$100 less than usual. Now suppose that a home game is about to be played and that the teams are so evenly matched that they have equal chances of winning. The restaurant owner is exposed to a risky situation with a possible variation in returns of plus or minus $100.

To protect himself against this risk the restaurant owner devised the following technique. Before the game he seeks out a local football fan who likes to gamble and bets $100 *against* the home team. Now if the home team wins, he loses his football bet of $100, but he makes an extra $100 profit in his restaurant and thus experiences no net gain or loss because of the team's winning. Similarly, if the team loses, the restaurant owner wins his football bet for $100, but loses $100 in the restaurant business and again experiences no net gain or loss. Surveying the results of this bet, we see that the bet has eliminated risk for the restaurant owner. Even if the restaurant owner had to accept an adverse gamble, he might still have been willing to bet because of the risk protection it afforded.

The principle of betting against one's self underlies all insurance. For example, an individual takes out a fire insurance policy on his house and pays $100 to the insurance company for a year's protection. In return the insurance company promises to pay him $10,000 if his house burns down. The person taking the insurance bets against himself; he bets that his house will burn. If it does, he wins the bet and collects $10,000, which helps to cover the fire loss: if he loses, he receives nothing in exchange for his $100 premium.

Insurance: an adverse gamble

Before continuing a discussion of insurance, a few more definitions are useful.

Policy A contract between an insurance company and an individual; it provides that the insurance company will pay out money if a particular event happens.

Policyholder An individual who enters a contract with an insurance company; one who "buys" an insurance policy.

Premium The amount paid by the policyholder to the insurance company, in exchange for the company's providing insurance.

Not only is the purchase of insurance a bet, but a bet with an insurance company is, except for a few rare situations, an adverse gamble. An insurance company, like the casino, must indirectly charge a commission when it offers bets to the public. The company cannot expect to pay out to its policyholders all of the amount of premiums that it collects from them, since it must provide for the large costs of selling the insurance, the costs of maintaining records and other office expenses, and some profits for the insurance company's stockholders.

The fact that insurance is an adverse gamble does not make the purchase of insurance irrational. Insurance is likely to fill a very important role in most families' economic planning. However, the knowledge that insurance is an adverse gamble reinforces the general proposition that insurance should be purchased with great care. Insurance can provide very basic protection, but it does not *necessarily* reduce risk.

Consider another example. An individual owns a house which he values at $10,000, but he finds that he is able to insure it for $15,000. Of this insurance $10,000 could be regarded as the policyholder's bet against himself. The other $5000 represents a chance for the individual to improve his financial circumstances if a fire occurs. (Insurance companies try to avoid situations like this because of the incentive provided for house burning.) Thus this marginal $5000 insurance is just an ordinary bet; the policyholder bets the marginal premium for this extra insurance on the chance that if a given event happens he will gain $5000. Hence this extra $5000 should not be regarded as insurance but as a gamble (of an adverse nature) which should be compared with other ordinary gambling opportunities, such as poker games and racetrack betting.

Insurance as a bet

It is useful to think of an insurance policy as a form of bet, but one distinction should be kept in mind. The policyholder bets against himself. His bet with the insurance company is structured in such a way that he "wins" his bet only if some misfortune occurs. Thus, unlike conventional bettors, insurance policyholders usually do not want to win. They bet by buying policies only so that, if they suffer a misfortune, the simultaneous winning of their bet with the insurance company will help make up for the loss caused by the misfortune.

Insurable interest

The "bet against one's self" aspect of insurance is also essential from the insurance company's point of view. The insurance company, before issuing any policy, makes sure that the policyholder is insuring against an event that will be harmful to him. For example, if Peter Pyro attempts to buy a fire insurance policy on a building owned by the XYZ Corporation, the insurance company's representative will immediately become apprehensive. If Peter would suffer no loss in the event that the building burns down, because it does not belong to him, he would have considerable incentive to set fire to the XYZ building and collect a payment on his fire insurance.

In general, insurance companies will not issue policies unless they can ascertain that the policyholder has an *insurable interest* in the situation for which he is buying insurance. One cannot insure a building that he does not own, because he is not insuring against harm to himself and therefore he will wish to win his bet with the insurance company.

Life insurance

Life insurance policies promise to pay a specified amount upon the death of the individual whose life is insured. This individual may be the policyholder, but one may also, under some circumstances, buy a policy on someone else's life. For example, a wife may buy a policy on her husband's life. The person to whom payment is to be made at time of death (the beneficiary) is designated in the policy. Policies may be purchased in nearly any amount, with the premium varying proportionately.

The requirement of insurable interest extends to life insurance. A cannot insure the life of B, if the death of B would cause no harm to A.

If A is B's employer and B is regarded as a virtually irreplaceable skilled employee, A will have an insurable interest in B's life. On the other hand, if B is only a casual friend of A's, insurable interest will not exist. In this second case, allowing A to buy the life insurance on B would provide A with an incentive to commit murder. In the first case, in which A insures the life of his essential employee, he does not have that incentive, since A's business will be disrupted if B dies. The payment from the insurance company will only help to compensate him for the losses caused by B's death.

There is an extensive variety of life insurance policies sold, but we apply the principal of simplification and examine only a few basic policy types. However, the discussion is general enough to enable the reader to readily analyze other policies that he may encounter. At the beginning a basic point to remember is that many of the premiums collected by life insurance companies are not for insurance at all but for the purchase of assets. (The nature of these assets is discussed later.) Although the purchase of these assets, usually very safe but rather low-yielding claims, may be desirable, more careful planning can be accomplished if the decision to buy these claims is kept separate from the insurance purchase decision. To make this distinction one needs to view the premium required for any proposed insurance policy as

$$\text{Premium} = \text{payment for insurance} + \text{payment for assets}$$

He can then decide to accept the blend of insurance and asset accumulation offered in any proposed policy or search for one with a more desirable ratio.

A simple method may be used to identify the dollar amounts of these premium components. One can find the cost of "pure" insurance protection by obtaining the price on a policy with no asset accumulation feature. On any other type of policy, he can then solve the following equation.

Payment for assets = premium — payment for insurance

For example, if the Tender Care Insurance Company offers a $10,000 policy with a premium of $400, and if $10,000 of "pure" insurance can be purchased for $150, the asset purchase component of Tender Care's premium is $250. Unless one wishes to purchase a $250 asset of the type offered by Tender Care, he will wish to look for another policy.

Term insurance

To consider policy types we first look at a policy that provides insurance only, with no asset purchase component. Term insurance represents life insurance in its pure form. The word term in the title of this policy denotes that this is a policy purchase for a particular time period, although it can be adapted into a permanent form. The simple term policy might consist of the requirement that an individual pay a $70 premium in return for $5000 life insurance for one year. Thus the individual enters a bet against himself: If he dies, his family receives $5000, if he lives nothing is received.

The insurance company bases the premium for term insurance on the likelihood that the policyholder will die during the year of his coverage. For example, a company considers issuing one-year, $5000 policies to a large number of people who are the same age. On the basis of studies of this age group, the company finds that one out of every hundred of these policyholders is likely to die within the year. Thus the company can estimate a mean expected payment of $5000 per 100 policyholders, or $50 per policyholder. After adding on various allowances for costs and allowing some profit, the company might accordingly set its premium at $70.

The nature of the policyholder's adverse gamble is also illustrated in this example. The insurance company's mean expected payment per policyholder is the policyholder's mean expected return. Hence, in our example, the policyholder exchanges his $70 premium in exchange for a mean expected return of $50; his mean expected net return is — $20.

In premium determination companies attempt to discriminate between those individuals with greater and lesser chances of dying. Since past experience indicates that the chance of dying is related to both age and sex, term insurance premiums are lower for the young than for the old and for women than for men.

There are two ways in which term insurance can be extended for longer periods of time beyond the basic term policy of a year. Term insurance can be sold for longer time periods, such as five years; it is also sold with a provision for guaranteed renewability. Although there is an extra charge for this "guaranteed renewable" feature, payment of this extra premium is likely to be justified if an individual thinks he will want insurance for a very long period of time. Without this feature the insurance company has no obligation to renew the policy at the expiration of its term of coverage. An individual may develop a serious health problem during the time he is covered by term insurance. For example, suppose that he suffered a heart attack during the period. When his policy expires, the insurance company may decide that the individual's chance of dying had become extraordinarily great and can therefore refuse to offer additional term insurance. However, with guaranteed renewability the insurance company must reissue insurance at the normal premium, even to those policyholders whom it would prefer not to insure.

The amount of insurance

In considering the amount of life insurance that a family should buy, it is essential to first consider the consumption requirements that are to be maintained out of the potential insurance benefits. The most important economic consequences of a death interrupting family income is curtailment of consumption plans. As we present additional aspects of the formulation of an economic plan, we want to consider a careful projection of family consumption expenditures, based on the assumption of no untimely death. These projections can be revised to form the needed estimates for determining adequate life insurance protection.

Revision is necessary because a death changes a family's consumption needs. If a husband dies, his earnings are lost, but his expenses for food, clothing, commuting, and hobbies also cease. Perhaps his survivors may even wish to move to a smaller home. Some expenses may also increase if the family finds it necessary to hire for some services, such as painting or lawn mowing, previously performed by the husband. In general, though, the death of a husband is likely to bring about a reduction in overall expenses.

On the other hand, if a wife dies, consumption spending might increase; a housekeeper might have to be hired to undertake the wife's services. The death of a child is likely to result in a decrease in consumption requirements, perhaps substantially because of the potential education expenses for the child.

The loss of income from the salary of an employed family member could necessitate serious curtailments in family consumption. On the other hand, if a nonworking member of the family dies or if the family is receiving substantial flows of benefits from assets, the disruption may not be serious. There may also be substitute income possibilities available; for example, the wife may accept a job after the death of her husband. Additionally, involuntary benefits are likely to provide considerable help.

To explore the need for life insurance protection, consider the following example. A husband and wife have two children, ages eight and fourteen. The family estimates its basic consumption expenditures (see Chapter 16 for a discussion of this concept) as $450 per month for the next three years, $550 per month for the following ten years, when the children will be attending college, $400 per month for the following 17 years until expected retirement, and $350 per month during retirement.

Death of either child will only decrease prospective expenses. The family estimates that death of the wife would require a part-time housekeeper until both children have started college (nearly ten years) and that the *extra* cost of this, after deduction of the wife's expected consumption, would be $100 per month. Death of the husband would result in the loss of his earnings and in the reduction of estimated expenses by $75 per month. The family is obligated to make mortgage payments of $70 per month for the next ten years, but has no other liabilities. The family also has a checking account balance of $50 and $3000 in a savings account.

By supplementing from the savings account balance, the family feels it could meet the extra expense associated with the possible death of the wife out of the husband's regular income. Therefore life insurance is needed only on the husband. To decide the amount of needed insurance, the family first notes its revised basic consumption needs; it then deducts from these the estimated involuntary benefits it would obtain if the husband died. These estimates are shown in Table 12.1; all benefits are assumed to be inflation protected.

TABLE 12.1

	Years in future				
	1–3	4–10	11–13	14–30	Retirement
Basic monthly expenditures for entire family including mortgage payments	$ 520	$ 620	$550	$ 450	$350
Deduction of husband's expenses	75	75	75	75	50
Expenditures without husband	$ 445	$ 545	$475	$ 375	$300
Involuntary benefits					
Social security	$ 200	$ 180	$150		$150
Job-connected survivor benefit	100	100	100	100	100
Inheritance			140		
Total involuntary benefits	$ 300	$ 280	$390	$ 100	$250
Monthly needs (expenditures minus involuntary benefits)	$ 145	$ 265	$ 65	$ 275	$ 50
Annual needs (monthly needs × 12)	1740	3180	780	3300	600

In Table 12.1, along with involuntary benefits another expected benefit source is shown. This family is almost certain to receive an inheritance of *at least* $5000 within ten years. This anticipated minimum amount of the inheritance is included; to coincide with the time periods used for other purposes, the expected inheritance is estimated as a flow of $140 per month ($5000/36) during years 11, 12, and 13.

After annual needs are estimated, plans can be made for meeting them. Three major sources from which these needs may be met are (a) the wife who had planned to use her earning power in unpaid home activities may elect to work if her husband dies; (b) the family may have claims or other assets which yield money benefits; and (c) life insurance may provide for the needs.

Continuing our example, the family decides that the wife could accept paid employment after the youngest child has started college.

To consider the effect of her employment, income taxes and any reduction in involuntary benefit payments caused by the fact that she will have another income source, are deducted from her expected earnings. In this hypothetical case the net earnings available are estimated to be *at least* $1500 to $3300 per year while she works, with estimated pension benefits of $600 per year.

With the wife's expected earnings deducted from the family's expected needs, net needs can be identified. These are shown in Table 12.2. The remainder of the analysis in Table 12.2 consists of a reduction of these net needs to a present value. This present value is computed with a discount rate of 3%. The family assumes that *at least* 3% can reasonably be earned, after tax and inflation adjusted, on claims already owned by the family or from investment life insurance proceeds. Thus the family can assume that, upon the death of the husband, about $23,000 will be required.

Since the family has a $3000 savings account, it decides that $20,000

TABLE 12.2

	Years in future				
	1–3	4–10	11–13	14–30	Retirement
Annual needs (from Table 12.1)	$ 1,740	$ 3,180	$ 780	$3,300	$600
Wife's estimated after-tax earnings and retirement benefits			1,500	3,300	600
Net needs	1,740	3,180	−720	–	–
Present value at beginning of each period discounted at 3%	5,000	20,000			
Present values discounted at 3%	5,000	18,200			
Total present value of net needs	23,200				

of life insurance on the husband will met its expected basic consumption needs. Although it is true that there may be some slight chance of shortage (assets not yielding 3%, pension benefits not sufficiently inflation protected, and so forth), there are also some offsetting chances for relief of the shortage. The wife expects to earn more than her needs in years 11 to 13 and could repay a small amount of borrowing done in earlier periods. The inheritance could be more than expected, the children might obtain educational loans or scholarships in greater amounts than expected, or other fortunate events might occur.

In addition to this calculated $20,000, there is good reason for providing a little additional insurance. Some cash in reserve may be especially desirable for a widow, beyond the $20,000 which must be invested for future consumption requirements. Funeral expenses will also have to be met. There is no way of precisely estimating these needs, but $2000 would seem like a modest amount to add for these requirements.

Therefore the family decides that it requires a minimum of $22,000 insurance. However, it may already own some life insurance, perhaps without realizing this. Sometimes when a family borrows money, part of the borrowing transaction consists of the purchase of *credit life insurance.* This is a special type of insurance that discharges a debt owed by a family if the husband dies. Since the family in our example owes money on a mortgage, it should check to see if this mortgage is protected by credit life insurance. If it is, this amount of credit life insurance should be deducted from the family's estimated insurance needs before purchasing more insurance.

If our family has no credit life insurance, it ought to consider strongly the purchase of $22,000 of life insurance. This basic insurance need be bought only in the form of guaranteed renewable term.

Marginal analysis

The purchase of life insurance can be subject to marginal analysis. After providing for a minimum level of insurance benefits, the family can decide whether it wishes to add additional steps of insurance coverage to provide additional benefits. However, the family would have to remember that, because insurance is an adverse gamble, its mean expected pattern of consumption will be decreased by the increasing marginal insurance purchases. Eventually marginal insurance purchases would become so high that they were not protecting against financial difficulty and, in this case, marginal life insurance would be ordinary gambling. Extra life insurance purchases can be especially unfortunate if at the same time, the family is avoiding the purchase of other basic insurance protection because it "cannot afford" this.

Special situation life insurance

It is not possible to distinguish between the financial consequences of death caused by a sudden illness or by an accident except that a job-connected accident will probably afford some workmen's compensation benefits to survivors. There are, however, a number of insurance policies available that attempt to provide protection from death occurring from an accident or from some particular type of accident. Some life insurance policies are offered with a *double indemnity* feature, which provides that the death benefit will be twice as much if accidental death occurs. Special insurance for death caused by travel accidents, including the machine-dispensed variety often seen in airports, is also available.

Marginal analysis suggests that these special forms of insurance are likely to have undesirable gambling aspects. For example, suppose that an individual has a chance to buy a conventional term insurance policy for $100 or one with a double indemnity feature for $110. He ought to question whether the marginal $10 that he pays for the double indemnity could be more advantageously used for the purchase of other insurance or for other purposes. The $10 spent for the extra accident protection amounts to a gamble on a special type of death rather than provision for the needs that will arise from any type of death.

Life insurance plus assets accumulation

The guaranteed renewable term insurance policy is a pure form of insurance since it offers nothing more than the chance for an individual to engage in bets against himself. Many life insurance policies offer something more to the purchaser than insurance alone. The extra aspect offered is asset accumulation, and the return on these assets is readily identifiable by marginal analysis. Since term insurance is available, the payment of larger premiums for an asset accumulation feature is optional. The marginal premium is a purchase of a particular type of claim and could be compared with other investment possibilities by a rate of return calculation.

Ordinary life

A type of insurance policy closely resembling guaranteed renewable term is the ordinary or straight life insurance policy. Although there is some variation in ordinary life policies, they usually provide that an individual pay premiums on a single policy until some specified age, usually 65. The policy pays its face amount if the individual dies at any time during this period. It differs from guaranteed renewable term principally by having what is called a *level premium* feature. As an individual grows older the premium on term insurance increases, whereas in an ordinary life policy the premium remains the same throughout the individual's life.

Because the individual pays slightly more than a term premium during the early years of the ordinary life policy, he accumulates an asset. If he discontinues the insurance, he can normally reclaim some money by surrendering his policy.[1]

Endowment policies: insurance with substantial asset accumulation

Insurance policies are available with much greater degrees of asset accumulation. Consider the 20-year endowment policy. An endowment policy provides for the accumulation of a sum of money as well as providing insurance protection. The terms of endowment policies differ, but we will assume that the one in this example is taken out by a 30-year-old man who must pay level premiums for 20 years. It provides that he will have insurance coverage until he is 65, when he will then receive the face amount of his policy in cash.

The policy can be compared with term insurance using marginal analysis. The cost of the assets being accumulated is the difference between payments made on this policy during each of the first 20 years and the payments necessary on term insurance during that period. The benefits receivable from the policy are the term insurance premiums which do not have to be paid between ages 50 and 65 and the face amount of the policy received at age 65. Thus a rate of return can be identified on such a policy. In this case it is desirable for the individual to obtain an opinion about whether any part of the benefit from the policy will be subject to income tax. An estimated inflation rate should again be deducted from the rate of return.

As in an ordinary life policy, the endowment policy can normally be discontinued by the policyholder if insurance protection is no longer needed. When discontinued, the asset accumulated in connection with the

[1] The insurance company is able to offer this feature by charging more than the term insurance premium during the beginning years of the policy and buying assets such as bonds with the difference. Then these assets and the earnings from them are used by the company to meet expenses during later years. The company can, in turn, hold ordinary insurance premiums at a level lower than term insurance premiums during the later years of the individual's life.

The rate of return on the asset accumulation in this type of policy could be calculated by finding that rate which would cause the present value of the premium savings in later years (as compared to term insurance) to be equal to the present value of the extra premium cost in earlier years. This rate of return is nontaxable, but because it is not inflation protected, an estimated inflation rate should be deducted from it when making comparisons between it and other assets.

policy is usually returned to the policyholder. Asset accumulation through payment of insurance premiums on nonterm insurance may be desirable. Some people feel that regularly required premium payments "force them to save" and prefer this type of asset accumulation. Except for this feature, the claim accumulated is similar to other very safe claims, such as high quality bonds. However, one should always remember that the marginal premiums (above the cost of renewable term insurance) paid for these insurance-with-asset accumulation policies are not for insurance.

Annuities

In addition to offering protection against untimely death, life insurance companies also offer protection against the extra consumption requirements associated with extraordinarily long life. This second protection is accomplished in the form of an annuity. The purchase of an annuity really represents an opportunity to purchase a lifetime pension. Again, there is a betting element present. The individual pays a given amount of money to the insurance company in return for the insurance company's assurance of a series of payments for the rest of his life. The policyholder bets against himself in the sense that living a long time may represent a financial problem. If he does live a long time, he wins by collecting a long series of payments; if he lives a short time, he loses by collecting only a few payments.

Traditionally annuities have been paid in fixed amounts specified in the annuity policy. As we discussed in the section on pensions in Chapter 11, variable annuities have recently become popular because they offer inflation protection. In the development of a comprehensive financial plan, annuities may have a place if the individual making the plans is in danger of being unable to meet the extraordinary consumption requirements imposed by a long life.

Services of the insurance agent

Although an individual needs to understand the basic concepts underlying insurance, he will probably not be able to master all the technicalities associated with insurance coverage. Thus selection of an insurance agent should be carefully undertaken, for it is very useful to be able to rely on an agent's opinions. Many individuals buy insurance on the basis of high pressure sales pitches by door-to-door salesmen, and sometimes this insurance is very justifiable coverage. However, anyone undertaking serious financial planning should spend some time in selecting a reliable insurance agent if he does not already have one. Even then, he should realize that the agent's income depends on the amount of insurance that he sells and should carefully scrutinize any recommended purchases of marginal insurance that might move his policy out of the realm of basic protection and gradually into the realm of pure gambling.

Summary

Insurance may be regarded as a special form of bet. When one buys an insurance policy, he bets that some unfavorable event will occur. If the event actually occurs, he wins his bet and is partly compensated for the unfavorable circumstances in which he finds himself. If the unfavorable event does not occur, he receives nothing from the insurance company.

Virtually all insurance policies are adverse gambles; that is, the insurance company will pay a smaller amount to policyholders than the amount that has been paid in premiums. This relationship occurs because the insurance company must provide for the cost of selling the insurance, the cost of operating the insurance company, and some profit for the owners of the insurance company out of the premiums, as well as providing for payments to policyholders.

Because insurance is an adverse gamble, care should be taken to avoid purchasing unnecessary insurance. Basic levels of insurance can be highly beneficial, however, because of the risk protection that they provide.

Life insurance is available in a basic form called term insurance, which provides for no asset accumulation. Normally it is desirable to purchase this term insurance in guaranteed renewable form.

Other types of life insurance policies provide for asset accumulation together with insurance protection. Ordinary insurance provides for only a moderate amount of asset accumulation, whereas endowment policies may be of such nature that only a relatively small part of premiums paid is used for insurance protection.

When one accumulates an asset by paying insurance premiums above the premium for the same amount of renewable term insurance, the asset accumulated will typically be a very safe and relatively low-yielding asset. Some families find this type of asset accumulation desirable because of its semicompulsory nature.

A family buying life insurance needs to consider the financial consequences of a death in the family. Usually it is only the death of an income earner that has serious money effects. In the event that income is interrupted by death, the family will have some other possible income sources available. These sources include assets owned by the family, possible inheritances, and the family's involuntary benefit programs. Life insurance can then be purchased to provide for the needs of the family that are not covered in other ways.

Life insurance purchase should be subject to marginal analysis. Basic levels of life insurance may be highly desirable, whereas additional levels of insurance will progressively deteriorate in value until marginal insurance purchases come to be an ordinary gamble of an adverse type.

SUGGESTED READINGS

An excellent discussion of life insurance is published by the Consumers Union, the *Consumers Union Report on Life Insurance.* This is relatively short and very readable. It sells for $1.50 ($1.00 to Consumers Union members).

The *Changing Times* magazine frequently provides useful comments on purchase of insurance.

A widely used basic insurance textbook which covers both life insurance and some other type is *General Insurance*, 8th ed., by John H. Magee and David L. Bickelhaupt (Homewood, Ill.: Richard D. Irwin, 1970).

QUESTIONS

1. Carefully explain how a bet can be used as a form of insurance to protect against risk.
2. Why is an insurance policy regarded as an adverse gamble?
3. Why is it essential than an insurance policy be a "bet against one's self"?
4. Would you have an insurable interest in your own life? the life of your wife? of your parents? of your employer? in the building in which you work?
5. Will your need for insurance protection increase or decrease over the next ten years?
6. Does the social security program provide any life insurance?
7. What reasons would an unmarried individual have for buying life insurance?
8. Try to formulate some basic consumption requirements for your family.
9. Specifically, why may marginal benefit from life insurance decrease as increasing amounts of insurance are purchased? Describe the type of asset purchased when ordinary life insurance is bought instead of term insurance.
10. What are the possible consequences of buying nonrenewable term insurance?
11. What are the possible advantages and disadvantages of buying an endowment policy instead of term insurance?
12. Why can an annuity be described as life insurance in reverse (insurance against living too long) and why would someone wish to purchase this type of insurance?

PROBLEMS

1. You have the opportunity to bet $20 with even chances of either of the following.
   (i) A recovery of the original $20 plus another $15 or a total of $35.
   (ii) Nothing.
      (a) Is this an adverse gamble?
      (b) What is the mean expected loss?

(c) Can you compose an example of a situation in which it might be logical to undertake such a bet provided you could not find a similar bet with more favorable terms?

2. You desire insurance protection over a 20-year period and consider two types of policies. You can provide the protection with renewable term insurance; the premium on this is $150 per year during the first ten years and $250 per year during the second ten years. You could also buy a 20-year ordinary life policy with a premium of $190 per year.
   (a) If you buy the ordinary life policy, what is the amount of asset accumulation during each of the ten years?
   (b) What is the benefit that will be received from each of these asset purchases?
   (c) What is the rate of return on the asset component of the ordinary life insurance? (Is this a before-tax or after-tax return? Is it inflation protected?)

3. (a) Jim expects to live 20 years. He has $100,000 in savings that he feels he can safely invest at a 5% after-tax, inflation-protected return. How much money could he spend each year if he wanted his savings to last exactly 20 years?
   (b) Would he be able to buy an annuity of this same amount for $100,000? Why or why not?
   (c) What advantage would there be for Jim to buy an annuity rather than just to spend out of his savings?

chapter thirteen

Other insurance

Life insurance is principally used to protect against interruption in the earnings from human capital. There are two other types of insurance that are closely linked with people rather than claims and physical assets: health insurance and disability insurance. Because the needs covered by these two forms of insurance often occur at the same time, they are very closely related insurance types.

Health insurance

Health insurance, like life insurance, has been given its name by sales-conscious insurance companies. These names sound more positive and appealing than sickness insurance and death insurance. Basically, health insurance protects against expenses arising from sickness or accident. A policy does not specify a particular amount in dollars; instead it pays certain costs, such as hospital bills or doctors' fees, when they occur during the period the insurance is in effect. Health insurance policies, however, do not offer any protection against earning loss while a wage earner is unable to work (disabled). Therefore a complete program of sickness and accident insurance protection also includes disability insurance or, as it is sometimes called, salary continuation insurance.

Some expenses for health care are quite predictable. If a family has annual physical examinations, their cost can be planned for about as easily as the cost of the family's food. A family also knows with reasonable certainty that occasionally there are going to be additional visits to the doctor and dentist and expenses for items such as eyeglasses and medicines, and it can plan for these possibilities. However, the family never knows when some unusual health expenses will occur, such as those caused by a major accident or illness. Because these expenses may run into many thousands of dollars, the family is likely to desire protection against these extraordinary needs.

Insurance is available to help with this risk situation. Again the insurance involves the same principle as enunciated earlier: a bet against one's self. In this case the policyholder bets that he will become ill or injured. If these misfortunes occur, he wins his bet with the insurance company and receives benefit payments. If he does not incur the health expenses, he loses his bet and receives nothing for his premium.

Double Benefits

Any planning for the risk of medical expenses should consider involuntary benefits that may be available for health care. It is quite common for health care provisions to be a part of the fringe benefits associated with a particular job; some veterans are also eligible for health care. Individuals over 65 receive a great deal of protection from health care risk by Medicare.

If already available benefits are not considered, double insurance coverage may result. There are two consequences of double protection by insurance and both are likely to be undesirable. If one has arranged to receive benefits from two sources, these sources may, by virtue of laws governing insurance transactions or because of provisions written into their policies, be allowed to pay jointly only a single set of benefits. Since the policyholder has been paying premiums based on double benefits, premium money is obviously wasted. Even if double benefits can be collected, these benefits are probably in excess of need; when an individual carries insurance at this level, he is no longer betting against himself but engaging in conventional gambling. Thus there is a good chance that premium dollars used to provide this protection could have been more advantageously used elsewhere.

To avoid providing double benefits, insurance that does not duplicate involuntary benefits should be selected. There are two possible approaches to this problem. Insurance may be purchased in lower amounts (as in the life insurance example) when other benefits are available or policies may be selected that exempt the insurance company from payment under certain circumstances. An example of this second situation is disability insurance that will not pay full benefits when the policyholder is injured on the job and can obtain workmen's compensation benefits. Such an exemption allows the insurance to be sold at a lower premium.

Deductible Feature

Not only is it unwise to pay premiums for double benefits, but it is also usually undesirable to use insurance protection for small or readily predictable expenses. To avoid coverage of these expenses, insurance policies often offer a *deductible* feature. This provides that expenses under a specified amount will not be recoverable from the insurance company. For example, a health insurance policy might be offered in the form, "$500 deductible." In this policy the insurance company agrees, within the period of coverage, to pay all of the policyholder's medical expenses above $500. If medical expenses totaling $450 are sustained during the period, the individual receives no help from his insurance.

Marginal analysis can be employed on the deductible feature. Suppose that the premium on a $500 deductible policy is $100 per year and that the individual also has the opportunity to purchase a policy with no deductible feature for $200 per year. An individual can reason that for a $100 premium he is protected for all expenses above $500 and that, for an extra $100 premium, he is protected against expenses within the range of 0 to $500. This second step might appear desirable at first glance because an individual is reasonably sure that he is going to incur some medical expenses and hence is likely to get at least part of the marginal $100 premium back in benefit payments.

At this point recall a statement made in Chapter 12; except for minor exceptions, *insurance is always an adverse gamble*. The insurance company cannot set the marginal premium on the nondeductible insurance at $100 unless the mean expected benefits to be received from this marginal insurance are substantially less than $100. (Otherwise, the insurance company would not be able to stay in business.) Thus, although a policyholder may expect to recapture part of his marginal premium in the form of benefit payments, he ought to discard the notion that he is likely to recapture nearly all of the premium; adverse gambles do not work that way.

The individual needs to decide whether he wishes to undertake an adverse gamble with its attendant cost in order to secure marginal protection for potential losses between 0 and $500. Although losses up to $500 are unpleasant, for most families a loss of this magnitude is not catistrophic. A large automobile repair bill, the consequences of some frozen water pipes, or the failure to receive an expected bonus could also cause "losses" of about the same magnitude. Unless the family is buying insurance to cover some of these other risk possibilities (an impractical undertaking), it is probably protecting itself against these risks in other ways. One common way is the maintenance of some liquid assets. When nondeductible insurance is contemplated, the marginal analysis of this insurance ought to include the question: Is our family already equipped to cope with losses of this size and therefore should we avoid the cost of insurance in this situation?

Coinsurance and Maximums

A deductible feature exempts the insurance company from providing benefits in some situations. At this same time, a policy with this feature places the burden of major expenses on the insurance company.

Health and other insurance policies often contain features that exempt the insurance company from participation in other situations. One of these is called a *coinsurance* feature, which specifies that when expenses are covered by insurance, the insurance company will pay only a certain percentage of them. The second is a *maximum* feature in which the insurance company places a dollar limitation or some other ceiling on the total amount of benefits it will pay. Both features tend to pass on risk to the policyholder and both can be subjected to marginal analysis.

Suppose that A considers two $500 deductible policies, one with no coinsurance provision and another with a 25% coinsurance feature. The policy with the coinsurance feature will be lower priced and A can decide if the marginal premium spent for the policy without coinsurance will be worthwhile. Because in unusual cases a family's health expenses may be very high, a 25% participation in these expenses may be a severe financial blow. It is unusual for a family to incur medical and hospital expenses of $20,000, for example, but if this happened A's participation under the $500 deductible coinsurance policy would be determined as

Amounts to be paid by A	
First $500 of expenses borne entirely by family	$ 500
Remaining $19,500, borne 25% by family	4875
Total expenses to be paid by family	$5375

Thus A might well feel that the coinsurance policy exposed his family to an unacceptable level of risk and that paying the marginal premium necessary to avoid coinsurance would be desirable.

The rejection of coinsurance may not always be desirable. Marginal premiums for the avoidance of all coinsurance may be rather high, since coinsurance is believed to prevent some abuses of insurance protection. For example, with no coinsurance, a hospitalized individual has some incentive to prolong his stay in the hospital. His insurance is paying for all expenses, including items such as food which he would otherwise have to purchase. (His hospital and doctor may also have some financial incentive to keep him hospitalized.) To check these potential abuses, insurance companies in turn can afford to offer substantial premium reductions on coinsurance for some types of health insurance.

Although coinsurance inflicts a portion of risk on a family, a maximum amount of coverage in a policy inflicts all of the risk of expenses beyond a particular amount. Maximums on health insurance may be in dollar amounts or may be in the form of a time limit, such as "the first 60 days of hospitalization." Most health insurance policies, including the widely distributed Blue Cross and Blue Shield plans, contain a maximum feature. Marginal analysis can be applied to these maximums, but, in general, if the family desires health insurance at all, it is likely to want protection for extremely severe illnesses and accidents. Therefore it will usually be desirable to pay a marginal premium to obtain a policy with a high maximum or no maximum.

Any health insurance policy should be carefully examined for coinsurance and maximum features. Most individuals are likely to find it desirable to economize on health insurance premiums by purchasing policies with deductible features rather than ones with low maximums or with very large coinsurance participation. When an individual is considering an insurance program to supplement involuntary benefits, he ought to find out whether his involuntary benefits are subject to a maximum and consider providing supplemental insurance protection above this maximum. The maximum will only be important in unusual cases, but it is these unusual cases that represent the most severe risks.

Health Insurance Policies Available

A wide array of health insurance policies are available. These range from "major" medical and hospitalization policies, which typically have a large deductible amount and high maximums (though these must be checked for their maximum and coinsurance provisions), down to policies which offer very little risk protection. These latter policies have low maximums, but because of their usual lack of deductible features, they are still likely to have high premiums. Most policies do not cover routine dental or eye care; these expenses are usually fairly predictable and hence do not involve much risk. (It is desirable, however, to have a policy that protects against the possibility of major dental surgery or expensive treatment of eye problems.) The possibility of coverage for major drug expenses should also be investigated since these may sometimes be financial burdens.

Disability insurance

When an accident or illness affects a salary earner, the financial problems of the illness are compounded. The problems caused by the disability can be even more severe than the medical and hospital expenses; the disability may continue long after these other expenses have stopped. Disability insurance, which provides protection against income interruption, is therefore at least as important as the more conventional forms of health insurance. Similarly, when disability insurance is compared with life insurance, we observe that when a death occurs in a family, consumption expenses are likely to be reduced, but when a disability interrupts a family's income, there is no accompanying expense reduction.

Disability insurance, like life insurance, is purchased in dollar amounts. These amounts are usually expressed in dollars payable per month upon total disability. Proportionately smaller payments are usually provided when disability is only partial. The desirable amount of disability insurance coverage can be determined in a manner similar to that used with life insurance. Again the appropriate standard to use in making this decision is not the amount of income that will be lost but the amount of consumption that the family wishes to have guaranteed under an insurance program. If a family receives a large part of its income from physical assets and claims, the interruption of a salary may not be severe. Thus there are cases in which a family might choose to do without disability insurance, just as there are cases in which life insurance is not desirable.

In an economic sense disability does differ from death in one major way: It can occur partially. If an individual is only partially disabled or if he is disabled for only a short period of time, the family might be able to cope with the disability without hardship. To allow families to tailor disability insurance to their own needs, the equivalent of a deductible feature has developed in disability policies. This feature may take two possible forms: a limitation on payments in the case of partial disabilities and the specification of a waiting period before benefit payments. For example, a policy may be obtainable that does not provide benefits unless the policyholder is at least 30% disabled. Or a policy may provide that benefits will not start until six months after the beginning of disability.

These forms of deductible insurance can be marginally analyzed. One point worth noting is that these deductible features may be of much larger dollar amounts than the deductible features on other insurance. For instance, an individual may consider a choice between a three-month and a one-year waiting period on disability insurance. If his potential benefits are $300 per month, he is considering the difference between a $900 and a $3600 deductible feature.

Since payments received from disability insurance are normally tax exempt, a dollar of disability insurance benefit goes substantially further than a dollar in salary. Nearly everyone is eligible for some involuntary disability through social security. Other benefits may be provided through workmen's compensation, veteran programs, or employment "fringe benefits." Disability insurance protection should be supplemental in nature and designed to avoid double coverage.

Disability policies may state a maximum length of time over which benefits will be paid. For example, one policy provides two years of disability benefits when disability is created by illness and lifetime benefits for an accident-caused disability. (From the policyholder's point of view a reversed arrangement would be more desirable since accident-caused disabilities are more likely to be covered by workmen's compensation or other involuntary sources of accident benefits.) These ceilings placed on the liability of the insurance company are subject to the same commentary made about ceilings imposed on health insurance benefits; they fail to protect against the most serious risks.

Liability insurance

The previously discussed insurance protects against the financial effects of some physical event, such as untimely death or accident-caused disability. Liability insurance offers protection against the financial consequences of a legal event in which an individual is held accountable by law for financial damages originally sustained by someone else. For example, a court may determine that an individual is "at fault" in an automobile accident and require him to pay money to those injured in the accident. An architect designing a building may make a planning error and be required to pay the cost of correcting the resulting flaw in the building.

It might be argued that the liabilities of an individual can, at most, cause the loss of all his physical assets and claims. This argument is based on the existence of personal bankruptcy laws. When an individual's debts have become greater than his physical assets and claims, he may undertake a special, formal legal process, giving up all his physical assets and claims to be divided among those to whom he owes money. By the process of personal bankruptcy, his legal responsibility for all of his outstanding debts is discharged. Thus, if an individual held $40,000 in physical assets and claims and owed $100,000, he could go through personal bankruptcy proceedings and satisfy his $100,000 obligation by surrendering his $40,000 in assets. By this process, his future earnings could be left immune to the pressures of his creditors, so his human capital would be shielded from loss.

There are many who may not wish to include the possibility of bankruptcy in their planning on personal ethical grounds. Furthermore, the individual who undertakes personal bankruptcy is likely to suffer some unfavorable future consequences from his action. Although this action is legal, it lacks social acceptability. The person undertaking it may find that he is barred from some jobs and he may have difficulty in obtaining credit. As an additional note, since there are many situations over which the protection of personal bankruptcy laws do not extend, the person contemplating reliance on these laws is strongly advised to consult an attorney in his home state.

For any person whose basic consumption is dependent on returns from physical assets and claims and for all who wish to avoid exposure to possible personal bankruptcy, consideration of liability insurance is essential. Note that in some instances (for example, auto liability insurance in some states) the individual may be required by law to carry some liability insurance.

It may be difficult for an individual who regards himself as very careful and law abiding to imagine a situation in which he may be held liable for damages to another party. However, the concept of "fault" that is used to fix blame for accidents and some other financial misfortunes is something different from the usual concept of guilt or wrong-doing. Sometimes the law defines fault in such a way that an individual is responsible without any direct harmful action. For example, consider the protection afforded employees by workmen's compensation for on-the-job injuries. In these situations the courts have held that the employer is almost always liable for on-the-job accidents even though many of these accidents are caused by the carelessness of employees. The courts were really saying that employers were more likely able to pay the cost of these accidents or were more likely to insure to cover these costs (with a form of liability insurance). Therefore it was socially desirable that legal fault should lie with the employer.

There are other examples of rather unusual concepts of fault. Property owners are almost always liable for accidents that occur on their property, regardless of the actual cause of the accident. Sometimes individuals are held liable for large settlements in automobile accidents even though they have committed only a minor traffic infraction (which most of us have had the good luck to commit, on at least one occasion, without causing an accident).

Automobile Liability Insurance

The most common variety of liability insurance is automobile liability coverage. Because accident claims can run to hundreds of thousands of dollars and because legal fault in an accident is often extremely difficult to avoid, driving or owning a car represents a threat of financial calamity to most families. Therefore a family's risk control program will almost always contain automobile liability insurance—a bet that one of the family members will be held responsible for a traffic accident.

Because an individual may be held responsible when others are operating his car, this risk is usually included in car liability insurance policies. Policies also normally include protection for insured individuals who are driving someone else's car. Liability insurance policies usually do not contain deductible features. When an individual is in an accident, the extent of liability cannot be quickly ascertained. Insurance companies maintain skilled legal staffs, and it is convenient for the individual to have a legal staff immediately available to assume his problems when an accident or other liability-creating incident occurs, regardless of the potential damage amount that might be involved.

Liability insurance policies all contain maximums that are sometimes low enough to shift considerable risk back to the policyholder. Many individual holders still buy what is called 50/100/5 auto liability insurance which provides for maximum payment of $50,000 to any one person, $100,000 for any one accident, and $5000 for any property damage, in spite of the fact that accident settlements have been known to run over $1 million. Again, it is very important to consider the possibility of a higher maximum. The marginal cost of this additional protection is usually small relative to the risk protection involved.

A feature commonly offered in connection with the sale of liability insurance is *uninsured driver coverage.* A policyholder is the victim of an accident in which someone else is at fault, who lacks either insurance coverage or assets to compensate the policyholder for damages sustained. Under uninsured driver coverage, the policyholder's insurance company will pay to the policyholder the damages that would otherwise have been paid by the person at fault.

The uninsured driver feature may result in the provision of double benefits. If X is injured in an accident, the financial consequences that may occur are the interruption of his earnings by death or disability and medical and hospitalization expenses. If X has already protected himself against these possibilities with his regular insurance program, then uninsured driver coverage does not protect X against these possibilities but simply gives X or his survivors an opportunity to receive some extra cash if an accident occurs; thus for X the marginal premium paid for uninsured driver coverage would be an ordinary gamble.

Other Liability Insurance Coverage

The car is one important source of potential liability to the family; the dwelling is another. It is fairly safe to say that if someone is injured in an individual's home or on his property, the homeowner will be responsible regardless of actual cause. An individual renting a house or apartment is also subject to possible liability if someone is injured on the property he is renting. Damages for persons injured on someone else's property do not usually reach the spectacular heights of automobile damage settlements; the injuries are often not as serious and there is frequently only one person involved. However, they are still potentially large enough to be financially catastrophic for many families. Therefore most families want insurance protection against liabilities of this type.

Individuals also ought to consider their possible liability for job-connected damages. Physicians may be subject to malpractice suits, directors of corporations may be sued by disenchanted stockholders, and schoolteachers may be liable for student injuries. It is impossible to make any generalization about the need for liability insurance to protect against job-connected liabilities, but certainly many persons are likely to find this coverage desirable.

A new liability insurance coverage insurance policy called an *umbrella* policy may also be of interest. This policy attempts to cover liabilities that are not covered with other liability insurance. The policy is designed for very unusual risk situations, such as extraordinarily high damages in an automobile accident or damage caused by an errant golf ball. For an individual attempting very rigorous risk control, such a policy may be worth consideration.

Property insurance

Often people are quite dependent on the services of physical capital, such as a house, and would find their consumption seriously disrupted by the loss of this asset. Since physical assets can be burned, flooded, blown away, stolen, or subject to other calamities, an individual should consider protection against risks of this type. For most persons the home fire insurance policy is the major type of property insurance undertaken. Since homes and their contents may be destroyed by other causes than fire, so-called fire insurance policies normally also include coverage against damage by wind, hail, flood, and possibly earthquake and vandalism.

Deductible features are sometimes available on property insurance coverage and ought to be given consideration. Coinsurance may also apply in the case of property insurance, although its application is usually unintentional for the policyholder. If property insurance is bought with a maximum benefit less than the value of the property insured, a coinsurance relationship normally exists. The proportionate participation of the insurance company is determined by the ratio between the insured value and the actual value. For example, Y's house is worth $30,000 and is insured for only $20,000, two-thirds of its actual value. A fire does $10,000 damage to it. The insurance company will bear its share (⅔ of \$10,000, or \$6667) of the loss and leave the remaining \$3333 of the loss to be borne by Y.

Unless an individual desires to coinsure, he has an incentive to buy a policy with a maximum benefit close to the actual value of the insured property. If he fails to recognize increases in the market value of his property and its contents, he may inadvertently subject himself to coinsurance even though he was originally fully insured.

Other types of property insurance are available. Although the loss of a car is not as serious as the loss of a house, most people still carry protection against possible damage to their own automobile through collision or other misfortune. This is normally done with a policy that provides both collision and comprehensive coverage. Again, deductible features are available. If a family feels that property insurance on its car is desirable, it may still want to absorb the small risk associated with those losses under \$100 or \$200 deductible amounts rather than participate in an adverse gamble in these situations.

Individuals are often given the opportunity to purchase some very minor types of property insurance, such as insurance against the loss of a contact lens or a television picture tube. The desirability of participating in adverse gambles to protect against these minor risks is highly questionable.

Basic insurance protection

An insurance program is an important part of a risk control program, although not the entirety of such a program. As noted before, risk can be controlled through choice of job or through selection of assets, including the maintenance of liquid assets. However, for nearly all families these other risk control meansures still leave major elements of risk that can be controlled by insurance.

When a family protects its lifetime consumption flows by the purchase of insurance, it does so at the cost of decreasing the mean expected amount of consumption that it will be able to sustain. The decrease is attributable to the fact that insurance is an adverse gamble, always subject to the inescapable fact that insurance companies cannot pay out as much in benefits as they receive in premiums.

Some generalizations about a desirable insurance program are possible. One of these is that the insurance program should be carefully designed to avoid duplication of involuntary benefits. Second, a basic insurance program should be designed primarily to protect a basic level of desired future consumption; other insurance should always be given a lower priority.

A basic insurance program should include the following policies.

1. Life insurance on the wage earner. Although a separate decision may be made to buy a higher priced policy, basic protection requires only renewable term insurance in an amount necessary to provide for basic consumption needs which cannot be met from involuntary benefits, returns on claims and other family earnings, and expected transfer payments.
2. Health insurance, preferably with a high deductible amount and a high maximum.
3. Disability insurance, with at least some waiting period (deductible feature) and with a long period of potential benefit payment. As with life insurance, the amount of basic disability insurance should be determined by estimating basic consumption needs which cannot be met from other sources.
4. Liability insurance on the car and home, with high maximum payments. Additional liability insurance may be needed in special circumstances to provide basic protection; for example, professional liability insurance.
5. Property insurance on the home and contents, with a deductible feature if possible.
6. Possibly property insurance on the car, with a high deductible feature. This insurance is most desirable for a family that owns few claims and places a high degree of importance on having a good car. (Without these two conditions it might be fairly easy for the family to either absorb the repair bills or replacement cost of the car by selling other assets or else to buy a cheap secondhand replacement car.

Beyond this basic insurance coverage, the family can, through marginal analysis, decide whether it wishes to protect itself against additional risk. It should always guard against the possibility of overinsuring (unless it like this particular form of gambling better than other consumption alternatives).

Risk control through asset diversification

A further look at asset diversification is also in order since this is an element of risk control. As noted in Chapter 7, greater safety can often be attended in a collection of claims by selecting either very safe items, such as savings accounts, or a diversified collection of items. Both of these precautionary measures will be accompanied by a reduction in the mean expected return of the claims. Safe assets usually have lower yields. Direct diversification by the asset owner is costly because of increased commissions and information costs; if the diversification is accomplished through a mutual fund or similar institutions, mean expected return will probably be slightly lower because of charges made by the institution. These reductions in yields are quite comparable to insurance premiums and ought to be viewed as part of the entire risk control program. For many families the purchase of safety through the acceptance of a reduced asset return may be a more effective means of risk control than the paying of insurance premiums on some marginal insurance coverage, such as car collision insurance or extraordinary amounts of life insurance.

Summary

Health insurance provides for expenses that may arise from sickness or accidents. When health insurance is purchased, the purchaser should take into account the involuntary benefit programs which may provide health benefits. Deductible features, coinsurance, and maximum payment provisions should be considered when comparing health insurance policies.

Disability insurance protects against the disruption of income that may occur when an income earner is subject to illness or an accident. Analysis similar to that used for determining the amount of life insurance needed can be used to determine necessary disability insurance coverage. This coverage should be designed to supplement involuntary benefit programs. Disability insurance programs may have a deductible feature (waiting time) and a maximum provision (maximum length of time benefits will be paid).

Liability settlements may be the source of very large unpredicted expenses for families. Even very careful families may potentially be subject to these costs. Thus it is usually desirable for families to have at least automobile liability insurance and homeowners' liability insurance; some additional coverage may also be desirable in special situations.

Liability policies do not have deductible features, but they do have maximums. Care should be taken to see that the liability policy's maximum is not so low that it provides inadequate protection.

Protection against interruption in the services provided by property, with fire insurance and other forms of property insurance, may also be useful. Protection of the home is essential for most families. A family may also wish to protect its car with collision insurance.

A basic insurance program should include the following: a basic level of life insurance, health insurance, disability insurance, liability insurance on the car and home, property insurance on the home, and (possibly) property insurance on the car.

Insurance is only part of a risk control program. Other aspects of a risk control should not be neglected.

SUGGESTED READINGS

Some of the material cited at the end of Chapter 12 discusses other insurance issues as well as life insurance.

There is a very informative chapter entitled, "Health Property and Automobile Insurance" in *Personal Finance: Principles and Case Problems*, 3d ed. by Jerome B. Cohen and Arthur W. Hanson (Homewood, Ill.: Richard D. Irwin, Inc., 1964).

QUESTIONS

1. Provide examples of health expenses that are predictable and those that are unpredictable.
2. How can liquid assets be used to protect against some of the risk of health problems? What is the limitation of using liquid assets for this type of protection?
3. How does one apply marginal analysis to a deductible feature?
4. Explain coinsurance and discuss the reason why it is a common feature on health insurance plans.
5. Why can the financial consequences of a disability be more serious than those of a death?
6. Criticize the following statement: I do not need liability insurance because I am not the type of person who commits illegal acts.
7. An individual may be able to increase the maximum payment of his car insurance policy by $100,000 or more with the amount of premium he saves by lowering a deductible feature by only $50. How can the insurance company afford to offer this possibility?
8. What are the advantages and disadvantages of using liquid assets to provide for the possibility of minor automobile collision damage?
9. Why is it much more important for an individual to have automobile liability insurance than collision insurance?
10. What types of risk cannot be covered by insurance?

PROBLEMS

1. Art buys a health insurance policy with the following provisions: $500 per year deductible; 20% coinsurance; maximum payment $25,000. Art's family is then subject to some very serious medical expenses over a period of years: year 1, $6000; year 2, $7500; year 3, $8000; year 4, $11,000. How much would Art's insurance pay each year?
2. Collision insurance premium is quoted at $80 for a $50 deductible policy and $95 for a $200 deductible policy. The value of the car being insured is approximately $4000.
   (a) If a $200 deductible policy is purchased, what is the maximum payment that the insurance company would make? What is the amount of premium *per dollar of coverage* on the $200 deductible policy?
   (b) How much marginal coverage is obtained by buying a $50 deductible policy instead of the $200 deductible? What is the marginal premium charge for this additional coverage? What is the marginal premium *per dollar of marginal coverage*?

chapter fourteen

Personal borrowing

Borrowing is a word that often suggests emotional or moral viewpoints. It may imply irresponsibility: the prodigal living beyond his means. Sometimes it has wheeler-dealer connotations, with the image of a person getting rich by using someone else's money. Sometimes its use is linked with the concept of usury, in which the borrower is thought of as the prey of an unscrupulous lender. An absence of borrowing may even convey an impression of bleak, puritanical self-denial. If possible, we want to separate our view of borrowing from any notion of ethical right or wrong and concentrate on borrowing as a possible tool in the implementation of a personal economic plan.

Borrowing, or the issuance of a liability, creates an "asset in reverse," as discussed in Chapter 1. When an asset is formed, some present consumption is given up to achieve the opportunity for some future consumption. When a liability is issued, some future consumption is assigned to someone else in exchange for extra present consumption or extra present asset-purchasing power.

Before we discuss the question of whether borrowing is desirable in particular circumstances, it is useful to consider some facts about borrowing. To understand the different interest rates and other terms that are attached to various borrowing arrangements, it is particularly useful to consider the viewpoints of lenders that make various types of loans.

Borrowing for physical assets and claims

The everyday process of borrowing for asset purchase may at first seem somewhat self-contradictory. Why would an individual buy an asset, and thus postpone consumption, at the same time that he issues a liability which enables him to accelerate consumption? A reasonable explanation for this paradox lies in the possibility that the rate of return on the asset may be in excess of the rate of interest on the loan. For example, the purchase of a car, when compared to alternative methods of providing transportation service, might yield a return of 20%; therefore borrowing money at 10% to finance the purchase might seem quite sensible.

Certain types of assets are more readily financed by borrowing than others. The nature of some assets makes the opportunity to finance them more attractive from the point of view of the lender. A house, for example, can often be readily financed because of certain characteristics that it possesses. It cannot be moved away and its value can be protected from physical destruction by insurance. It is real estate and is subject to a formal, controllable process for transfer of ownership. Thus the lender, by lending on a mortgage, can be assured that the property will be available for the satisfaction of the promises made, even though it is sold by the borrower. Because many families have similar tastes in housing, a house can usually be resold without much loss. The lender, whose mortgage gives him the right to sell the house if default occurs, can be reasonably sure that the sale price will enable him to recover his money.

Claims are another type of asset that can be readily financed. Claims do not yield their return in physical services and hence do not need to be in the physical possession of their owner; they can be held by the lender as an assurance that promises will be executed. Furthermore, claims are often readily salable; in the event of default, the lender can normally sell them and recover the amount of his loan.

Although it is very common for families to borrow for a car purchase, lenders do not find the financing of cars as attractive as houses or claims. Cars are anything but immovable and they cannot be readily placed under the lender's control. Their resale value is also not usually as certain as that of houses or claims, particularly because the resale value of a car is quite dependent on the care given the car by its owner. Because of these factors, it should be no surprise to find, as is discussed later in this chapter, that lenders usually insist in higher interest rates when they are financing cars than when they are financing houses or claims.

Similarly, smaller physical assets, such as appliances and furniture, are not as attractive to lenders, especially because of their lack of resale value. (Secondhand furniture, particularly, is usually worth only a small fraction of its original price.) Again, loans made directly for the purpose of financing these items are likely to carry high interest rates, even higher than those on cars.

Borrowing for consumption and human capital formation

Borrowing for consumption may occur even though a family has very few claims or physical assets. Sometimes the family may have substantial accumulations of human capital which will generate large amounts of future earnings, and it may wish to hasten the consumption that would otherwise be achieved later out of its future human capital returns. In other instances, a family may have no assets of any kind, but may still wish to consume out of expected future earnings.

For example, a family which is quite sure of a substantial increase in income may decide that it is willing to give up $2000 in anticipated luxury consumption two years in the future in order to have $1500 worth of convenience items now. If the family could borrow $1500 for two years at 10%, the required repayment including compound interest would be only $1815. Therefore, by borrowing, present goods subjectively valued at $2000 future dollars can be obtained in return for a promise to pay $1815 future dollars.

Lenders are likely to be apprehensive about lending in situations in which salable assets are lacking. (Human capital cannot be sold as an asset to satisfy a debt.) Increasing recognition, however, is being given to future earning power as a basis for lending. Implicitly, this policy also accords recognition to stocks of human capital, since these stocks are important sources of future earning power. Nevertheless, families who wish to borrow for consumption without having unusually secure future earning prospects are likely to find borrowing possible only at the cost of rather high interest charges.

Unplanned borrowing

Not all borrowing is carefully planned. Some occurs almost by accident. A family spends its paycheck early in the month, or buys a car which requires large monthly payments, and then finds that it does not have sufficient money to purchase bare necessities. It then borrows to fill the gap.

Such borrowing, which arises from unplanned spending, may have undesirable consequences, as illustrated in the following example. Dick receives $600 per month take-home pay; he is paid at the end of the month. On April 1 after pay day, Dick and his wife take some friends out to dinner and spend $50. They also buy some costly new clothes during the first week in April and eat expensive steaks nearly every night. By April 7, they have spent $300. This means that they have less than $100 per week to spend during the rest of the month. If they feel that they require $135 per week for basic consumption requirements, and if they have no previously accumulated money, they must borrow over $100 before the end of the month. This will impose strain on the budgets of future months as the borrowing is repaid; although this strain may be postponed by the use of additional borrowing in future months, eventually all the unplanned debt will have to be paid back.

The undesirable aspect of Dick's policy, or lack of policy, lies in the "feast or famine" consumption pattern that results. The family may spend some dollars frivolously at one time and be deprived of expenditures that it regards as important at another time. This deprivation may be especially acute if the unplanned debt rises to a large amount and if Dick's creditors then take steps to force Dick to repay his obligations.

This does not imply that all impulsive purchases are undesirable or that there was something morally wrong about Dick's unplanned borrowing. The point is that Dick was led "accidentally" into a consumption pattern that was most likely undesirable by his own standards. He ends up with regrets about his earlier actions when the time comes to pay his bills. One of the purposes of this chapter's analysis is to try to illustrate the nature of borrowing as part of an overall consumption plan so that unplanned borrowing with its usually unwanted consequences can be avoided.

Borrowing for the unexpected

Some "unplanned" borrowing may actually be part of an economic plan. We discussed in Chapter 10 how a cash reserve could serve as a cushion for unexpected expenditures. Most families like to have some extra money available to meet needs such as unusual car repairs, extraordinary dental bills, and other uncertain spending requirements which are too small to be economically covered by insurance.

Borrowing is another way to handle these extra items. A family may decide that it can readily borrow some particular amount, such as $2000. It then may decide to use this $2000 like a $2000 bank account. When unexpected needs arise, instead of dipping into a bank account, it borrows. The family then repays its loan out of its regular earnings just as it would otherwise replenish its bank account.

For example, Jill expects unusual expenses to average about $50 per month, but these items may be much higher than $50 in any particular month. If she followed the cash reserve method for handling unexpected situations, she would put $50 in a bank deposit (or other liquid asset) each month and, as the unusual expenses occurred, she would pay them by reducing her deposit balance. If she did not previously have any money on deposit, she might decide to set aside an extra $25 per month (or some other amount she thought she could afford) until she had built up a balance she regarded as adequate.

If Jill followed the borrowing method, she would not try to build up a bank balance. Until expenses actually occurred, she might, if she wished to save, use her $50 or $75 per month to purchase stocks, make extra payments on her house, or make other asset purchases or liability reductions.

When the unusual expenses actually occurred, she would borrow to meet them. She could then apply $50 per month plus the interest on her borrowing (or more) to repay her loans. Most of the time she would probably be in debt, but if her planning was correct, her regular repayments would always keep the debt from getting excessively large.

There are pros and cons to the policy of using borrowing instead of liquid assets. The advantage of the method probably lies in the fact that the family does not need to deny itself consumption by building up a sizable bank account. The disadvantages are twofold. It is easy for borrowing of this type to get out of control and become unplanned, with the result that serious future consumption denials may be necessary to reduce the too large level of debt.

Furthermore, it is nice to have some borrowing power remaining as an extra cushion. When a family follows the policy of building up and maintaining a cash reserve, it really has double protection against emergencies. If unexpected expenditures become so high that the cash reserve is exhausted, it can then draw on borrowing for those extreme cases. This double protection is not available to individuals who rely on borrowing for extraordinary needs and who never build up a cash reserve.

In practice, a compromise between the two methods may be useful. Borrowing for the unexpected may be especially helpful to a family which is just in the process of building up an adequate cash reserve. The family may also not need to build quite as large a cash reserve as it would if borrowing was unavailable. In general, however, it would seem that a policy of trying to rely solely on borrowing, without building any significant stock of liquid assets, would not be desirable.

Borrowing agreements

When a borrower gives his promise to pay he enters a legal contract for repayment that is normally enforceable in the courts. This contract may be an oral agreement, but it is usually in writing. The simplest form of written agreement is the *promissory note*, which contains a promise in approximately the following form:

December 20, 19__

Ninety days after date I promise to pay to Pinkeye Optical Company the sum of two hundred dollars, with interest at the rate of 8% per year.

Signed
Mary Myopic

Loan contracts can be distinguished between those that are secured and those unsecured. When a contract is secured, it conveys to the lender some rights in an asset or assets of the borrower. Specific assets are designated within the contract and the lender is often entitled to seize these assets, almost immediately and with a minimum of legal formality, if default occurs. In some cases the lender initially becomes the legal owner of the assets designated as security, with ownership passing to the borrower only upon the complete fulfillment of his contractual obligation. It is important for the borrower to fully understand all terms of the contract in a secured loan.

Some loans are made without explicit security, or *collateral*, as those assets used to support a borrower's promise are sometimes called. The previous example of a promissory note listed no collateral. However, these liabilities, too, are still claims against the borrower's assets. If a borrower defaults on an unsecured loan, the lender can bring action against him in the courts to enforce the promises. In most circumstances the court will then order payment of the obligation and direct that, if necessary, the assets of the borrower be sold to fulfill the borrower's promises. Thus seizure of assets is still possible on an unsecured borrowing contract, although the process of seizure may be more formal and complicated than for secured obligations.

One should also note that the claims of a lender on a secured obligation are not limited to the assets listed as collateral. If the sale of these assets is not sufficient to discharge the promises of a defaulted obligation, the secured lender can then usually proceed against the borrower in the same manner as the unsecured lender.

Consider an example of the rights of lenders. Charlie buys a car on a time payment plan and agrees to pay $100 each month to the Friendly Finance Company for 36 months. After a year Charlie tires of the car, and especially of his car payments, and decides to "let the car go back." He stops making payments and Friendly Finance takes ("repossesses") his car. Charlie now thinks his problems with the car are over.

Friendly Finance, however, finds that the car is in very poor condition and can be sold for only $1500. Friendly Finance then calculates that Charlie, at the time the car was repossessed, owed $2000 on the car. (Part of the payment he had made would have been for interest rather than reduction of his "unpaid balance.") Consequently, Charlie soon receives a bill for $500.

This amount is due immediately, the bill alleges. If Charlie were to read his original borrowing agreement, he would find a provision (a typical one by the way) that, if any payment is missed on his obligation, the entire amount of his debt is due. Since Friendly Finance received $1500 from selling Charlie's car, he still immediately owes $500.

Probably Friendly Finance will allow Charlie to pay off the $500 with more monthly payments, usually at a very high rate of interest. If Friendly Finance does not make this offer, or if Charlie does not wish to accept it, Friendly Finance can sue Charlie. The court, satisfied that Friendly Finance has a perfectly legal claim, will then order Charlie to pay the $500. The court may even require Charlie's employer to withhold money from Charlie's paycheck and turn this money over to Friendly Finance until the obligation is discharged with interest.

Some Unpleasant Terms

Several actions available to lenders are described by legal terms. A consideration of these terms will help provide some "feel" for the seriousness of borrowers' obligations.

FORECLOSURE The seizure of real estate, such as a house, that has been used as collateral.

ATTACHMENT Taking control of property under court order to satisfy a debt obligation. For example, the borrower's bank account may be attached and used to discharge his debt.

GARNISHMENT The setting aside of a portion of a borrower's pay, by court order, to satisfy a debt. Wages are withheld by the borrower's employer.

ACCELERATION CLAUSE This part of a loan agreement provides that all of the debt becomes immediately due if the borrower fails to meet any payment on the debt.

JUDGMENT A court order that a debt must be repaid.

DEFICIENCY JUDGMENT If collateral has been seized by a lender and sold for an amount that is insufficient to discharge a debt, the lender can obtain a judgment for the remaining amount of the debt.

This is not a comprehensive list of lenders' rights. The purpose of this chapter is to discuss planned borrowing; the borrower who plans can usually expect to meet his obligations as they become due. Therefore refer to standard business law texts (several are noted at the end of Chapter 6) for further discussion of the legal consequences of loan default.

Long-term borrowing

Borrowing arrangements can be classified by the length of time for which promises are made. No neat distinction is possible, but generally contracts running more than five years are regarded as long term. The most common form of long-term borrowing for the household is the *home mortgage.* A mortgage is a secured loan in which the home and the lot on which the home is situated provide collateral. Although home mortgages may be of shorter duration, many of them run for 20 to 40 years and occasionally longer. Usually home mortgages promise the payment of equal monthly installments; these payments are sufficient to discharge all of the mortgage, with interest, by the date of the final monthly payment (maturity date). The amount of monthly installment required can be approximated by solving for A.

P = amount originally borrowed
n = number of years over which mortgage is to be paid
r = annual interest rate on mortgage
A = unknown
Monthly payment = about $A/12$

After a home has been mortgaged, an additional loan in the form of a second mortgage is sometimes obtained. This loan is secured by the difference between the actual value of the house and the amount of the first mortgage. Because the position of the second mortgage lender is not as well secured, second mortgages require higher interest rates than first mortgages. Second mortgages are often used by families who wish to buy a home but are unable to obtain a large enough loan from financial institutions that specialize in first mortgage lending.

A home purchase financing arrangement which has many characteristics of the mortgage is the *contract-for-deed.* This type of contract is often used when the seller of a home is providing financing for the buyer. These contracts are usually long term and payable in monthly installments. They differ from mortgages in that the formal rights of the lender are somewhat greater. In a contract-for-deed the lender remains the legal owner of the house until the promises under the contract have been discharged. He can usually seize the home more easily than a mortgage holder if default occurs. Since the contract-for-deed is used in place of a first mortgage, it would be appropriate in analyzing a home purchase decision to treat payments on such a contract in the same way as first mortgage payments when determining net benefits before FMP (as described in Chapter 8).

Some types of special education loans may also fall into the long-term category. Usually these are made directly by a government or else are government-subsidized or guaranteed, since private lenders are commonly reluctant to make long-term loans for purposes of human capital acquisition. Because loans of this type are available only to students, home financing is likely to be the only feasible form of long-term borrowing for most families.

Intermediate-term borrowing

Intermediate-term loans mature between one and five years from the date the original borrowing takes place. There are three common varieties of these loans: mortgages, conditional sale contracts, and unsecured personal loans. The first two usually discharge through monthly payments; unsecured loans may be paid in this manner, but other patterns of payment may also be used.

Homes can be mortgaged for an intermediate term as well as a long-term basis. Home improvement loans for remodeling and major repairs are often secured by intermediate-term mortgages. Another type of intermediate-term mortgage is the chattel mortgage. This is a loan that is secured by a mortgage on a car, appliances, or other physical assets (but not by a home or other real estate).

When physical assets other than real estate secure intermediate-term loans, another type of contract is much more common than the mortgage —the *conditional sale contract.* A conditional sale contract is the nonreal estate counterpart of a contract-for-deed and is used extensively in the financing of cars, appliances, and furniture. In the conditional sale contract the lender becomes the temporary owner of the collateral until the loan is paid in full. This legal arrangement makes it relatively easy for the lender to seize the property in the event of default.

Unsecured intermediate-term loans may also be available. Because of the absence of security, loans of this type often command rather high interest rates. This generalization, however, is not entirely true; sometimes individuals with large asset holdings or excellent credit records are able to borrow on an unsecured basis simply because the lender feels that no security is required. In this instance the rate of interest charged is likely to be close to that charged on the first mortgage on a home.

Short-term borrowing

Some conditional sales contracts run for less than a year and unsecured loans are often made for short terms. Charge accounts provide a convenient source of very short-term credit (commonly one month). These accounts may often be extended to a longer term under a "revolving charge" arrangement. In effect this converts part of a charge account balance into either an unsecured loan or a conditional sales contract.

Credit cards offer short-term credit and are beginning to offer the opportunity for converting their monthly billings into revolving charge arrangements.

Banks have often discouraged a form of credit used by some of their customers—the *overdraft*. An overdraft occurs when an individual writes checks in excess of the amount he has on deposit in his checking account. Sometimes banks cash these checks anyway, thus creating the form of credit called an overdraft by implicitly extending an unsecured loan to the individual who has overdrawn his account. More commonly they refuse to make payment and return overdrawn checks marked NSF (not sufficient funds).

Recently some banks have started to view the overdraft as a possibility for a new source of business and extend automatic overdraft privileges to their customers. The customer accorded this privilege has the right to overdraw his account up to a specified amount. The automatic overdraft in effect assures the customer in advance that an unsecured loan will be granted. Interest charges on automatic overdrafts are likely to be comparable to those charged on revolving charge accounts (the common current figure is 18%), but the convenience of this form of loan may be attractive to some families.

Borrowing costs: prepayment

The actual interest rate on a loan may be identified by finding an appropriate value of r, as discussed in Chapter 3. On most loans, truth-in-lending legislation now requires that this rate must be disclosed by lenders to prospective borrowers. When the lender does not make loans as part of his regular business (for example, when a homeowner sells his home and extends financing), disclosure is not required.

There is one instance in which the rates disclosed under truth-in-lending laws may be inappropriate from the borrower's point of view; this occurs when the borrower contemplates repaying a loan in advance of the promised payment schedule. The truth-in-lending rate is calculated on the assumption that prepayment will not occur. The difference in interest cost on a prepaid loan may arise from two possibilities: prepayment penalties and fixed charges.

Prepayment penalties are extra charges which, if included in a loan contract, must be paid by a borrower who repays the loan in advance of the payment schedule required by the contract. The penalty is imposed by the lender to discourage the borrower from *refinancing* a partly paid obligation with a different lender. (Refinancing is the replacing of an existing loan with a new one.) If a loan with a prepayment penalty is prepaid, the result is an actual cost of borrowing above the stated interest rate required by truth-in-lending legislation.

Consider an example. Joe borrows \$10,000, repayable in \$100 monthly installments (\$1200 per year), at a stated rate of 6%. Suppose he decides to pay off his loan at the end of two years, when his unpaid balance is about \$8700 and his loan is subject to a 5% prepayment penalty. The total amount he must pay to discharge his obligation would be \$8700 plus \$435 (5% of \$8700). More completely, his total payments on the loan will have been

Year 1		\$1,200
Year 2	\$1,200 8,700 435	
		\$10,335

If he solves for r, where $P = \$10{,}000$, he will find his actual rate of interest to be about 8% in this situation.

Fixed charges, the second source of possible higher interest on prepaid loans, are lump sums added to the amount borrowed at the time a loan is made. For example, a home buyer who borrows \$20,000 on a 20-year mortgage may find that the lender levies a fixed charge of \$1000 for credit investigation and other items and then charges 7% interest. The lender bases his calculation of the required monthly payment on $r = 7\%$ and $P = \$21{,}000$, the amount of the loan plus fixed charges. However, since he is only providing \$20,000 to the borrower, the required truth-in-lending disclosure (use $P = \$20{,}000$) will show a rate of about 7⅔%.

If the loan is prepaid in, say, five years, the \$1000 fixed charge will have been paid, not for the use of money over a 20-year period but for only five years. We will not show the exact calculation here, but this prepayment would change the actual interest cost on the loan to over 8% on a five-year basis.

Borrowing costs: taxes

Interest payments are deductible for tax purposes. Accordingly, it would appear that interest payments would result in a lowering of income taxes. Unfortunately, this conclusion is not *necessarily* correct. The problem lies in the nature of the standard deduction. (See Chapter 4 for review of this concept.) Unless deductible expenses exceed the amount of the standard deduction (10% of total income up to \$1000 when this book was written), these deductions do not reduce tax.

For example, the Brown family earns \$12,000 per year. It pays \$600 interest annually and also incurs \$300 in other deductible expenses, such as certain medical costs, state taxes, and charitable donations. Thus the deductible expenses are \$900 per year, *but* the standard deduction is \$1000. Therefore the family does not list its individual expenses, such as interest, and in fact would pay the same amount of taxes whether or not it was paying interest.

On the other hand, consider the Smith family, who also earns \$12,000 per year. It pays interest of \$1300 per year and has other deductible expenses of \$600. The Smiths therefore have deductible expenses of \$1900. Instead of taking their standard deduction, \$1000, they list their deductions of \$1900 on their tax form.

For the Smiths, borrowing affects tax payments. If the Smiths paid off all their debt, they would reduce the expense deduction on their tax form from their current \$1900 to the standard deduction of \$1000. If their marginal tax rate was 20%, this reduction of \$900 in deductible expenses would increase taxes by \$900 × 20%, or \$180.

Thus the Smiths may regard their after-tax cost of borrowing as

Total interest paid	\$1300
Tax saving because of interest	−180
After-tax interest cost	\$1120

There is no easy way to resolve the problem of interest deductibility. Families with high incomes are likely to have deductible expenses other than interest which exceed their standard deduction. For them, interest payments are fully tax deductible. Lower income families, on the other hand, are much more likely to use the standard deduction and not get any extra tax reduction from making interest payments.

Fortunately, the problem is not quite as serious as it first seems. If a family has a low income, its marginal tax rate will be low and the benefits from the tax deduction of interest will not be very great in any event. Therefore we will probably not expose ourselves to very serious error possibilities if, throughout the rest of this book, we simply regard interest as tax deductible. We can then identify the following.

$$\text{After-tax interest rate} = \text{before-tax interest rate} \times (1 - \text{marginal personal tax rate})$$

Any reader who thinks most of his interest would not be tax deductible can then simply regard his after-tax interest rate as equal to his before-tax interest rate, or else work out some compromise that seems to fit his personal situation.

Inflation adjustment

Most readers will wish to make some tax adjustment for interest as discussed above. For all readers an inflation adjustment will be appropriate.

Recall from our previous analysis of bonds and other fixed dollar claims that the purchaser of one of these claims (who is in effect a lender) would consider the consequences of inflation by deducting the expected inflation rate from the after-tax rate of return on his claim.

What the lender loses, the borrower gains. If inflation occurs, the money amount that a family is required to repay on a debt does not change. Therefore, the burden of the repayment changes, since the family's money income is likely to increase with inflation. Put another way, the real value of the dollars repaid declines during an inflation.

For example, Nancy borrows $1000 at 6%, after tax, for one year. A year later she must repay $1060. She expects that without inflation her income a year hence will be $7000 after tax and her consumption requirements $5940; she expects to set aside $1060 to repay the loan with interest.

In fact, inflation occurs at a rate of 3%. We assume this inflation affects both Nancy's income and her consumption spending. Her income rises by $210 ($7000 × 3%) to $7210. Her consumption needs increase by $178.20 ($5940 × 3%) to a total of $6118.20 ($5940 + $178.20). Nancy then finds herself with the following amount available for debt repayment.

Inflated income	$7210.00
Inflated consumption	6118.20
Amount available for debt repayment	$1091.80

Since the amount of her loan repayment is a fixed number of dollars ($1060), inflation makes the loan easier to repay.

Inflation may not always work this way. When one speaks of a 3% inflation, he speaks of a 3% average price increase. Some incomes and prices may rise more than 3% and others less. However, for most people there is little reason to believe in advance that all income and prices will not be affected at about the same rate. It makes more sense to guess that money incomes and expenses will rise by the inflation rate than it does to ignore the problem (and thus implicitly assume that neither will rise).

The approach toward inflation in this text assumes that incomes and expenses will rise at the inflation rate. Since we are interested in the ability of families to meet future expenses when we formulate economic plans, we do not worry about inflation except for certain situations. If some of a family's income is in fixed dollar amounts (bond interest, for example), we reduce this by an inflation adjustment to recognize that this is one form of money income that we know will not keep up with the overall inflation rate. (This process is discussed in Chapter 9.)

Similarly, when we know that an expense is in the form of a fixed number of dollars and will not increase during inflation, it is appropriate to make another inflation adjustment. In this case we reduce the expense by the inflation rate. Thus we note:

Inflation-adjusted, after-tax interest rate =
after-tax interest rate — expected inflation rate

Notice that the inflation rate is deducted *after* tax adjustment has taken place. Any gains that the family makes from inflation are not taxable. This process is equivalent to the inflation adjustment on interest received by the family; in that case the adjustment was based on the fact that inflation losses were not tax deductible.

After-Tax, Inflation-Adjusted Mortgage Payments

In Chapter 8, which dealt with home purchase decisions, we identified net benefits after first mortgage payments (FMP) without considering the tax deductibility of interest on the payments or the effects of inflation. Thus a revision is in order. The procedure for this change is:

1. Identify the after-tax, inflation-adjusted interest rate on the first mortgage. (The stated rate, minus tax and inflation adjustments.)
2. Using this rate as r, find A, where P is the amount borrowed originally on the mortgage and n is the number of years the mortgage will run.
3. Use this value of A as an adjusted FMP in identifying net benefits after FMP.

For instance, Joe borrows \$20,000 on a 7% mortgage that runs for 20 years. (His approximate annual payments are \$1900.) His marginal tax rate is 30% and all his interest payments are fully tax deductible (he was not going to use the standard deduction even if he paid no interest on his house). Joe expects a 2% annual inflation rate. He reduces the interest rate from 7% to 5% because of tax benefits and then to 3% because of inflation.

To revise his payments, Joe solves for A as follows.

$$P = \$20{,}000$$
$$n = 20$$
$$r = 3\%$$
$$A = \text{about } \$1350$$

Because of his relatively high marginal tax bracket, he reduces his FMP from \$1900 per year to \$1350 per year (by \$550). He increases his net benefits after FMP by \$550 to adjust for taxes and inflation. By considering the tax and inflation effects of borrowing, his home purchase becomes a more attractive possibility.

The Cost of Borrowing: An Example

To review the processes of tax and inflation adjustment, another example is useful. A borrows \$4000 at 1% per month (12% annually). His marginal tax rate is 25% and he expects an inflation rate of 2%.

To arrive at a tax-adjusted rate, we solve:

$$\begin{aligned}\text{After-tax rate} &= \text{before-tax rate} \times (1 - \text{marginal tax rate})\\ &= 12\% \times (1 - 0.25)\\ &= 12\% \times (0.75)\\ &= 9\%\end{aligned}$$

His after-tax rate is 9%. Subtracting the inflation rate leaves 7% as an after-tax, inflation-adjusted interest rate which is most appropriate for use in considering his personal planning.

Borrowing costs in total dollars

We have been expressing interest costs as annual percentages; sometimes these costs are also expressed in the total dollar amounts of interest obligations. In general these total dollar amounts are not very useful to the planner, although they do have one important application. To examine the reason for their general lack of usefulness, consider the following example.

In some foreign countries a special type of bond, called a *consol,* is issued by governments and corporations. A consol has no maturity date and is a promise to perpetually pay interest of a given amount. Suppose a company had the unusual opportunity to issue a \$1000 consol at an interest rate of 1%. Its only promise would be to make a \$10 payment to the bondholder every year. No one would be likely to dispute the fact that this would be an attractive borrowing arrangement. However, if one tried to add up the total interest to be paid on the loan, he would find that his addition problem would never finish—the total dollar amount of interest would be infinite because the loan has a perpetual life.

This illustration shows the flaw in the total dollar interest cost approach This approach fails to recognize the time over which money is being used. Dollar interest costs may be very large on a long-term loan because a long period of service (in the form of "the use of money") is being extended by the lender. The dollar cost is therefore not an appropriate measure either for considering the cost of loans from alternative sources or in deciding whether or not to borrow at all.

The one valuable aspect of total dollar cost calculations lies in evaluating small loans of short duration. For example, suppose an individual plans to finance merchandise valued at \$300 over a three-month period.

He is offered credit by a department store at an 18% annual rate (1½% per month); the store's finance charge will be \$300 × 1½% × 3, or \$13.50 in total dollar amount of interest. Perhaps the borrower feels that if he "shopped" for credit at other sources he might be able to borrow \$300 for three months at a 10% annual rate, or a total interest cost of \$300 × 10% × ¼, or \$7.50. He can now identify the possible saving by shopping around as \$13.50 — \$7.50, or \$6 before any reduction for tax and inflation. He could now decide whether the inconvenience of "shopping" was justified when the potential saving was so small.

Total dollar cost calculations are useful when interest costs or differences in these costs may be trivial in amount. On these small, short loans the interest rate, though high, may not be important. However, if the small, short loans are used regularly, the total interest amounts over a longer period of time may no longer be trivial. In this case interest rate comparisons will still be important; shopping around may be advantageous.

Sources of difference in interest rates

We have already noted that lenders are likely to offer better interest rates on loans that can be secured by houses and claims than on loans that use other physical assets as collateral or are unsecured. We also noted, however, that an individual with many assets might be able to borrow on an unsecured basis at a comparatively low interest rate. Thus collateral is not all that matters; another important factor is to be found in the family balance sheet. If the family's liabilities are very low in comparison to its total physical assets and claims, lenders are much more likely to be confident of repayment than if the ratio of liabilities to assets is high. Similarly, lenders will often compare the amount an individual wishes to borrow to his prospective income, and if the borrowing is relatively small in comparison to the amount of income, preferred treatment may be accorded. As noted before the introduction of income into the lender's evaluation implicitly recognizes the borrower's stock of human capital.

Another factor that will be given consideration is the family's record of performance on past borrowings. If the family has defaulted before or, worse yet, gone through bankruptcy, lenders are likely to be prejudiced. Lenders exchange information about the repayment habits of borrowers; therefore an individual's repayment history is usually available to a lender. This repayment history plus other information which provides an indication about the honesty and stability of the individual (a criminal record, for example) become part of the overall evaluation or "credit rating" applied by a lender to a borrower.

Marginal borrowing costs

If a young family is considering the possibility of financing a car and other physical assets which will result in a total indebtedness of $5000, it may survey various possibilities for borrowing this amount. Since the family does not own a home, a home mortgage cannot be arranged. One possibility, usually readily available, is to finance the assets with conditional sale contracts with the sellers of the assets. Suppose this credit is obtainable at a rate of 15%. The couple also discuss this financing with a small loan company but find that its interest rate is just as high as the conditional sale contract. They then talk over their prospective purchase with a banker. The banker offers to make them a chattel mortgage loan at a rate of 10%, but he is only willing to make a loan in the amount of $3500.

The couple, after talking the matter over, decide that the best way to finance their purchase is to obtain $3500 from the bank and the remaining $1500 from one of the other sources. They return to the banker to obtain the loan only to have him explain that he will grant the loan only if they have no other major liabilities, including the other $1500 of prospective borrowing.

To analyze their problem, marginal analysis is appropriate. If only $3500 of credit is used, the annual cost at 10% will be $350 per year. If the $5000 is borrowed at a rate of 15%, the annual cost will be $750 per year. Thus the family can reason that in order to increase the amount of its borrowing from $3500 to $5000 its annual interest payment is increased from $350 to $750, or by $400 per year. Therefore the interest charge on the marginal $1500 of borrowing ($5000 — $3500) is $400 per year/ $1500, or about 27% per year.

The couple may consider their borrowing in two steps: an initial $3500 at 10% and a further $1500 at 27%. If their marginal income tax rate were 20% and they expected 2% annual inflation, these marginal rates would be reduced to a marginal 6% on the first $3500 and a marginal 19% on the next $1500. They can now decide whether they wish to revise their plans for immediate asset purchase down to an amount they can manage with $3500 credit or whether they are willing to pay the high marginal rate to procure the additional $1500.

As a family's liabilities increase, the ratios between its liabilities and assets, and between its liabilities and income, also increase. These increasing ratios may deter some low cost lenders from providing funds, with the result that high amounts of borrowing must be done entirely with high cost lenders who are willing to accept more risks. If this happens, the marginal cost of the increase in borrowing is likely to be very substantial.

Borrowing costs and asset selection

A reasonable explanation noted earlier for an individual's simultaneous undertaking of both asset purchase and borrowing would be that the asset afforded a rate of return greater than the cost of borrowing. Does this imply that an asset should be purchased if the rate of return identified on the asset exceeds the marginal cost for borrowing for the asset? For example, an individual may have the opportunity to purchase common stock on which he estimates an after-tax return of 7%. He finds that he is able to borrow at an after-tax, inflation-adjusted rate of 5%. The comment that first suggests itself is that these two rates are too close for comfort. The return estimated on the stock is only an estimate; its actual return may be greater or less than 7%.

The 5% interest that is going to go to the lender is a much more certain proposition. The burden of debt may be subject to some variation because of inflation rates being greater or less than those expected, but at least the lender is quite sure of the amount of money that he is promised. Even if the stock actually proves to be a bad investment, the borrower is still responsible for the full amount of his obligation to the lender.

Because the lender usually assumes much less risk than the family who is purchasing an asset, the returns on assets are not strictly comparable with the cost of borrowing. A better test for the acceptability of a particular asset is its comparability with other asset opportunities of comparable risk. For example, if the family thinks it can obtain a 7% after-tax, inflation-protected return on common stock, this ought to constitute the *minimum* acceptable level of return for investments such as a home purchase, which probably are fairly comparable in their degree of risk.

If the original question posed in this section had been, should an asset be rejected if its return is less than marginal borrowing cost?, our answer could have been more definite. If an asset fails to meet this test, it should be rejected out of hand for it will do more harm than good. The source of financing for the asset will require the surrender of more future consumption than benefits generated by the asset.

Another viewpoint may also aid in understanding the relationship between borrowing cost and asset returns. A family's liabilities are usually significantly less than its assets. If, for example, the family's liability to asset ratio is 30%, the assets owned by the family have been financed principally with the family's own savings; every $10 asset is financed by $7 in savings and only $3 in borrowed money. Even lenders who have provided 100% financing on some individual assets can take comfort in the cushion of protection provided by the fact that the family owns other assets far in excess of its liabilities. Even if misfortunes should occur that caused default and the assets of the family were seized and sold in an attempt to cover the promises to the lenders, the family would still have to discharge any remaining obligation out of its remaining future earning power unless it wanted to undergo personal bankruptcy.

Because of the great risks borne by the family in comparison to the risks undertaken by lenders, it is only appropriate that the family should have a much larger rate of return on its own investment in its assets. If the family wanted to calculate the full cost of acquiring assets, it would be appropriate to do so by considering not only the cost of the $3 provided by creditors for each $10 of assets purchased but also the fact that a higher return ought to be required on the $7 provided by savings. This approach again suggests that no asset should be acquired by borrowing unless its rate of return is considerably above the borrowing rate.

Choice of borrowing term

It at first seems obvious that long-term borrowing is appropriate for the family that wishes to obtain financing over a long period of time and that short- and intermediate-term borrowing is appropriate for more temporary financial needs. Sometimes, however, temporary needs have a way of turning into a long-term requirement. If a family almost always has some short- or intermediate-term loans outstanding because of the repeated financing of new cars, appliances, and so forth, borrowing is really being done on a rather permanent basis, even though short-term financial arrangements are being used. Sometimes it may be possible and advantageous to substitute some long-term borrowing for a series of short-term loans.

To illustrate, suppose a family usually has between $2000 and $3000 in car and appliance financing outstanding. Even though the family is regularly meeting the promised payments on its loans, as it reduces some obligations it incurs others by trading cars or purchasing new appliances. An alternative arrangement for this financing might be for the family to increase its house mortgage by $3000.

Such a step may result in obtaining lower interest costs since mortgage financing is likely to carry a lower interest rate than some short-term financing alternatives.

Sources of borrowed money: long term

Occasionally a family may borrow from a relative or other individual, but much more commonly, borrowing will be done from a financial institution, that is, a business or government agency that specializes in financial services. Among financial institutions further specialization exists, so that various institutions concentrate on the performance of particular types of services. For example, commercial banks provide some mortgage financing, but are specialists in the provision of short- and intermediate-term financing, usually under conditions of limited risk. An explanation of this policy can be found by recalling the nature of a typical bank balance sheet (shown in Chapter 10) which contains many liabilities in the form of demand deposits and a small net worth position. Because banks have many obligations which may have to be met on short notice and because their liability:asset ratios are so high, banks require a high degree of safety on their investments and prefer to make many loans which are repayable in a fairly short time.

Mortgage financing is available from a number of sources. Savings and loan associations specialize in this type of financing. They are able to provide long-term loans more readily than banks because they have no demand deposits outstanding in their balance sheets. Certain specialized types of banks, called mortgage banks and savings banks, also do not accept demand deposits, enabling them to concentrate on making long-term loans. Life insurance companies are important suppliers of mortgage money, and again, the institutions' balance sheet can offer an explanation for this. Life insurance companies have many obligations which they do not expect to pay until long into the future since they often sell "permanent" life insurance policies to relatively young policy holders.

In discussions of mortgages the names of the Federal Housing Administration (FHA) and Veterans Administration (VA) are almost certain to emerge. The Federal Housing Administration does not directly serve as a source of funds to families desiring credit, although it indirectly enables many families to obtain mortgages on favorable terms. It does this by providing insurance for institutions that make mortgage loans. If a family's mortgage is approved by the FHA, this approval will guarantee to the lender that the promises made under the mortgage will be kept. If the borrower does not meet his promises, FHA will fulfill these obligations, although it will then undertake legal proceedings against the defaulting borrower. Because lenders are offered a guarantee from FHA, they compete more vigorously for the mortgage business of FHA-approved borrowers and offer them preferential interest rates. In the past the Veterans Administration made many direct mortgage loans to families. Now it principally offers an FHA-type guarantee on mortgages made to those veterans who are eligible for its services, as well as providing some other benefits to these veterans.

Families in rural areas have access to some programs of direct mortgage lending by the Federal Government and government-supported agencies. The Farmers Home Administration is now the most important of these sources. An individual living in a rural area should consider this organization as a possible source of mortgage financing, since its mortgages usually carry a very low interest rate.

Sources of borrowed money: short and intermediate terms

Commercial banks are important sources of intermediate- and short-term borrowing. As noted previously, they are likely to prefer lending under circumstances in which there is little chance of default. To attract safe loan customers they usually offer fairly low interest rates. Credit unions are likely to offer loans under conditions very similar to those of banks. Because credit unions do not have quite as urgent obligations in their own balance sheets, these institutions are sometimes willing to accept a little more risk and, correspondingly, they sometimes charge a slightly higher interest rate than banks.

Finance companies are also a very important source of short- and intermediate-term credit. The balance sheets of these companies contain a lower liabilities:net worth ratio than banks, and the liabilities of the finance companies do not include the pressing deposit liabilities that banks have. Because of these differences, finance companies are able to accept loans with considerably greater chance of default than those accepted by banks. Finance companies also specialize in making loans of very small amounts. In return for their willingness to lend under these conditions, they charge substantially higher interest rates than banks.

Another important source of short- and intermediate-term credit is through the sellers of physical assets and consumer goods. Some of these sellers extend the credit themselves; others provide credit to their customers and then sell the loan contracts executed by their customers to financial institutions. The rates charged on seller-provided credit vary greatly. Short-term credit in the form of 30-day charge accounts normally carries no charge. Revolving charge account credit is often priced somewhat above credit supplied by banks, but may be lower than finance company credit. Credit under conditional sales contracts extended by sellers to purchasers of cars and appliances may vary from a little above bank rates up to, or even greater than, finance company rates.

Borrowing policies

A very important point to remember when undertaking borrowing is that money obtained from one source of borrowing is a very good substitute for money obtained from another source. For example, even though the car dealer offers financing in connection with a sale of a new car, the buyer always has the option of paying for the car with cash that he obtains from a loan at a finance company or a bank. Also, loans on securities, as discussed in Chapter 7, may be limited by government-imposed margin requirements, but there is nothing to stop an individual from borrowing for other purchases that would have been paid for in cash and using this released cash to finance the securities.

To the borrower the major differences between various financing sources are likely to be interest rates, the term of financing offered, and convenience. If a family anticipates long-term financing needs such as those connected with a purchase of a house or continuing purchases of other physical assets, institutions offering mortgages should normally be considered first for two reasons: (a) the interest rate on mortgages may be as low or lower than that offered by other sources and (b) long-term financing offers a convenience in that the borrower is freed from periodically searching for new financing.

For short-term financing requirements both convenience and interest rates are likely to be significant. Charge account credit, including the occasional use of revolving charge plans, may be convenient even though the interest rates on revolving credit charge arrangements may be rather high. When a family is obtaining more than a few hundred dollars of short- or intermediate-term credit, however, the interest rate will probably outweigh convenience and some shopping around is desirable. As noted previously, banks and credit unions are likely to constitute rather low cost sources, but these institutions in their efforts to shun risks may be willing to lend only moderate amounts. In this case finance companies and other higher cost sources will have to be investigated. The investigation of higher cost sources, however, should be accompanied by a marginal analysis of interest rate differences. This analysis identifies the full cost of obtaining additional credit from higher cost sources and losing the opportunity to use a smaller amount of lower cost credit.

Amount of Borrowing Desirable

No easy formula is available for determining how much borrowing a family should undertake. Most families borrow for the purchase or retention of assets; their loans should not be undertaken unless the asset return appears to be comfortably above the borrowing cost. Beyond this rule the family should also be concerned with the effect of loan repayment on future consumption. To consider this issue it is first necessary to examine other aspects of planning for future consumption. Therefore the discussion of borrowing policy reappears in the following chapters in the context of the lifetime financial plan.

Amount of Borrowing Possible

In the formulation of a financial plan a large amount of borrowing might seem appropriate. A recent college graduate, who anticipates a high future income, may decide that he wishes immediately to begin a fairly high level of consumption and asset acquisition. Suppose, for example, that Tom, a 23-year-old college graduate with a wife and two children, has a car, paid for, and a $1000 bank account, but virtually no other assets except the family's clothing, dishes, and other small items. The family currently lives in a furnished apartment.

In working out a financial plan Tom decides that it would be desirable for him to buy a house, financed with a $20,000 first mortgage and a $4000 second mortgage. He also would like to finance about $3000 of furniture and appliances by borrowing. Furthermore, he decides that rather than try to reduce this initial amount of debt ($27,000) during the next five years, he would like to borrow increasing amounts and bring his debt up to $35,000. After that he would expect to gradually reduce this debt.

This policy may appear perfectly reasonable to Tom. He may feel that his family will benefit greatly with a higher standard of living now and that his income prospects are so good that repayment of the debt will be easy. Let us assume that Tom has based this desire for borrowing on very careful planning.

Tom must still confront another question. Will he and his wife be able to borrow this much? Although Tom may not be worried about the amount of his proposed debt, the lenders whom Tom expects to provide this borrowed money may not share his optimism. Perhaps Tom, after consulting with various possible lenders, finds out that it will not be possible for him to borrow more than a total of $28,000. In this case Tom must "go back to the drawing board." His first plan based on $35,000 debt will not work. Tom will either have to find a way of earning more during the next five years or he will have to settle for a lower standard of living.

It is hard to provide any general guideline for identifying the maximum amount of credit an individual can obtain. However, one estimate that might possibly be used is the following:

1. The family will not be able to have total debt greater than three times its annual take-home pay.
2. The family will not be able to have debt, other than its first mortgage on its home, greater than half of one year's take-home pay.

These are not rules that will always apply. Many families may be able to bend these rules a little by being willing to pay very high interest rates. Families with poor credit records or very low incomes may not be able to obtain this much credit. Families with large amounts of claims or other readily salable assets may be able to do better. This is also true of families with obviously good income prospects such as young, highly trained professional people. However, we will make use of these rules in our subsequent analysis. If one wishes to find better guidelines for his own personal situation, he would find it very useful to discuss this problem with financial institutions in his own locality.

Consider an example of the application of these rules. John is formulating a financial plan. His take-home pay five years from now is expected to be about $10,000. John should not plan to have more than $30,000 in total debt outstanding, or $5000 more than the first mortgage on his house. Thus, if John expects that his house mortgage will be $26,000, he could not plan on owing more than $4000 on such forms of debt as a second mortgage or a car. (This would make a total of $30,000, three times his pay.) If John expects his house mortgage to be only $10,000 at the end of five years, he could not plan on owing more than $15,000. (Borrowing could not go more than $5000, one-half year's pay, above the first mortgage.)

Summary

House mortgages offer the lender a great deal of protection, and therefore a low interest rate is common on loans of this type. Other physical assets are usually not financed under as favorable terms as houses. Borrowing for the purpose of financing human capital is often relatively difficult because of the lack of protection for the lender. Similarly, borrowing for consumption may be difficult to arrange, with credit available only at relatively high rates.

Although borrowing is often useful, unplanned borrowing may lead to unfortunate results. A family may unintentionally overspend in one time period and subject itself to deprivation during a later time period when the borrowing must be repaid.

Borrowing may be used to handle unexpected cash requirements. However, a stock of liquid assets may also be useful for this purpose; then borrowing can be reserved for these emergency situations when the stock of liquid assets is exhausted.

Loans may be made on a secured or unsecured basis. Secured loans may require that assets be pledged in support of the loan; these supporting assets are called collateral. Borrowing on an unsecured basis does not normally protect the borrower from the unfavorable consequences of default.

Borrowing arrangements can be classified according to their length, or term. Long-term financing is most often extended in connection with house mortgages, though some types of educational loans may fall into this category. Intermediate-term loans (between one and five years) are associated with such purposes as home improvements and the financing of smaller physical assets. Conditional sale contracts are instruments commonly used on the intermediate-term financing of small assets. Intermediate-term borrowing may also be done on an unsecured basis.

Short-term borrowing (less than one year) may often be done under very informal arrangements such as a "revolving charge" account or a bank automatic overdraft. Conditional sales contract and unsecured borrowing are also often used on a short-term basis.

Truth-in-lending legislation requires the disclosure of interest rates. However, under some circumstances, a loan which is prepaid in advance of maturity may have a higher interest rate than that disclosed by the lender.

The burden of interest payments may be lessened because of two factors. Interest, especially in large amounts, usually results in a marginal income tax reduction because of its tax deductibility. Furthermore, a shrinking of the value of the dollar because of inflation reduces the real cost of repaying a loan. Therefore it is desirable in planning to convert interest rates to an after-tax, inflation-adjusted basis in the same manner as the interest adjustment that is made by the holder of money-yielding claims.

If an individual, to increase his total amount of borrowing, must do all of his borrowing at a higher interest rate, the result may be an extremely high marginal borrowing cost.

When an individual borrows for an asset purchase, he should only undertake this if the rate of return on the asset appears to offer a comfortable margin above the interest cost associated with financing the asset. This constitutes an attempt to compensate for the fact that an individual will be responsible for repaying his loan even if the asset financed by the loan proves unsatisfactory.

Banks, credit unions, and finance companies are specialists in providing short- or intermediate-term credit. Finance companies usually charge a higher interest rate and are willing to undertake a greater risk.

Long-term financing, such as for house mortgages, is available through such institutions as mortgage banks, life insurance companies, and savings and loan associations.

Mortgage financing is often made easier for individuals because of government guarantees of mortgage credit. The Federal Housing Administration is the most important of these guarantors who protect the lender against default and therefore make lenders willing to extend more favorable terms to borrowers.

Especially on small amounts of credit, interest rates may not be as important to the borrower as the convenience of the credit arrangement, since the dollar cost of borrowing in small amounts may be relatively insignificant.

In formulating a lifetime economic plan, an individual may want to consider the possibility of increasing current consumption through borrowing. However, even though he feels that repayment will be feasible, a ceiling may be imposed by lenders on the amount of borrowing that he is able to undertake.

SUGGESTED READINGS

Excellent descriptions of various types of financial institutions are found in the *American Financial System* by James Ludtke (Boston: Allyn and Bacon, Inc., 1967). Information about borrowing policies is obtainable from banks and other financial institutions.

Descriptive material about financing practices is found in a *Finance Facts Yearbook* which may be obtained free from the National Consumer Finance Association, 1000 16th St. N.W., Washington, D.C. 20006.

QUESTIONS

1. Why do first house mortgages typically carry a relatively low rate of interest?
2. Carefully explain how unplanned borrowing can lead an individual into actions which are in conflict with his own tastes and goals.
3. Consider the following three facts.
   (a) A family owes $15,000 on a house mortgage.
   (b) The family has $2000 in cash above its normal liquid asset requirements.
   (c) If the family uses this $2000 to repay part of its mortgage in advance of the required repayment schedule, it anticipates that in a year or two it may need to do some additional borrowing to send a daughter to college.

   Discuss the pros and cons of using the $2000 to repay part of the mortgage as opposed to holding this $2000 in liquid assets.
4. Will borrowing on an unsecured basis offer much protection to a borrower in the event that he defaults? Discuss.
5. As part of a financial plan, a family desires to build up its level of borrowing from $1000 to $3000 and to maintain its level of borrowing at $3000 for several years. The family finds, however, that it cannot arrange to borrow increasing amounts of money on a permanent basis but instead must make periodic repayments on any amount borrowed. How can the family succeed in building up and maintaining a $3000 borrowing level?
6. Why is the privilege of prepaying without penalty desirable from the point of view of the borrower? Why may a lender be reluctant to offer this privilege?
7. Make a case for the statement that under present tax laws it is reasonable for middle income families that owe substantial amounts on house mortgages to regard the interest payment on these mortgages as marginally tax deductible (in spite of the standard deduction argument).
8. Why is it appropriate to deduct the expected inflation rate from borrowing costs?
9. Suppose that you live in a state in which the maximum interest rate on small loans permitted by law is 36%. Explain how it would be possible for

you to incur marginal borrowing costs above this rate without any breach of the law on the part of the lender.

10. What are the arguments for and against legal ceilings on interest rates (usury laws)? Do you agree that usury laws discriminate against poor people who are often regarded as poor credit risks and who will not be offered credit unless it is possible to charge an interest rate high enough to compensate for a high rate of expected default?
11. What help does the Federal Housing Administration provide to individuals borrowing for home purchases when the FHA does not actually make loans to individuals?
12. Try to find out from your local financial institutions if they have any formulas or "rules of thumb" to determine the maximum amount of borrowing that they think an individual should undertake.

PROBLEMS

1. Suppose you are considering the purchase of a house and the owner of the house has offered to extend financing in the form of a contract-for-deed. You can either buy the house for a $15,000 cash price or you can buy it for $17,000 on the following terms: $3000 down and a $14,000 balance to be paid off in equal installments over a ten-year period "with interest at 8%." When an individual extends financing on a home that he is selling he does not normally need to conform to the truth-in-lending laws and disclose the actual interest rate being charged. Therefore, if you are purchasing a home under terms of this type, you will need to calculate your own effective interest rate.
   (a) First identify the approximate amount you will have to pay each year to discharge a $14,000 loan with 8% interest in equal payments over a ten-year period.
   (b) How much credit is actually being extended by the seller of the house?
   (c) What actual interest rate is being charged. [Find the internal rate of return that equates the annuity identified in (a) with the amount of credit noted in (b).]
2. In purchasing a house you arrange to borrow $20,000 payable in $1320 annual installments over 30 years. The financial institution issuing the mortgage deducted $1000 from the amount of the mortgage to cover various charges and actually provides you with $19,000 in cash in exchange for your $20,000, 30-year mortgage.
   (a) Calculate the rate of interest that will have to be disclosed under truth-in-lending legislation.
   (b) Suppose the mortgage allows prepayment and you in fact expect to pay off the mortgage at a rate of $4000 per year. How long will it take you to pay off the mortgage with interest?
   (c) If you prepay, as set forth in (b), what will your actual rate of interest be?
   (d) If your marginal tax rate is 25% and you expect an inflation rate of 2%, what will your actual rate of interest be on an inflation-adjusted, after-tax basis?

3. An individual finds that if he wants to borrow \$2000, he can obtain this amount from a bank at an 8% interest rate, but if he wishes to increase his total borrowing to \$4000, he must borrow the entire amount from a finance company at a 20% interest rate. Find the marginal after-tax, inflation-adjusted borrowing cost for increasing this individual's borrowing from \$2000 to \$4000. Use a 30% marginal tax rate and a 2% inflation rate.

chapter fifteen

Information for planning

In this chapter a fundamental planning tool, the lifetime personal economic projection, is applied. This plan does not involve an entirely new technique, since it will be similar to the cash flow projection made for a short period of time in Chapter 10. Furthermore, we have already previewed simplified versions of the overall economic plan in the last part of Chapter 3 and at the beginning of Chapter 10. The reader may wish to review these versions before going further into this chapter.

The reasons for making a lifetime plan are quite straightforward. The plan should serve to compare the family's economic objectives with its means for obtaining them. The plan may reveal that the family is presently following patterns of earning and spending that allow for the achievement of its objectives. It may also show, however, that the family's current economic patterns are not leading in the long-term direction that it wishes to follow. In this case the plan should initiate a new reconciliation of the family's present actions and its future objectives; if they are to be reconciled, one or both will have to be changed.

The plan is expected to be a guide for present actions. It is not reasonable to believe that a family could or would want to develop a plan that would guide all its future actions. Instead the important aspect of the plan is its answer to the questions: Are the actions that we plan to undertake now or in the next few years in conflict with our currently held long-term goals? If there is a conflict, what can we do about it now?

In this chapter, the plan formulation emerges in a particular form. However, the reader should not think of this as the "one right way" of personal economic planning. If this text is successful, it will succeed in relating the logic of planning and provide the reader with a "way of looking at things" which will help him to prevent a personal plan that is better suited to his own personal needs and objectives. If the plan is being developed for a family, it is very desirable for both husband and wife and perhaps children also to participate in the plan development. Unless a plan influences actions, it is futile. Since spending decisions are often made by several members of the family, the cooperation of all these members is necessary if the plan is to be translated into action.

A review of some introductory concepts

The means for meeting personal economic objectives lie in the earning power of the individual or family. Recall from Chapter 1 that earning power may be used to produce money income, but that it may also produce such nonmoney services as housewife labor and the benefits from home ownership. In addition, earning power can be diverted to self-improvement, resulting in accumulation of human capital. Earning power can also be left unused, that is, used for leisure.

The division of earning power among the four alternatives is controlled by the individual. This control of the uses of earning power can, in turn, be used to control future earning power. If present earning power is used for self-improvement or for the attainment of money income which is then saved, the resulting accumulation of assets will confer flows of earning power in the future.

Consumption can be regarded as the objective of personal economic activity. Consumption may be attained in the form of currently used goods and services that are purchased with currently earned money income and in nonmoney benefits provided by physical capital and to some extent by human capital. Leisure is also a form of consumption. For our purposes we define money consumption expenditures broadly enough to include gifts and bequests which are not directly "used" by the family. Consumption also includes unwanted expenditures such as those required by illness or lawsuit.

Some consumption may be derived from transfer payments, in the form of public assistance programs or the gifts of relatives. Otherwise, consumption requires earning power. All or part of current earning power can be used up in consumption as can assets accumulated from the earning power of previous periods (dissaving). Because consumption restricts asset accumulation or uses up existing assets and because assets produce future earning power, the capacity for future consumption is arrested by present consumption. In its most basic form personal economic planning is the balancing of present and future consumption into a blend that most nearly fits the desires of the planner.

Consumption and asset accumulation can jointly exceed current earning power if borrowing takes place. Borrowing shifts consumption from the future to the present. Also, because it may be used to acquire assets with a high potential for increasing earning power, borrowing may allow the attainment of an increase in future consumption.

Through the use of insurance and other risk control devices, the individual tries to avoid interruption in his flow of desired consumption which might otherwise occur because of a reduction in earning power or unwanted consumption requirements. In a sense insurance expenditures may themselves be a form of unwanted consumption. However, inclusion of insurance and other risk control measures in an economic plan lends stability to the consumption pattern.

Planning information requirements

Plan development requires two major types of information—future purchases and future receipts. Purchases refer to the family's desires and needs for spending to obtain consumption. A purchase may be for direct consumption spending, such as food, or for assets that yield flows of non-money services, such as housing or furniture. Receipts refer to a number of sources of money for the family. Money income earned by the family, expected inheritances, transfer payments, and involuntary benefits all are means for meeting the wants of the family.

Some money to be spent and to be received is *not* included in the projections of purchases and receipts. Any money spent for or received from claims is not included nor is money received from borrowing or spent for borrowing repayments (one exception is noted later).

These exclusions are necessary because part of the purpose of the plan is to investigate the amount of claims the family should purchase and the amount of borrowing it should undertake. The purchases and receipts projections are made first; then these other items are brought into the analysis.

Dealing with risk

Obviously the estimation of purchases and receipts for a series of future time periods is going to be an inexact process. Mean expected amounts can be projected, but there is a risk dimension in these projections. Some risk can be guarded against with insurance and other risk control devices, but there are types of major risk that cannot be insured away. For example, insurance will not protect against the failure of career expectations to materialize. Ralph may expect to be earning $15,000 a year in 20 years, but because he originally overestimated his abilities or he is "passed over" in promotion for various other reasons, he may actually have to get along on $10,000 in earnings during that time period. Not only receipts but also purchases may prove to be erroneously estimated. Ralph may fail to anticipate that he and his wife will develop a strong desire to travel.

To incorporate risk into this analysis, our approach is to estimate two separate projections for purchases and two for receipts. Purchases are estimated as realistically as possible in the form of mean expected figures. Then a second set of basic purchase requirements is estimated. These last amounts are estimates of the floor below which the family feels it would be very undesirable for its standard of living to fall. Thus for any period a family may estimate that its purchases will be $9000 per year, but it may also estimate that it could "squeeze by" on $6000 a year without being subject to (by its standards) undue hardship.

To investigate whether the family can meet its basic consumption requirements under all foreseeable circumstances, minimum estimates of receipts should also be developed. These are estimates of the worst employment earnings that it is reasonable to expect. These estimates can then be compared with the family's basic purchase projections while the family's mean expected receipts are compared with mean expected purchases.

The purchases and receipts estimates should be developed with the assumption that a basic insurance plan will be used for protection against large unwanted spending requirements, such as extraordinary medical expenses, and against major interruptions in receipts, such as the possible loss of employment earnings by disability or death.

Because risk is explicitly taken into consideration in the form of basic consumption and minimum receipts estimates, and assumptions about insurance, it does not need to be also considered implicitly. Therefore the mean expected estimates of purchase and receipts should be as realistic as possible and should not be set low or high "just to be on the safe side."

Timing of purchases and receipts

When projections of purchase and receipts are to be made, time becomes an integral part of the projections. It is not necessary to know the total amount of purchases or receipts during a lifetime but the pattern of these flows over a lifetime. A detailed projection would include estimates for each year in the expected lifetime of the members of the planning family.

There are two reasons for not developing a very detailed plan. First, working with so much information would be very difficult. Second, future projections, especially those far into the future, cannot be made precisely enough to estimate meaningful differences from one year to the next. Instead a simplified approach can be employed. It may be useful for a family to make year-by-year estimates for a few years into the immediate future. These estimates are easier to make and since difficulties that are foreseen in the near future are, in one sense, more serious, precision is more important.

The seriousness of near-future difficulties arises from a problem that may be described as one of correction time. If the family anticipates money shortages far in the future, slight modifications of its spending habits or its level of receipts over a long period of time may be sufficient to correct the problem. However, difficulties foreseen within a year or two may require both prompt and drastic action to correct them.

Beyond projections for a few years (three year-by-year projections are included in our examples), future projections may be made for multiyear periods of time. These longer time periods can be selected by trying to find periods of time when major changes in the family's needs or income are likely to occur. For most families these periods are:

1. Period before children are born.
2. Period when children are growing up.
3. Period when children are in college (if college educations are planned).
4. Period after children require no support and before retirement.
5. Retirement period.

The single person who plans to marry might also want to include a period before marriage. If he does not plan to marry, he might use other periods: before age 30, age 30–45, age 45–65, retirement.

If a family with children is formulating a plan it obviously would not include period 1. For a family which has or expects to have several children, the boundaries between periods 1, 2, 3, and 4 will be rather hazy; the family may wish to define period 1 as the period before *most* of the children are born, period 2 as when *most* of the children are growing up, and so forth. Families who do not expect to have children might use a method similar to that used by someone who expected to stay single.

Even though these time classifications do not perfectly reflect the family's changing levels of purchases or receipts, they allow the family to set forth an approximate lifetime pattern of money to be obtained and spent. A family might want to use more classifications. However, it is important to remember that a simple plan has many advantages; if one makes a plan too complex, he may be more likely to discontinue planning completely because it becomes too much work.

For the typical family the necessary purchase and receipts estimates might be represented by Table 15.1. Each blank space in the table would have to be filled in by the family to begin the planning process. (The year-by-year estimates may, in many instances, coincide with our earlier definition of period 1.)

The blanks to be filled in after period 2 to period 5 refer to years from the present. For example, if a family with three children was preparing a plan in 1970 and expected two children to be finished with high school in 1982, it might denote the time of period 2 as 4 to 12. It will make year-by-year estimates for the first three years, but then will provide a single set of estimates for the period from year 4 until the children leave school in year 12.

Similarly, the family may expect to have two of its three children in college for the six years after year 12, and therefore would identify period 3 as 13 to 19. If it expects that the husband will retire in year 40, it indicates period 4 as 20 to 39. Period 5 might be estimated to last about 15 years, 40 to 54. (Of course the family would also have to consider the possibility of living longer than expected; if necessary, this risk might be taken care of by the purchase of an annuity.)

The estimates required in Table 15.1 are discussed in subsequent sections.

TABLE 15.1

Years into the future		Mean expected purchases	Basic purchases	Mean expected receipts	Minimum expected receipts
Initial	1	____	____	____	____
year-by-year	2	____	____	____	____
estimates	3	____	____	____	____
Period 2	___ to ___	____	____	____	____
Period 3	___ to ___	____	____	____	____
Period 4	___ to ___	____	____	____	____
Period 5	___ to ___	____	____	____	____

Receipts projection

Receipts projections should include estimates of the following flows:

1. Take-home pay from employment.
2. Pensions and old-age benefit payments.

Interest should not be included nor should any other money received from physical assets or claims.

Take-home pay includes estimated earnings from employment minus income taxes and other deductions. Other deductions include estimated social security taxes (see Chapter 11), estimated state or local income tax if any, and estimated payroll deductions for employee's contributions toward pension funds, involuntary insurance programs, and so forth. This last item should not be overlooked, for it may be of considerable size; it is not uncommon for these deductions to be about the same as the social security tax, or even higher in some instances.

For example, Bill expects to be employed after graduation at a salary of $10,000 per year. He is married but has no children. Therefore he expects to claim two exemptions ($600 each) and to use the standard deduction ($1000); his taxable income is computed as follows.

Total income		$10,000
Deduct		
Exemptions	$1200	
Standard deduction	1000	
		−2,200
Taxable income		$ 7,800

Checking the tax table he finds his Federal income tax on a joint return to be about $1300. He also estimates that his social security tax will be $450 and that other deductions for involuntary programs will be another $450. Finally, he estimates state income taxes at 2% of taxable income, or about $150. Thus his total income reductions are:

Federal income tax	$1300
Social security tax	450
Involuntary programs	450
State income tax	150
Total	$2350

He subtracts the $2350 from his total income of $10,000 to arrive at total take-home pay of $7650.

Note that he based his tax estimate on his employment income and the use of the standard deduction. This would be appropirate even if he expected to receive extra income in the form of interest, or to have extra deductions because of interest expense. The tax effects of interest are taken into consideration when after-tax interest rates are identified; they do not need to be considered in making the receipts projection. The appendix at the end of Chapter 9 may provide some guidelines for making take-home pay projections.

Take-home pay estimates should be based on current pay levels for expected employment situations. For instance, if Miguel, age 21, expects to be an insurance agent, he should find out what insurance agents in different stages of their careers are earning now. He might find that capable insurance agents who have worked for five years are now earning $10,000 and those who have worked for 20 years are earning $15,000. Miguel could base his own estimates of his future earnings on these figures.

To review, by using this method we attempt to handle the problem of inflation. If an insurance agent with 20 years experience is earning $15,000 take-home pay now, Miguel, 20 years later, will probably have a much larger dollar amount of take-home pay because of inflation. The things Miguel has to buy then, however, will be higher priced too. Rather than try to estimate the effect of price changes on Miguel's future receipts and on his future purchases, it is easier, and probably just as accurate, to use current figures for both.

For estimates of receipts during the retirement period, current levels of old-age benefit payments can also be used, provided that these benefits are inflation protected, that is, that they are likely to rise if prices rise. Social security benefits appear to be inflation protected and many other pension benefits may also be; however, a review of Chapter 11's discussion of the problem of nonprotected benefits might be useful at this point. Since pension plans differ greatly from employer to employer, it is difficult to generalize about benefits expected from them. Current benefit payments under social security are presented in Chapter 11.

Both mean expected and minimum projections of receipts are required. Although the projection of minimum receipts is difficult, it is necessary to try and estimate the lowest take-home pay that can reasonably be earned if a job is not as successful as anticipated. This minimum estimate of take-home pay is likely to be rather close to mean expected take-home pay during the first few years but diverge more further in the future. Since pension benefits may be based on previous earnings, minimum projections should consider the possibility of a lower pension. These estimates should all be made on the basis of current prices.

Purchase projections

The formulation of consumption spending estimates is discussed in Chapter 17. Data describing spending patterns of different types of families are also included in that chapter as a guideline for planning.

In addition to spending on regular items such as food, utilities, clothing, and insurance, the family will also normally spend money on physical assets—cars, furniture, appliances, and recreational equipment. This spending, too, should be incorporated in the purchase estimates. Even though the family expects to buy some of these items on installment plans, the full cost of each asset should be included in the purchase estimates made for the time of the expected asset purchases. In this way the family can first look at the question, "Will financing actually be necessary or desirable?"

Purchase projections include three major categories.

1. Regular consumption spending.
2. Physical assets.
3. First mortgage payments on existing house, if any.

Some use of simplification is desirable on the estimates of asset purchases. Small assets can be estimated in a "miscellaneous" category. As one projects further into the future, approximate annual spending estimates can be used for all physical asset purchases. (Housing is excepted.)

For example, Ben's family estimates that it will purchase a new car, a refrigerator, and $300 worth of miscellaneous assets in the next three years. It may estimate time of the purchase for that period of its plan as follows.

	Year 1	Year 2	Year 3
Miscellaneous	$100	$100	$100
Car		2500	
Refrigerator	400		
Regular spending	5000	5000	5500
First mortgage	1500	1500	1500
Total	$7000	$9100	$7100

Ben's family also realizes that it will continue making asset purchases in the future. However, it is not sure just when each individual purchase will be made. Accordingly it may wish to make an estimate for years further into the future. Totals from this estimate can then be used to supply data for mean expected purchases per year as shown on p. 269.

Note that the asset purchase estimates are likely to vary over time. A family with a new house probably wants to accumulate more miscellaneous items such as pictures and small appliances. At some time the family may anticipate a need for two cars or a desire for a higher priced car. Children leaving home may reduce the need for recreational equipment or the rate at which some appliances need to be replaced. Since physical asset purchases typically constitute a rather large portion of total spending, it is important to make these estimates with some care.

	Years 4–10	Years 11–20	Years 21–35
Miscellaneous	$200	$150	$150
Car	800	1,900	1,000
Appliances	200	200	100
Furniture	100	100	100
Recreational equipment	100	100	—
Regular spending	7,000	10,000	7,000
First mortgage	1,500	1,500	—
Total	$9,900	$13,950	$8,350

Additionally, payments on the family's existing first mortgage, if any, should be included in the purchase estimates. Future expected house purchases, and their associated financing, will be handled separately. The payments on the existing mortgage should be expressed in yearly rather than monthly form. These payments should be tax and inflation adjusted as discussed in Chapter 14.

A note on projecting basic purchases

The purpose of projecting basic purchases and minimum receipts estimates is to see whether the family is prepared for adverse circumstances. To serve this purpose, one important notion needs to be considered when estimates are prepared. The family cannot reduce its spending to a basic level until it knows that receipts are going to be lower than originally expected.

The O'Byrne family, for example, expects to receive $10,000 next year and increasing amounts in the future; it plans to spend $9000 next year. If the family knew that its income was going to remain at $10,000 in future years, it might want to spend less next year; perhaps it could "get by" on $8000. However, until it *knows* that Mr. O'Byrne's career is not going to turn out as well as expected, it will not want to cut back its spending to a basic level.

Therefore in estimating basic purchase levels in the plan it is probably safe to project for at least several years that basic purchases will equal expected purchases. Only after a family knows it is in trouble can it be expected to adopt a "defensive" purchasing policy. Thus we can begin supplying the needed information on receipts by noting that in at least years 1, 2, and 3 and perhaps even through period 2 basic purchases will be equal to expected purchases.

Additional information needed

In addition to receipts and purchase projections, several other (fortunately less burdensome) pieces of information are needed. These fall into three classes: current balance sheet information, information on unusual purchases and receipts, and two interest rate estimates.

The following balance sheet information is required.

Current amount of claims owned	$________
Current amount of money-yielding physical assets, if any	$________
Current amount of liabilities, except first house mortgage	$________

This information is needed in estimating whether the family will be able to provide for its projected levels of purchase.

The following information is needed on unusual purchases and receipts.

For each expected future home purchase	
Number of years from present	________
Expected difference between price of new house and previous one	$________
For each estimated receipt from gifts or inheritances	
Number of years from present	________
Amount	$________

Finally, the family needs an estimate of the rates of interest which it can obtain from claims and the rates that it must pay on borrowing. After-tax, inflation-adjusted (or protected) rates should be used. There may be a question as to whether one rate is enough for each situation. Will not claims return different rates of interest?; may not debts require differing rates of interest payments? True, but simplicity is also desirable in our planning process. Therefore an estimated average rate of interest received and of interest paid may be justified.

The average rate of interest expected should be set with the understanding that not all claims will earn high returns. Some claims will no doubt be in the form of liquid assets which may even yield negative returns. Perhaps an appropriate compromise return on claims would be something like 3 or 4% to recognize that although some higher-yielding assets, such as common stocks, may be held, these returns will be partly offset by the lower yields on claims such as bank deposits, bonds, or the saving feature of insurance policies.

Interest rates paid may be somewhat similar. If a family expects to pay borrowing rates between 6% and 12%, for example, and if a 30% marginal tax rate and 2% inflation rate were expected, the family's adjusted borrowing rates would range from about 2% to 7%. Perhaps, here, a mid-way rate of around 5% would be appropriate.

Net receipts

Our list of mean expected purchases and the information just noted are adequate for the first step of the planning process. For each period purchases are subtracted from receipts to obtain net receipts. This subtraction is made twice, for both mean expected receipts and purchases and for minimum expected receipt and basic consumption needs. Thus from our initial information we identify the net money inflows or outflows that a family may expect from receipts and purchases in each period. These projections are exemplified in Table 15.2.

TABLE 15.2

	Years from present						
	1	2	3	4–10	11–20	21–40	41–55
Expected receipts	$9,000	$9,300	$9,600	$10,000	$14,000	$16,000	$5,000
Expected purchases	9,000	9,500	9,500	10,500	11,000	10,000	8,000
Net receipts	0	—200	100	—500	3,000	6,000	—3,000
Minimum receipts	9,000	9,000	9,000	9,000	10,000	10,000	4,500
Basic purchases	9,000	9,000	9,000	9,000	9,500	9,000	6,000
Net minimum receipts	0	0	0	0	500	1,000	—2,000

The unusual receipts and purchases—inheritances, gifts, and purchase of different houses—can now be considered. Suppose the family expects an inheritance of $30,000 in about 20 years; also it would like to move to a better house at the end of ten years. If purchased, the house is expected to cost an extra $12,000.[1] It estimates that the inheritance could be as little as $15,000. If necessary the family could do without the better house. This information is included in Table 15.3.

TABLE 15.3

	Years from present								
	1	2	3	4–10		11–20		21–40	41–55
Expected net receipts (from Table 15.2)	$0	—$200	$100	—$500		$3000		$6000	—$3000
Unusual items									
Inheritance							$30,000		
House					—$12,000				

[1] One might ask, "What happens if the old house is not paid for before the new one is purchased?" This problem can be handled in a simple way by assuming that the family will continue to make payments equal to its old house payments until the time when the old mortgage would have been paid off. For example, Dick lives in a house on which payments are $2000 per year for the next 20 years. He plans to "trade up" to a house costing $10,000 extra at the end of ten years. With our method, we will only worry about how Dick will obtain the extra $10,000. His previous house is not paid for, but, by assuming that Dick will continue to make payments of $2000 per year for the following ten years, we have provided for the unpaid debt on the old house.

Note that the —$12,000 and $30,000 amounts (house purchase and inheritance) occur *between* time periods. It will be very convenient in planning if it can be assumed that unusual information will "fit" the time period already used. Even if the unusual information does not exactly fit, "forcing" it a little may be a justifiable simplification. For example, if the new home purchase was actually expected to be made 12 years hence, one might still treat it as occurring in 10 years. This treatment would be much easier and probably would be quite safe: If the plan shows the family cannot afford the house in 10 years, it probably will not be able to afford the house in 12 years either.[2]

Similar changes can be made for extraordinary minimum receipts; these are shown in Table 15.4.

TABLE 15.4

	Years from present							
	1	2	3	4–10	11–20		21–40	41–55
Net minimum receipts (from Table 15.2)	$0	$0	$0	$0	$500		$1,000	—$2,000
Unusual items								
Inheritance (minimum)						$15,000		

The family is now in the position to ask itself, on the basis of Tables 15.3 and 15.4, will it be able to spend the amounts it is currently planning to spend, and will it be protected from hardships if things go wrong? The answers to these questions are discussed in Chapter 16.

Summary

Summaries are omitted from Chapters 15, 16, and 17. These chapters deal principally with processes rather than with facts and in a sense the chapters themselves represent distillations of previously presented material.

[2] In the event that unusual information is of an important amount and cannot be "forced" into the time periods used, one recourse may be to reconstruct receipts and purchase estimates for a different set of time periods. Another possibility is to discount expected purchases to the beginning of a time period (find P where $r =$ assumed rate of return on claims, $n =$ number of years between time of purchase and beginning of time period, and $F =$ amount of expected unusual purchase). Expected unusual receipts could, to impart a little extra safety, be compounded to the end of the period (find F, where $r =$ rate on claims, $n =$ years till end of period, and $P =$ amount of expected unusual receipt). Hopefully, however, it will not be necessary to employ these techniques; most unusual information can probably, with a little judgment, be "forced" into existing time periods.

SUGGESTED READINGS

The material in Chapters 15 and 16 relates to previous material for which readings have already been cited. Procedures used in these chapters are not extensively discussed in other literature.

For an academic example of the concept of forming an optimal distribution of consumption over an individual's lifetime, see the article entitled "The Optimum Lifetime Distribution Expenditures," by L. C. Thorough in *American Economic Review*, June 1969.

QUESTIONS AND PROBLEMS

Questions and Problems are intentionally omitted from Chapters 15, 16, and 17. Instead the author strongly recommends that readers attempt to develop their own financial plans and budgets. There really is no acceptable substitute for this personal involvement in the planning process.

Appendix

One might ask, how does the concept of net receipts differ from the previously discussed concepts of saving and dissaving? There are differences arising mainly from simplifications made in the development of the planning process.

To cast the concept of net receipts in terms previously used:

1. Net receipts = money income from employment + transfer payments − money consumption spending, except nonfirst mortgage interest − purchases of physical assets

One may also recall:

2. Saving = earning power − consumption
3. Earning power = money income + leisure + nonmoney services + self-improvement
4. Consumption = money consumption spending + leisure + nonmoney services

Therefore, by subtracting consumption from earning power:

5. Saving = money income + self-improvement − money consumption spending

Equations 1 and 5 can now be compared:

		(a)		(b)		(c)		(d)
5. Saving	=	money income			−	money consumption spending	+	self-improvement
1. Net receipts	=	money income from employment	+	transfer payments	−	money consumption spending, except non-first mortgage interest	−	purchase of physical assets

Differences between equations 5 and 1 in column (a) arise because net receipts do not include interest; this is remedied in later analysis. Differences in column (c) are of the same nature and are also remedied in later analysis. Differences in column (b) are attributable to a previous simplification in which transfer payments were not originally included. A nonsimplified definition of saving should have included transfer payments.

The differences in column (d) are more basic. Self-improvement as defined in Chapter 1 does not require direct money spending. Therefore it is not necessary to plan to provide money for this type of expenditure directly. If self-improvement is to be undertaken by, say, quitting work to go to school, the indirect effect of this will show up in planning in the form of a lower estimate of money income from employment.

Purchase of physical assets has been separated from other types of saving because these assets are so interconnected with the consumption process. These assets do not yield money benefits which in turn can be used to buy other assets or reduce liabilities; the benefits from a physical asset must be consumed. Therefore, even though the purchase of these assets represents a type of saving, they are included among purchases and separated in the analysis from claims.

chapter sixteen

Lifetime economic planning

In Chapter 15 the information necessary for planning was discussed. This chapter deals with the use of this information in planning. The main purpose of the plan developed is to find out whether the family's estimates of purchases are possible or desirable. If they are not, the family will have to either change its planned purchases or try to change its receipts.

We have already considered net receipts (receipts — purchases) in particular time periods. These may be either positive or negative. If the family has no liabilities to start with and if net receipts (both mean expected and minimums) are positive in all time periods, the family's purchase plans are not excessive. If the family has liabilities at the beginning of the plan or anticipates negative net receipts in some time periods, we need to examine whether positive net receipts from other periods are sufficient to repay the liabilities and/or provide for the periods in which net receipts are negative.

We may find that the family has planned to

spend too much. On the other hand, the family could be spending too little. The plan shows not only the consequences of extravagance but also of frugality. The end result of thrift may be the possession of large, unneeded amounts of claims as the family members near the end of their lifetimes. Perhaps a family envisioning such a result would decide that denying itself marginal purchases earlier in life is not very beneficial and that it should spend more in the immediate future.

Before going further in plan development, it may be helpful to examine another example—one that continues through the entire chapter. Simplified information about a hypothetical family is presented; then this information is used to illustrate the subsequent discussion of planning.

An example of purchase projection

Our projection is for Sam and Sandra Seer who have been married two years and have one child. The purchase estimates are set forth in Table 16.1. Sam is 22 years old and Sandra is 21. They plan to have one more child after a year or two and they would like to buy a $25,000 house within three or four years. They have some recently purchased furniture and they own a new washer and dryer. They own a modest amount of claims and have several liabilities. They own a compact car which they

TABLE 16.1
PURCHASE ESTIMATES: SEER FAMILY

	Years from present									
	1	2	3		4–17		18–23	24–38		39–58
Age of husband	23	24	25		26–39		40–45	46–60		61–80
Age of wife	22	23	24		25–38		39–44	45–59		60–79
Age of first child	2	3	4		5–18		19–24			
Age of second child			1		2–15		16–21			
Expected purchases	$7,500	$8,500	$7,500		$9,000		$12,000	$11,000		$10,000
Unusual purchases										
Houses				27,000		10,000			−5,000	
Basic purchases	7,000	7,000	7,000		8,000		11,000	7,000		7,000
Unusual (basic) purchases				20,000						

purchased second hand at the time they were married; they expect that this will provide for their transportation needs for the next two years. At the end of that time they would like to trade for a new compact station wagon.

Looking ahead the Seers also see other asset needs. For example, next year they would like to buy a dishwasher for $300. They also estimate that at the time they move into their home they will want to buy $2000 worth of furniture and appliances. (For simplicity they add this rather large purchase to the $25,000 estimated house cost, thus treating $27,000 as a single purchase.)

The Seers are currently making purchases of about $600 per month including the $150 per month rent on their apartment. This $600 cash outlay includes the premiums they pay for basic insurance protection. Their purchase estimates fluctuate over the next few years because of their anticipated purchases of specific physical assets. After their second child is born they expect that their level of purchases will rise and continue rising in future periods as the children progress through primary and secondary school and go on to college. After their children have finished college, they would like to maintain a reasonably high standard of living. They are willing to curtail some of their purchases during their expected retirement period. They also anticipate the possibility that after they have lived in their new home for ten years or so, they might like to move to a better house. Accordingly, they estimate a $10,000 expenditure for that purpose.

Looking further ahead the family decides that it might wish to move to a smaller home at the time of its retirement and therefore anticipates the possibility of releasing some money by this $5000 "trade-down." This amount is shown as a negative unusual purchase requirement. (It could also be shown as another form of unusual receipt; the choice of method will make no difference in our analysis.)

In addition to projecting expected purchases, it is also necessary to estimate the minimum tolerable level of basic purchases. (These estimates are also needed for the planning of an insurance program.) The estimates shown in Table 16.1 note that the Seers place a high priority on maintaining a substantial level of purchases during the years their children are growing up and in college, but that they are willing to accept a considerably lower living standard, if necessary, during the immediate future and during the years after their children have finished college. Their unusual purchases are also reduced to the basic level of only one house purchase for $20,000 at the end of year 3. They feel that if necessary they could live all their lives in this more modest home.

The inclusion of basic purchase estimates in an economic plan poses some difficulty, however. This is the level of purchases that a family will make only if unfavorable circumstances occur. How does the family know when it will become necessary to restrict spending to the basic level? Its career may appear to be progressing well during early years only to suffer downturns in later periods. In its planning the family cannot expect that it will be able to adjust its spending in anticipation of specific future economic woes.

To handle this problem for the Seer family, we resort to simplification. We make the assumption that in early years the Seers will not be able to predict the actual future pattern of its earnings—whether they are to be above or below the mean expected income. Therefore we assume that, even if income does not materialize as fast as expected during early years, the family will have an insufficient basis for reducing its standard of living. In the early years of its plan the Seer family will maintain its expected purchases even if its receipts are only minimum during that period. (For the Seers' planning we define this early period as years 1–17.)

An example of receipt projection

A projection of receipts for the Seers is shown in Table 16.2. The projections are on take-home pay basis and include transfer payments during retirement. The income projections include projections both for Sam Seer's anticipated business career and for Sandra Seer's assumption that she is likely to take a part-time job for a while after the children are out of high school. No unusual receipts are expected.

Minimum incomes have also been estimated; these are based on the possibility that Sandra might not be able to find a suitable job after the children were grown up and on observations of others in Sam's occupation whose careers did not fulfill their anticipation. Of course, Sam knows that things might even turn out worse than these minimums, but he has tried to make his minimum estimates realistic and not take extremely far-fetched possibilities into consideration. (He might, for example, turn into an unemployable alcoholic.)

TABLE 16.2
RECEIPTS PROJECTIONS: SEER FAMILY

	Years from present						
	1	2	3	4–17	18–23	24–38	39–58
Husband's take-home pay and retirement benefits	$7,500	$8,000	$9,000	$11,000	$14,000	$16,000	$5,000
Wife's take-home pay and retirement benefits						2,000	1,000
Totals	7,500	8,000	9,000	11,000	14,000	18,000	6,000
Minimums	7,500	8,000	9,000	10,000	12,000	12,000	4,000

TABLE 16.3
EXPECTED NET RECEIPTS: SEER FAMILY

	Years from present									
	1	2	3		4–17		18–23	24–38		39–58
Expected receipts	$7,500	$8,000	$9,000		$11,000		$14,000	$18,000		$ 6,000
Expected purchases	—7,300	—8,500	—7,500		—9,000		—12,000	—11,000		—10,000
Unusual purchases				—27,000		—10,000			+5,000	
Expected net receipts	+200	—500	+1,500	—27,000	+2,000	—10,000	+2,000	+7,000	+5,000	—4,000

Net receipts

Table 16.3 is based on Tables 16.1 and 16.2 and shows the net receipts that are expected for the Seer family. These mean expected projections predict two early periods of receipt deficiency: a modest difference in year 2 and a large and very normal shortage between years 3 and 4 when a house is to be purchased. An additional shortage is foreseen at retirement.

Table 16.4 repeats the process of net receipts determination using minimum receipts. Expected purchases are used during years 1–17 to indicate that the family might not realize that it should veer from its normal purchase plans during this period. Basic purchase estimates are used during years 18–58.

TABLE 16.4
MINIMUM NET RECEIPTS: SEER FAMILY

	Years from present							
	1	2	3		4–17	18–23	24–38	39–58
Minimum receipts	$7,500	$8,000	$8,500		$10,000	$12,000	$12,000	$4,000
Basic purchases	—7,300	—8,500	—7,500		—9,000	—11,000	—7,000	—7,000
Unusual purchases				—27,000				
Minimum net receipts	+200	—500	+1,000	—27,000	+1,000	+1,000	+5,000	—3,000

Claim purchase and borrowing

If positive net receipts are generated in any period, they can be used either for repaying liabilities or for accumulating claims. If negative net receipts occur, they will require either borrowing or the disposal of previously accumulated claims.

A family may wish to borrow even if it owns some claims. It is usually desirable for the family to try to maintain some liquid assets. Even if it is borrowing, the family should probably try to keep a small liquid asset "cushion" of a few hundred to a few thousand dollars to provide against unexpected needs.

The purchase of claims and the use of borrowing provide the family with the opportunity to shift consumption over time, using the surpluses of one period for the deficiencies of another. To find out whether the projections for receipts and purchases comprise a satisfactory outlook for a family, we assume that any net receipts are used in the following order.

1. Build up minimum acceptable level of liquid assets (such as bank account).
2. Repay liabilities.
3. Build up additional claims.

For example, a family has $300 in liquid claims, $1500 in debts, and regards $1000 as the minimum acceptable level of liquid assets. If it receives $800 in net receipts, we assume that it buys $700 of liquid assets ($1000 − $300) and repays $100 of debt. If it instead receives $3000 in net receipts, it would buy $700 in liquid assets, repay its $1500 debt, and buy $800 of additional claims.

Similarly, negative net receipts are handled in the following order.

1. Sale of claims, except those necessary for maintaining minimum acceptable level of liquid assets.
2. Borrowing.

In this case, a family owns $1500 of claims and regards $1000 as the minimum level of claims acceptable. If it experiences $300 in negative net receipts, it sells claims to cover the deficiency. If its deficiency was $1200, it would sell $500 in claims (down to $1000) and borrow the remaining $700. By applying these assumptions and using the estimated borrowing rate and rate of return on claims discussed in Chapter 15, we can analyze the effects of a family's net receipts, whether positive or negative, in any period.

The analysis must first begin with information on the family's current holdings of claims (and other money-yielding assets) and its existing debt. The family's existing first mortgage, if any, is not included in this existing debt since its payments will already have been incorporated in the family's projected purchases.

A claims and debt projection

Net receipts and other information discussed previously can be used to develop a projection of a family's claims and debt. In this statement (shown in Table 16.5) year 0 is used to designate the present for purposes of showing the family's current claims and debts.

TABLE 16.5
CLAIMS AND DEBT

	Years from present			
	0	1	2	3
Net receipts				
New borrowing				
Repayments				
Debt balance				
New claims				
Claim disposals				
Claims balance				

New borrowing or claim disposals arise from negative net receipts. Repayments or claim purchases result from positive net receipts. Debt and claims balances begin with existing amounts of these items in year 0. The debt balance rises when new borrowing takes place and falls when repayment takes place. The accumulation of interest on the debt is also included in the debt balance. Similarly, the claims balance rises with new claim purchases and interest accumulation, and falls with claims disposals.

The preparation of this statement can be discussed more effectively with an example. Therefore we return to the Seer family.

Claims purchase and borrowing: an example

The Seer family owns the following claims in year 0:

Checking account	$ 310
Savings account	400
Common stock	800
Total claims	$1510

It owes the following liabilities:

Minor charge account balances, not yet due, totaling less than $100[1]	—
Time payment balance on appliances	$150
Total debt	$150

It regards its $700 combined savings and checking accounts balances as an adequate level of liquid assets. It estimates that it will pay an average rate of 6% (adjusted) when borrowing and earn 3% (adjusted) on claims.

This information along with the Seers' expected net receipts can be incorporated into an uncompleted claims and debt statement (Table 16.6).

TABLE 16.6
CLAIMS AND DEBT: SEER FAMILY

	Years from present							
	0	1	2	3	4–17	18–23	24–38	39–58
Expected net receipts		+$200	−$500	+$1,500	+$2,000 −$27,000	+$2,000 −$10,000	+$7,000	−$4,000 +$5,000
New borrowing								
Repayments								
Debt balance	$150							
New claims								
Withdrawals								
Claims balance	$1,510							

Our next step is to complete this statement. Beginning in year 1 we assume the family will repay its debt out of net receipts. The debt repayment with 6% interest is assumed to require $150 + ($150 × 6%), or $159. This reduces the debt balance to 0. Since $41 of the $200 net receipts is left over, this can be recorded as new claims. The year 1 claims balance then consists of

[1] For simplicity these balances will be ignored since the family will probably always have a few small charge balances which are not yet due.

Year 0 claims balance	$1510
Interest on year 0 balance at 3%	45
New claims bought in year 1	41
Year 1 claims balance	$1596

Accordingly, the Seers could fill in the following information in the claims and debt statement.

	Year 1
Net receipts	+$200
New borrowing	0
Repayments	159
Debt balance	0
New claims	41
Withdrawals	0
Claims balance	1596

To continue, in year 2 expected receipts are —$500. This will require claims disposals of $500. The new balance will be

Year 1 claims balance	$1596
Interest on year 1 balance at 3%	48
Total	$1644
Deduct withdrawals	−500
Year 2 claims balance	$1144

For year 2 they can then fill in

	Year 2
Net receipts	−$500
New borrowing	0
Repayments	0
Debt balance	0
New claims	0
Withdrawals	500
Claims balance	1144

For year 3 net receipts are $1500; this can be used for buying new claims. The family's claims balance at the end of year 3 will have reached

Year 2 claims balance	$1144
Interest at 3%	34
New claims	1500
Year 3 claims balance	$2678

For year 3 the family can fill in

	Year 3
Net receipts	+$1500
New borrowing	0
Repayments	0
Debt balance	0
New claims	1500
Withdrawals	0
Claims balance	2678

Between year 3 and year 4 (end of year 3) the family plans to buy a house which imposes a net cash receipt of —$27,000. The claims balance can be reduced by about $2000, leaving a balance of approximately $700 ($678), but the rest of the —$27,000 will have to be covered by borrowing. Thus the Seers may project

	Between years 3 and 4
Net receipts	−$27,000
New borrowing	25,000
Repayment	0
Debt balance	25,000
New claims	0
Withdrawals	2,000
Claims balance	678

From years 4–17 net receipts of $2000 per year are expected. These can be used to reduce the family's debt balance. To find out the amount by which the debt will be reduced, we can solve for the amount of debt that would be owed at the end of year 17 if no repayments were made.

$P = \$25,000$
$n = 14$ (years 4 to 17)
$r = 6\%$ (family's borrowing rate)
$F =$ unknown

Solving from Appendix Table A.1, $F = \$25,000 \times$ about $2.26 =$ about $56,500. From this we may deduct the future value of the debt repayments that can be made during years 4–17. (For this purpose, the borrowing rate of interest is used.)

$A = \$2000$
$n = 14$
$r = 6\%$
$F =$ unknown

Solving from Table A.3, $F = \$2000 \times$ about $21 =$ about $42,100.

Deducting the future value of the payments, \$42,100, from the future value of the debt, \$56,500, we find that about \$14,400 of debt will be owed at the end of year 17.

Thus for years 4–17 the Seers can fill in

	Years 4–17	
Net receipts	+\$2000	(per year)
New borrowing	0	
Repayments	2000	(per year)
Debt balance	14,400	
New claims	0	
Withdrawals	0	
Claims balance	1000	

The last claims balance was determined on the basis of 3% interest being earned on the claims balance of \$678 after the home purchase. The approximate future value of \$678 is \$1000, where $r = 3\%$ and $n = 14$.

Between years 17 and 18 the Seer family plans to buy a house for \$10,000. The family's claim balance is already near its minimum level, but \$300 could be withdrawn from claims for the house purchase. The rest must be financed by additional borrowing. Therefore between years 17 and 18 the Seers must borrow another \$9700 (\$10,000 — \$300). The Seers may fill in

	Between years 17 and 18
Net receipts	−\$10,000
New borrowing	9,700
Repayment	0
Debt balance	24,100
New claims	0
Withdrawals	300
Claims balance	700

From years 18–23 the Seers will continue to generate net receipts of \$2000 per year, all of which can be used for debt repayment. To find the amount of debt owed at the end of year 23, we can again deduct the future value of the \$2000 per year repayments from the future value of the beginning debt of \$20,100.

$$
\begin{aligned}
P &= \$20{,}100 \\
n &= 6 \\
r &= 6\% \\
F &= \text{unknown} = \text{about } \$34{,}200
\end{aligned}
$$

$A = \$2000$
$n = 6$
$r = 6\%$
$F = \text{unknown} = \text{about}$ 14,000

Debt at end of year 23	$20,200

For years 18–23, the Seers may project

	Years 18–23	
Net receipts	+$2000	(per year)
New borrowing	0	
Repayments	2000	(per year)
Debt balance	20,200	
New claims	0	
Withdrawals	0	
Claims balance	850	

During years 24–38 the Seers expect to generate large net receipts of $7000 per year. All of this amount can be applied to debt repayment until the Seers' debt is all repaid; then the $7000 per year can be used for claims accumulation.

To find the length of time necessary to repay the debt

$P = \$20{,}200$
$r = 6\%$
$A = \$7000$
$n = \text{unknown} = \text{about 3.3 years}$

Thus the debt will be repaid early in year 27. After that the Seers can buy claims at a rate of $7000 per year foralmost 12 years (years 27–38). To find the accumulated value of these new claims at the end of year 38

$A = \$7000$
$n = 12$
$r = 3\%$
$F = \text{unknown} = \text{about } \$99{,}000$

The claims balance will also be enhanced by the compounded value of the previous $850 balance. Therefore the Seers may fill in the following estimates.

	Years 24–38	
Net receipts	+$7,000	(per year)

New borrowing	0	
Repayments	7,000 (24–26)	(per year)
Debt balance	0	
New claims	7,000 (27–38)	(per year)
Withdrawals	0	
Claims balance	\$100,000	

Between years 38 and 39 \$5000 can be added to the claims balance from the anticipated sale of a house. This balance now reaches \$105,000. During anticipated retirement (years 39–58) net receipts of —\$4000 are expected. These deficiencies can be covered by drawing on the Seers' large claims balance. To check that the claims balance is sufficient we can solve for the claims balance that will remain in year 38. To do this, we follow a procedure similar to that used for identifying a remaining debt balance. We find the future value of the \$105,000 and then deduct the future value of the \$4000 per year claims disposals.

This process yields

$P = \$105{,}000$
$n = 20$ (years 39–58)
$r = 3\%$
$F =$ unknown $=$ about \$189,000

$A = \$4000$
$n = 20$
$r = 3\%$
$F =$ unknown $=$ about 108,000

Year 58 claims balance \$81,000

To complete the Seers' projection of debt and claims, they can note

	Between years 38 and 39	Years 39–58	
Net receipts	+\$5,000	−\$4,000	(per year)
New borrowing	0	0	
Repayments	0	0	
Debt balance	0	0	
New claims	5,000		(per year)
Withdrawals	0	4,000	(per year)
Claims balance	\$105,000	\$81,000	

The entire claims and debt statement for the Seers is now presented in Table 16.7.

TABLE 16.7

CLAIMS AND DEBT: SEER FAMILY

	Years from present										
	0	1	2	3		4–17		18–23	24–38		39–58
Net receipts		+$200	−$500	+$1,500	−$27,000	+$2,000	−$10,000	+$2,000	+$7,000	+$5,000	−$4,000
New borrowing		0	0	0	25,000	0	9,700	0	0	0	0
Repayments		159	0	0	0	2,000	0	2,000	7,000 (24–26)	0	0
Debt balance	150	0	0	0	25,000	14,400	24,100	20,200	0	0	0
New claims		41	0	1,500	0	0	0	0	7,000 (27–38)	5,000	0
Withdrawals		0	500	0	2,000	0	300	0	0	0	4,000
Claims balance	1,510	1,596	1,144	2,678	678	1,000	700	850	100,000	105,000	81,000

The Seers' outlook: a preliminary view

The initial impression given by Table 16.7 is that there is nothing wrong with the Seers' current spending pattern. They appear to be consuming at a sufficiently low present level to provide for desired levels of consumption throughout their lifetime. In fact they may feel that they do not want to build up an $80,000 estate (more or less, depending on their actual lengths of life).

Their projection also does reasonably well on another test. They reach a peak level of borrowing at the end of year 3 when they project a debt balance of $25,000. This can be compared with their net expected receipts (Table 16.3) in year 3 of $9000. If total debt can be no more than 3 times take-home pay, their maximum possible debt level at year 3 will be $9000 × 3, or $27,000.

Thus the maximum loan limit does not appear to pose any problem. They should be able to convince lending agencies that they are worthy of $25,000 in credit at year 3, especially with their bright future prospects. If not, they may simply have to wait a year to buy a house when some increase in income will have increased their estimated levels of permissible debt and year 4's net cash receipts will have reduced the need for borrowing by an estimated $2000.

Their next major amount of new borrowing will occur at the end of year 17. Since this need is not as great and their take-home pay by then should be greater, this should impose no strain.

Minimum net receipts and the claims and debt statements

Although the Seers' projections in Table 16.7 have so far suggested no difficulties, this table was based on expected net receipts. The family should also address the question: What are the implications of our current spending plans if the future does not turn out as favorable as we expect? Estimates of minimum net receipts were developed in Table 16.4 to indicate the amount of net receipts the family would have available if (a) only minimum receipts were forthcoming in future periods and (b) the family did not allow its purchases to drop below its "basic consumption requirement."

A new claims and debt table, called Claims and Debt: Minimum, can be developed from minimum net receipts information in exactly the same way as Table 16.7 was calculated. We do not present the details of this calculation, but simply present the table in completed form (Table 16.8).

Table 16.8 shows both impossibly high borrowing requirements and an inability to provide for desired retirement spending. There would actually have been no need to complete all of Table 16.8. It was apparent after

TABLE 16.8
CLAIMS AND DEBT: MINIMUM: SEER FAMILY

	Years from present								
	0	1	2	3		4–17	18–23	24–38	39–58
Minimum net receipts		+$200	−$500	+$1,000	−$27,000	+$1,000	+$1,000	+$5,000	−$3,000
New borrowing		0	0	0	25,500	0	0	0	Plan Fails
Repayments		159	0	0	0	1,000	1,000	5,000	
Debt balance	150	0	0	0	25,500	36,600	45,000	0	
New claims		41	0	1,000	0	0	0	0	
Withdrawals			500	0	1,500	0	0	0	
Claims balance	1,510	1,596	1,144	2,178	678	1,000	800	12,500	

considering the home purchase that the family would be in trouble. Even if it could obtain the necessary loans to buy the house, it would not be able to pay the required interest ($25,500 at 6%) of over $1500 per year out of its estimated net receipts of +$1000 during years 4–17.

The Seers' outlook: a second look

The Seers now have two possible lifetime consumption prospects: a happy one if their income expectations materialize and a dour one if they do not. On the basis of these two prospects, modifications of spending plans need to be considered. The prospects pose a general issue that must be resolved in nearly all planning situations: How can a line of defense be provided against misfortunes without excessive frugality?

Consider one possible approach. The Seer family could decrease its expected purchase estimates by $500 per year during years 1–17. This would still leave its expected purchases somewhat above its basic purchase estimates for those years. (See Table 16.1.) It could also reconsider its plans and buy a somewhat more modest home at an estimated cost, including furniture, of $24,000.

The effect of the modification can be examined by reconstructing the claims and debt:minimum statement (Table 16.9). Particularly if the Seers' home purchase can be financed mainly with a quite long-term mortgage (30 years perhaps), the family should be able to meet its basic consumption needs even in the face of adverse income.

Other modifications might also be possible. Sam might want to try to increase receipts by "moonlighting" at the expense of leisure. He might

TABLE 16.9

CLAIMS AND DEBT: MINIMUM (MODIFIED)

	Years from present								
	0	1	2	3		4–17	18–23	24–38	39–58
Minimum net receipts		+$700	$ 0	+$1,500	−$24,000	+$1,500	+$1,000	+$5,000	−$3,000
New borrowing		0	0	0	21,000	0	0	0	0
Repayments		159	0	0	0	1,500	1,000	5,000 (24–26)	0
Debt balance	$150	0	0	0	21,000	16,000	15,000	0	0
New claims		541	0	1,500	0	0	0	5,000 (27–38)	0
Withdrawals			0	0	3,000	0	0	0	3,000
Claims balance	1,510	2,096	2,159	3,724	724	1,000	800	70,000	45,000

even reconsider his choice of job and try to do something that might be more demanding but would also be higher paying. Sandra might try to work for a few years at the start of the planning period even if this meant that the family would have to do without some of the nonmoney services she was providing in the home.

Had the expected financial strain been even greater, the Seers might have had to consider more stringent policies. They might have had to revise their whole way of thinking about the minimum standard of living they considered acceptable. A basic consumption level is something that is very much dependent on the attitudes of the family; most of us could survive on a level of purchases much below that which we have come to regard as "necessary."

Excess frugality

It should not be inferred from this analysis that only the family's minimum receipts really matter in its planning. The Seer family, although it wishes to protect against contingencies, should also be concerned about a spending policy that will not overconcentrate its spending in the retirement period or result in a much larger estate than the Seers wish to leave.

The claims and debt: minimum statement can be used as a test to see if contingencies are adequately provided for. Although this statement counsels for caution in the next few years, the Seers ought to periodically reexamine their receipts prospects. Perhaps after five or ten years they will be quite sure that their receipts will not drop as low as the originally predicted minimum. As soon as they are confident that the old minimum receipts estimates do not apply, they can reconsider their spending plans. Perhaps they can then move to a better house or expand their spending on other things. Although self-discipline is extremely important to the family, there is no point in practicing unnecessary self-denial.

The urgency of action

The purpose of planning is to influence action. It might have been easy for the Seer family to respond to the initial suggestion of troubles in its economic plan (Table 16.8) by deciding to reduce spending only in the future. With this intention it could have made plan modifications that on paper would have avoided trouble. However, if the Seers cannot begin to restrict their spending promptly, their intentions to restrict future spending are probably illusions. Unless one is prepared to let his plan influence what he does right away, the planning is probably just an academic exercise.

Estate planning

In the financial planning of the Seer family, the possible accumulation of a substantial estate was projected. The family might not wish to have this occur; that is, it might prefer to consume more during its lifetime rather than pass on a large bequest at the time of death. However, if it anticipates having an estate of significant size and if it is at all concerned about what becomes of this estate, a special type of planning, which is commonly called estate planning, should be undertaken. Estate planning incorporates both the objectives of exercising control over the disposition of the estate and lessening the amount of the estate that will be absorbed by special taxes.

This text does not attempt to discuss estate planning at any length; it can be an extremely complicated topic. However, we extend two advisory statements. To facilitate controlling the disposition of an estate, almost everyone can advantageously make use of a will. This is usually a formal legal document drawn up with the aid of a lawyer in which an individual or married couple specify directions for the disposal of the estate. Without this document, the estate is divided up among the survivors of the individual or family according to formulas established under the laws of various states; sometimes this division may be quite contrary to the desires of the persons who have accumulated the estate.

If an estate of substantial size is expected and if the family desires control over its disposition, planning the disposal of the estate should probably start long before the anticipated time of death. Sometimes it is desirable to give part of the estate away before death occurs. There may also be an advantage to having part of the estate received by the survivors in the form of a life insurance settlement rather than a direct inheritance. On large estates both taxes levied on the estate itself (estate taxes) and those levied when portions of the estate pass to survivors (inheritance taxes) can be quite large. Early actions may be important in controlling the amount of the estate diverted into these taxes. Again, consultation with a lawyer, the trust department of a bank, and/or a trusted insurance agent should be undertaken at the time the accumulation of a sizable estate is first anticipated.

Experimentation

Once a plan has been developed a variety of modifications can be "tried on," if one is willing to do the extra calculations. How much would the plan be affected if the rate on borrowing was decreased by 1%, for example? If the difference appears significant, the family may devote more care to choice of borrowing sources.

What would be the effect of giving up some early receipts to form human capital and increase later receipts? Job choice decisions may often be of this form. The possibilities for experiments can go on and on.

Saving and borrowing

In Chapter 5, in introducing the discussion of asset selection, we noted three basic issues relating to assets—choice of individual assets, total amount of assets to be acquired, and means of financing the assets. The first issue was treated in some detail and the third has also been partially discussed in Chapter 14. We have not directly considered the second issue, how many assets should be acquired nor the extent to which these assets should be financed by saving as opposed to borrowing. Stated another way, we have not directly faced the question, "What is the right amount of saving and consumption for the family to undertake?"

Although these issues have not been confronted directly, we have nevertheless been reaching for their answers in an indirect way. The use of the lifetime financial plan enables the individual or family, through consideration of various financial possibilities, to seek their own answers to these questions. Saving and borrowing are nothing more than shifts in consumption, or potential consumption, from one time period to the next. "How much shall I save or borrow?" The correct answer must consider the consequence of any action on the pattern of consumption that is expected to result. If an individual is saving "too little" and/or borrowing "too much," this can alternatively be expressed by saying that his present consumption is at a level that is likely to undesirably affect future consumption.

Another issue, previously discussed in Chapter 8, can be reviewed in the context of the lifetime plan. Assets, such as houses, which yield nonmoney benefits can be regarded as unacceptable if their after-tax rate of return is below that available on money-yielding assets. However, we noted that on these service-yielding assets a superior return did not necessarily make them acceptable. Their acceptability can now be tested in the lifetime plan. When a family considers the purchase of a house or other physical asset with nonmoney benefits, it can, by fitting the initial cost into its plan, determine whether the purchase will have an undesirable effect on its lifetime consumption pattern. If the house purchase results in the family's inability to obtain adequate consumption in some future periods, some marginal house expenditure may have to be foregone. The alternatives to buying a house are usually an increase in the holding of claims or a reduction in potential borrowing. Even though the house yields benefits that are greater than either the cost of borrowing or the return available on claims, the house, because it is providing nonmoney benefits, may result in the family's being short of money in future periods as disclosed by the plan.

chapter seventeen

Budgeting

In Chapters 15 and 16 we considered a type of financial planning which would enable a family to examine the effects of its present actions on its future pattern of consumption. In developing this plan, estimates of present and future requirements for purchases of consumption goods and physical assets were required. The preparation of these estimates is now considered more carefully. The problem of controlling actual expenditures is also examined in an attempt to insure that the family which formulates a plan does not inadvertantly depart from it. Unless the family is prepared to keep its actual spending in line with its plans, the plan itself will be of little value.

To aid in the formation of expenditure estimates and in the control of these expenditures, another more detailed plan should be considered. This plan, the budget, concentrates only on purchases. Thus it differs from the cash flow statement in Chapter 10 as well as the long range plan of Chapters 15 and 16.

It excludes consideration of borrowing and repayment, the buying and selling of money-yielding assets, and the general issue of the relationship between consumption and saving. Many other forms of budgets also exist, but the one we prepare here will be used as a supplemental part of a larger plan, so that the total amount of spending on consumption and physical assets can be viewed in the perspective of a lifetime plan.

Form of the budget

Since the major purpose of a budget is to control expenditures, the budget should cover a rather short time period, often a month. A budget consists of a set of expenditure plans and, by keeping its period short, the actual expenditures made by the family can be more promptly compared with the budgeted expenditures. In this way, if actual spending starts to deviate from planned spending, quick remedial action can be attempted.

TABLE 17.1
BUDGET FOR MAY

Consumption spending		
Food		$120
Clothing		30
Rent (or first mortgage payment)		150
Utilities		35
Gas and other car expenses except insurance and car purchases		40
Other asset maintenance		10
Insurance		30
Medical and dental expenses		50
Recreation		25
Beverages, tobacco		20
Gifts, donations		15
Haircuts, cosmetics		15
School expense, children's allowances		15
Vacation		25
Interest, other than on first house mortgage		20
Miscellaneous		30
Emergencies		15
	Total	$645
Asset purchases		
Furniture and appliances		30
Car		50
	Total	$ 80
Total budgeted spending		$725

A typical budget is shown in Table 17.1; it consists of various categories of expenditure. The budget draws on the principle of simplification in that it uses only a limited number of broad categories of expenditure. If the budget becomes too complicated, not only will the budget itself be difficult to prepare, but very detailed record keeping will also be required to compare actual expenditures with budgeted expenditures.

The use of a monthly budgeting period poses some problems because not all of a family's expenditures are made on a monthly basis. Rent payments, food purchases, utility expenses, and a number of other items are required in regular and rather predictable amounts each month. On the other hand, some items occur sporadically, such as medical and dental expenses, and can only be included in a monthly budget on a mean expected basis. Other items, such as car purchases or vacation spending, occur in "lumps" rather than an even flow each month.

These irregularly occurring items are included in the monthly budget for two reasons. If the monthly budget is to be a family's principal expenditure estimate, it needs to be complete. Additionally, averaging these expenditures into a monthly figure enables the comparison of their size with other regular expenditures and thus may lead to the reconsideration and possible revision of the spending plans for these items.

However, care has to be taken with these irregular items if the budget is to serve as an instrument of control. In the preceding example, the family budgeted $50 per month for car purchases. It is not appropriate for the family to congratulate itself if its car purchase expenditures are under $50 in a particular month or to condemn itself if they are over $50. Instead, when the family considers irregular expenditures, it should see whether these are in line with the overall budgeting pattern for the year or even a longer period. For example, when a family buys a car it wants to inquire whether or not the cost of the car purchase is going to mean that, over a longer period, the car purchase expenditures are going to exceed the budgeted average.

Why not all monthly payments?

Monthly house payments (on the first mortgage) were included in the family's purchase estimates as discussed in preceding chapters. This was justified on the grounds that houses are such large purchases and are so frequently financed with first mortgages that this may be regarded as the normal way of purchasing a house.

Many families have other loan obligations, such as second mortgages and conditional sale contracts, that require monthly payments and yet these amounts have not been included in the proposed budget. The reason for this lies in the fact that these discharges of debt, although they require cash payments, are not really a part of the family's current spending. They are, instead, payments for past asset purchases.

Suppose the family whose budget appeared in Table 17.1 had recently purchased a new car without any trade-in of a previous car. The monthly payments on this car purchase are $120 per month. However, the family expects from now on that it will be able to trade cars at an average cost of $600 per year ($50 per month). The family is already committed to its debt payment of $120 per month, but it can consider a change in its policy for acquiring future new cars. Thus it can plan for an average annual purchase requirement of $50, or some other amount, and control its spending to conform to this amount. The family can do nothing about its promise to pay $120 per month on its previous car purchase except perhaps to extend the term of financing, a separate issue.

Again, the planning purpose and the supplemental role of the budget need to be stressed. A budget is a device for planning and controlling the family's current and future spending. It is not an attempt to predict what the family's current cash requirements are actually going to be. The family may borrow for part of its expenditures or finance these expenditures from the sale of assets and thus may require little current cash outlay. On the other hand, cash outlays may be greater than the spending predictions in the budget if the family must repay previous indebtedness or is buying other assets. To keep the budget in conformity with its intended purpose, it must not serve to take the place of either the lifetime projections discussed in Chapters 15 and 16 or the short-term predictions of cash requirements discussed in Chapter 10.

Bases for budget predictions

Two major sources of information can be used in developing the spending predictions that comprise a budget. One of these is records of past expenditures. The family may have a complete set of spending records. If not, it may be able, on the basis of check stubs, receipts, and other information, to reconstruct its approximate pattern of spending.

If the family lacks expenditure records, it should consider undertaking some record keeping so that the budget will be of greatest usefulness. Unless some spending records are maintained, the family will have difficulty comparing its actual spending with budgeted amounts. If this comparison cannot be made conveniently, the budget is likely to be an ineffective device for controlling the level of spending.

In addition to records, budgeted estimates can also be based on the experience of others. This may be particularly necessary with a newly married couple. Banks and other financial institutions often provide budget suggestions based on their experience. Friends and relatives may be consulted. In addition, the U.S. Bureau of Labor Statistics has prepared some guideline budgets representing the average spending of families in various living standard categories. Estimates for 1971 based on these figures are shown in Table 17.2.

Records of past spending and experience of others cannot be the sole basis for budget preparation, however. A budget by its very nature is a forward-looking analysis which seeks to anticipate forthcoming expenditures. If the family plans to increase its number of children, send children to college, move to a different location, or go into retirement, it will have to rely very heavily on its own judgment. It will need to look at its proposed expenditures, category by category, and try to predict how they could be affected by change in its future circumstances. In comparison with the spending habits of others, each family will have to recognize that its taste and plans are distinctive; it will probably not achieve a satisfactory budget by attempting to imitate the spending patterns of someone else or the average spending patterns of some group.

Control at the time of budget preparation

The budget can begin to control family expenditures immediately at the time it is prepared. Ideas about expenditures can be discussed and various spending proposals can be increased or decreased. For example, when the family considers the purchase of physical assets, it ought to consider whether the services yielded by these assets will be worth the implicit rent involved. When the family thinks about its food, clothing, and educational expenditures, it may wish to discuss the possibility of

TABLE 17.2
ESTIMATED 1971 MONTHLY PURCHASES FOR FAMILY OF FOUR

	Lower standard of living	Moderate standard of living	Higher standard of living
Food	$170	$210	$260
Housing[a]	130	220	330
Transportation[b]	50	90	110
Clothing and personal care	70	100	150
Health care[c]	60	60	60
Insurance[d]	20	30	40
Miscellaneous	30	30	100
	$530	$740	$1050

[a] Includes estimates of rent or mortgage payments, taxes, insurance, utilities, and repair costs, and purchase and maintenance of household appliances.
[b] Includes car insurance as well as other car ownership and maintenance costs.
[c] Includes cost of health insurance.
[d] Includes life and disability insurance, but excludes insurance purchased under an involuntary benefit program.

limiting the size of the family since it will be difficult to control future spending unless family size is itself controlled. However, this preliminary budgeting control should not be of a totally negative nature. At the time the budget is prepared, ideas for travel or other possibilities of increasing certain classes of consumption spending can also be discussed and perhaps fitted into the family's future consumption plans.

Reality in budget estimates

Budget estimates should be as realistic as possible and should not be prepared with an attempt to be either optimistic or pessimistic. Even when a family prepares estimates of its minimum consumption requirements in order to plan its lifetime consumption and develop its basic insurance program, these estimates should be realistic expectations of the degree to which the family will be able to curtail its expenditures without undue hardship.

A good test for the realistic budget is that it should appear just as likely to be underspent as overspent. To accomplish this end a budget must literally attempt to predict the unpredictable. It is difficult to tell what actual expenses are going to be in any particular month, especially for items such as automobile repairs, children's eyeglasses, or travel necessitated by the illness of a relative. Although these particular items cannot be readily predicted, most families can be reasonably sure that such items will occur from time to time. Therefore budget estimates should be large enough to attempt to cover these "unpredictable" items.

The various regular expenditure categories should be large enough to allow for an average of unusual expenditures. For example, the medical and dental category should be large enough to cover some dental expenses besides routine examinations. Beyond these regular categories, two more distinctive expenditure categories are also likely to be useful. In the budget shown in Table 17.1 both a miscellaneous and an emergency category were included.

The miscellaneous category is intended to cover regularly recurring small expenditures which do not fit other categories and hence, are rather difficult to predict: the payment of a lawyer's fee, the charge for help in filling out an income tax form, "coffee money" for work, or other small items that cannot be neatly fitted into other categories. The use of a miscellaneous account makes allowances for items that are not easily classifiable and also eliminates some budgeting detail. If categories had to be developed for every possible expenditure, the budget would become a maze of trivial classifications. A budget is a useful tool; if it becomes too complicated, however, it is not likely to be used.

In addition to miscellaneous items, occasional emergency expenditures occur, such as those caused by acts of vandalism, an emergency trip as mentioned previously, or a truly unusual repair bill. Insurance can protect against many unusual cash outlays, but it is usually not economical to insure against small contingencies even if insurance were available for all of them. Therefore some extra allowance for these purposes make the budget more realistic. Even though these emergency items cannot be readily controlled, an allowance for them in the budget is very useful in planning.

Relating the budget to other plans

We have noted that the budget is only a part of personal economic planning and budget estimates need to be related to other plans. The budgeted expenditure predictions can be included as current spending predictions in the development of a lifetime consumption plan. These current spending predictions can also serve as a basis for making the future predictions required in the lifetime statement. In turn, if the analysis of lifetime consumption reveals that current spending should be curtailed or that a higher level of current spending would be readily permissible, the budget can be revised on the basis of these long-term implications.

Just as the budget needs to be coordinated with the lifetime cash projections, it also needs to be accompanied by short-term cash flow projections. For example, despite the fact that the family is going to spend an average of $600 per month, it may concentrate $1000 or more of cash outlay in one month when, for example, the purchase of a major appliance and the payment of annual insurance premiums coincide. Overall, the budget really tells very little about the inflow and outflow of cash, since cash may be required to meet previous commitments and some current purchases may be financed by borrowing. Thus cash planning along the lines discussed in Chapter 10 needs to be undertaken separately.

These separate plans may seem to entail a rather burdensome amount of "book work." Admittedly the initial development of both a budget and a lifetime consumption plan will take some time. However, after these are once developed, the necessary revisions and associated record keeping should not be very time consuming. In fact, if a planning process becomes burdensomely time consuming, attempts should be made to simplify the process. Even a very simple process is preferable to one that has been completely abandoned.

Who should administer the budget

When an unmarried person budgets or engages in other planning, he has no problem about who should undertake this responsibility. However, in the family situation this issue needs to be faced. In most families spending is not done solely by one person in the family. A husband and wife both may make major expenditures and children may also spend a significant portion of the family's budget. In general a good rule to follow is that all persons involved in spending should be involved in planning. As we noted in Chapter 16, planning is ineffective unless some action follows from it. In the case of budgeting, not only are the predictions included in the budget likely to be more realistic if all spenders participate, but conformity of actual expenditures to the budget is likely to be improved if this preliminary involvement of all parties has taken place. Each one can then view his own spending as part of a related spending pattern and can be made aware of the implications that overspending can have on the attainment of other economic goals.

Reviewing and revising

Budgets are seldom perfect. The budget preparation may have neglected to include expenditures which subsequently become necessary. It may have allowed too small an amount for some expense categories and too much for other expenditures. If a family finds that a budget is difficult to live with, the budget should be reexamined. Perhaps the total amount of expenditures budgeted is satisfactory, but this amount needs to be reallocated among categories. More importantly it may be difficult for the family to stay within the total amount budgeted.

If the second difficulty occurs, the review of the budget must be related to the family's lifetime cash flow projections. Perhaps this will show that the consequences of raising the current amount of expenditures will not be unfavorable. On the other hand, an examination of the long-term implications may indicate to the family that it needs to try more firmly to conform to its budgeted expenditure amounts. Reconsideration of a budget does not necessarily have to lead to revision. If revision does not result, the reconsideration may still have been desirable, for it reemphasizes the need for controlling expenditures.

Even though a budget seems to be working well and conformity to it seems to be occurring without much difficulty, the budget should still be reconsidered occasionally together with the rest of the family's lifetime financial plan. Perhaps some circumstances have changed which now require the family to restrict its expenditures. Or perhaps the family has been disciplining its spending with unnecessary rigor and can afford to relax. Unless the budget is kept alive by periodic reexamination, there is danger of it either becoming unnoticed and irrelevant or else it may bind the family to a pattern of expenditures that is no longer appropriate when viewed in the light of long-term considerations.

SUGGESTED READINGS

Information about consumer spending and borrowing patterns is provided in the annual *Survey of Consumer Finances* published by the Survey Research Center, Institute for Social Research, University of Michigan, Ann Arbor, Michigan.

Current information on spending patterns of the type estimated for 1971 in this chapter is obtainable from the U.S. Department of Labor.

Financial institutions make information about budgeting available. An example is *The Family Money Manager*, obtainable free from the Institute of Life Insurance, 277 Park Ave., New York, N.Y. 10017. Another is the *Family Financial Planner*, available free from the Prudential Insurance Company of America, Prudential Plaza, Newark, N.J. 07101.

Appendix
Compound Interest Tables[1]

TABLE A.1
COMPOUND SUM OF $1

Year	1%	2%	3%	4%	5%	6%	7%	8%	9%	10%	15%
1	1.010	1.020	1.030	1.040	1.050	1.060	1.070	1.080	1.090	1.100	1.150
2	1.020	1.040	1.061	1.082	1.102	1.124	1.145	1.166	1.188	1.210	1.322
3	1.030	1.061	1.093	1.125	1.158	1.191	1.225	1.260	1.295	1.331	1.521
4	1.041	1.082	1.126	1.170	1.216	1.262	1.311	1.360	1.412	1.464	1.749
5	1.051	1.104	1.159	1.217	1.276	1.338	1.403	1.469	1.539	1.611	2.011
6	1.062	1.126	1.194	1.265	1.340	1.419	1.501	1.587	1.677	1.722	2.313
7	1.072	1.149	1.230	1.316	1.407	1.504	1.606	1.714	1.828	1.949	2.660
8	1.083	1.172	1.267	1.369	1.477	1.594	1.718	1.851	1,993	2.144	3.059
9	1.094	1.195	1.305	1.423	1.551	1.689	1.838	1.999	2.172	2.358	3.518
10	1.105	1.219	1.344	1.480	1.629	1.791	1.967	2.159	2.367	2.594	4.046
11	1.116	1.243	1.384	1.539	1.710	1.898	2.105	2.332	2.580	2.853	4.652
12	1.127	1.268	1.426	1.601	1.796	2.012	2.252	2.518	2.813	3.138	5.350
13	1.138	1.294	1.469	1.665	1.886	2.133	2.410	2.720	3.066	3.452	6.153
14	1.149	1.319	1.513	1.732	1.980	2.261	2.579	2.937	3.342	3.797	7.076
15	1.161	1.346	1.558	1.801	2.079	2.397	2.759	3.172	3.642	4.177	8.137
20	1.220	1.486	1.806	2.191	2.653	3.207	3.870	4.661	5.604	6.728	16.367
25	1.282	1.641	2.094	2.666	3.386	4.292	5.427	6.848	8.623	10.835	32.919
30	1.348	1.811	2.427	3.243	4.322	5.744	7.612	10.063	13.268	17.449	66.212
40	1.489	2.208	3.262	4.801	7.040	10.286	14.974	21.725	31.409	45.259	267.860

[1] Adapted from J. Fred Weston and Eugene F. Brigham, **Essentials of Managerial Finance** (New York: Holt, Rinehart and Winston, Inc., 1968).

TABLE A.2
PRESENT VALUE OF $1

Year	1%	2%	3%	4%	5%	6%	7%	8%	9%	10%	12%	14%	15%	16%	18%	20%	24%	28%	32%	36%	40%
1	0.990	0.980	0.971	0.962	0.952	0.943	0.935	0.926	0.917	0.909	0.893	0.877	0.870	0.862	0.847	0.833	0.806	0.781	0.758	0.735	0.714
2	.980	.961	.943	.925	.907	.890	.873	.857	.842	.826	.797	.769	.756	.743	.718	.694	.650	.610	.574	.541	.510
3	.971	.942	.915	.889	.864	.840	.816	.794	.772	.751	.712	.675	.658	.641	.609	.579	.524	.477	.435	.398	.364
4	.961	.924	.889	.855	.823	.792	.763	.735	.708	.683	.636	.592	.572	.552	.516	.482	.423	.373	.329	.292	.260
5	.951	.906	.863	.822	.784	.747	.713	.681	.650	.621	.567	.519	.497	.476	.437	.402	.341	.291	.250	.215	.186
6	.942	.888	.838	.790	.746	.705	.666	.630	.596	.564	.507	.456	.432	.410	.370	.335	.275	.227	.189	.158	.133
7	.933	.871	.813	.760	.711	.665	.623	.583	.547	.513	.452	.400	.376	.354	.314	.279	.222	.178	.143	.116	.095
8	.923	.853	.789	.731	.677	.627	.582	.540	.502	.467	.404	.351	.327	.305	.266	.233	.179	.139	.108	.085	.068
9	.914	.837	.766	.703	.645	.592	.544	.500	.460	.424	.361	.308	.284	.263	.226	.194	.144	.108	.082	.063	.048
10	.905	.820	.744	.676	.614	.558	.508	.463	.422	.386	.322	.270	.247	.227	.191	.162	.116	.085	.062	.046	.035
11	.896	.804	.722	.650	.585	.527	.475	.429	.388	.350	.287	.237	.215	.195	.162	.135	.094	.066	.047	.034	.025
12	.887	.788	.701	.625	.557	.497	.444	.397	.356	.319	.257	.208	.187	.168	.137	.112	.076	.052	.036	.025	.018
13	.879	.773	.681	.601	.530	.469	.415	.368	.326	.290	.229	.182	.163	.145	.116	.093	.061	.040	.027	0.18	0.13
14	.870	.758	.661	.577	.505	.442	.388	.340	.299	.263	.205	.160	.141	.125	.099	.078	.049	.032	.021	.014	.009
15	.861	.743	.642	.555	.481	.417	.362	.315	.275	.239	.183	.140	.123	.108	.084	.065	.040	.025	.016	.010	.006
16	.853	.728	.623	.534	.458	.394	.339	.292	.252	.218	.163	.123	.107	.093	.071	.054	.032	.019	.012	.007	.005
17	.844	.714	.605	.513	.436	.371	.317	.270	.231	.198	.146	.108	.093	.080	.060	.045	.026	.015	.009	.005	.003
18	.836	.700	.587	.494	.416	.350	.296	.250	.212	.180	.130	.095	.081	.069	.051	.038	.021	.012	.007	.004	.002
19	.828	.686	.570	.475	.396	.331	.276	.232	.194	.164	.116	.083	.070	.060	.043	.031	.017	.009	.005	.003	.002
20	.820	.673	.554	.456	.377	.319	.258	.215	.178	.149	.104	.073	.061	.051	.037	.026	.014	.007	.004	.002	.001
25	.780	.610	.478	.375	.295	.233	.184	.146	.116	.092	.059	.038	.030	.024	.016	.010	.005	.002	.001	.000	.000
30	.742	.552	.412	.308	.231	.174	.131	.099	.075	.057	.033	.020	.015	.012	.007	.004	.002	.001	.000	.000	.000
40	.672	.453	.307	.208	.142	.097	.067	.046	.032	.022	.011	.005	.004	.003	.002	.001	.001	.001	.000	.000	.000

TABLE A.3

SUM OF AN ANNUITY OF $1 FOR *N* YEARS

Year	1%	2%	3%	4%	5%	6%	7%	8%	9%	10%	12%	16%	20%
1	1.000	1.000	1.000	1.000	1.000	1.000	1.000	1.000	1.000	1.000	1.000	1.000	1.000
2	2.010	2.020	2.030	2.040	2.050	2.060	2.070	2.080	2.090	2.100	2.120	2.160	2.200
3	2.030	3.060	3.091	3.122	3.152	3.184	3.215	3.246	3.278	3.310	3.374	3.506	3.640
4	4.060	4.122	4.184	4.246	4.310	4.375	4.440	4.506	4.573	4.641	4.779	5.066	5.368
5	5.101	5.204	5.309	5.416	5.526	5.637	5.751	5.867	5.985	6.105	6.353	6.877	7.442
6	6.152	6.308	6.468	6.633	6.802	6.975	7.153	7.336	7.523	7.716	8.115	8.977	9.930
7	7.214	7.434	7.662	7.898	8.142	8.394	8.654	8.923	9.200	9.487	10.089	11.414	12.916
8	8.286	8.583	8.892	9.214	9.549	9.897	10.260	10.637	11.028	11.436	12.300	14.240	16.499
9	9.369	9.755	10.159	10.583	11.027	11.491	11.978	12.488	13.021	13.579	14.776	17.518	20.799
10	10.462	10.950	11.464	12.006	12.578	13.181	13.816	14.487	15.193	15.937	17.549	21.321	25.959
11	11.567	12.169	12.808	13.486	14.207	14.972	15.784	16.645	17.560	18.531	20.655	25.733	32.150
12	12.683	13.412	14.192	15.026	15.917	16.870	17.888	18.977	20.141	21.384	24.133	30.850	39.580
13	13.809	14.680	15.618	16.627	17.713	18.882	20.141	21.495	22.953	24.523	28.029	36.786	48.497
14	14.947	15.974	17.086	18.292	19.599	21.051	22.550	24.215	26.019	27.975	32.393	43.672	59.196
15	16.097	17.293	18.599	20.024	21.579	23.276	25.129	27.152	29.361	31.772	37.280	51.659	72.035
16	17.258	18.639	20.157	21.825	23.657	25.673	27.888	30.324					
17	18.430	20.012	21.762	23.698	25.840	28.213	30.840	33.750					
18	19.615	21.412	23.414	25.645	28.132	30.906	33.999	37.450					
19	20.811	22.841	25.117	27.671	30.539	33.760	37.379	41.446					
20	22.019	24.297	26.870	29.778	33.066	36.786	40.995	45.762					
25	28.243	32.030	36.459	41.646	47.727	54.865	63.249	73.106					
30	34.785	40.568	47.575	56.085	66.439	79.058	94.461	113.283					

TABLE A.4
PRESENT WORTH OF AN ANNUITY OF $1

Year	1%	2%	3%	4%	5%	6%	7%	8%	9%	10%	12%	14%	16%	18%	20%	24%	28%	32%	36%
1	0.990	0.980	0.971	0.962	0.952	0.943	0.935	0.926	0.917	0.909	0.893	0.877	0.862	0.847	0.833	0.806	0.781	0.758	0.735
2	1.970	1.942	1.913	1.886	1.859	1.833	1.808	1.783	1.759	1.736	1.690	1.647	1.605	1.566	1.528	1.457	1.392	1.332	1.276
3	2.941	2.884	2.829	2.775	2.723	2.673	2.624	2.577	2.531	2.487	2.402	2.322	2.246	2.174	2.106	1.981	1.868	1.766	1.674
4	3.902	3.808	3.717	3.630	3.546	3.465	3.387	3.312	3.240	3.170	3.037	2.914	2.798	2.690	2.589	2.404	2.241	2.096	1.966
5	4.853	4.713	4.580	4.452	4.329	4.212	4.100	3.993	3.890	3.791	3.605	3.433	3.274	3.127	2.991	2.745	2.532	2.345	2.181
6	5.795	5.601	5.417	5.242	5.076	4.917	4.766	4.623	4.486	4.355	4.111	3.889	3.685	3.498	3.326	3.020	2.759	2.534	2.339
7	6.728	6.472	6.230	6.002	5.786	5.582	5.389	5.206	5.033	4.868	4.564	4.288	4.039	3.812	3.605	3.242	2.937	2.678	2.455
8	7.652	7.325	7.020	6.733	6.463	6.210	5.971	5.747	5.535	5.335	4.968	4.639	4.344	4.078	3.837	3.421	3.076	2.786	2.540
9	8.566	8.162	7.786	7.435	7.108	6.802	6.515	6.247	5.985	5.759	5.328	4.946	4.607	4.303	4.031	3.566	3.184	2.868	2.603
10	9.471	8.983	8.530	8.111	7.722	7.360	7.024	6.710	6.418	6.145	5.650	5.216	4.833	4.494	4.193	3.682	3.269	2.930	2.650
11	10.368	9.787	9.253	8.760	8.306	7.887	7.499	7.139	6.805	6.495	5.988	5.453	5.029	4.656	4.327	3.776	3.335	2.978	2.683
12	11.255	10.575	9.954	9.385	8.863	8.384	7.943	7.536	7.161	6.814	6.194	5.660	5.197	4.793	4.439	3.851	3.387	3.013	2.708
13	12.134	11.348	10.635	9.986	9.394	8.853	8.358	7.904	7.487	7.103	6.424	5.842	5.342	4.910	4.533	3.912	3.427	3.040	2.727
14	13.004	12.106	11.296	10.563	9.899	9.295	8.745	8.244	7.786	7.367	6.628	6.002	5.468	5.008	4.611	3.962	3.459	3.061	2.740
15	13.865	12.849	11.938	11.118	10.380	9.712	9.108	8.559	8.060	7.606	6.811	6.142	5.575	5.092	4.675	4.001	3.483	3.076	2.750
16	14.718	13.578	12.561	11.652	10.838	10.106	9.447	8.851	8.312	7.824	6.974	6.265	5.669	5.162	4.730	4.033	3.503	3.088	2.758
17	15.562	14.292	13.166	12.166	11.274	10.477	9.763	9.122	8.544	8.022	7.120	6.373	5.749	5.222	4.775	4.059	3.518	3.097	2.763
18	16.398	14.992	13.754	12.659	11.690	10.828	10.059	9.372	8.756	8.201	7.250	6.467	5.818	5.273	4.812	4.080	3.529	3.104	2.767
19	17.226	15.678	14.324	13.134	12.085	11.158	10.336	9.604	8.950	8.365	7.366	6.550	5.877	5.316	4.844	4.097	3.539	3.109	2.770
20	18.046	16.351	14.877	13.590	12.462	11.470	10.594	9.818	9.128	8.514	7.469	6.623	5.929	5.353	4.870	4.110	3.546	3.113	2.772
25	22.023	19.523	17.413	15.622	14.094	12.783	11.654	10.675	9.823	9.077	7.843	6.873	6.097	5.467	4.948	4.147	3.564	3.122	2.776
30	25.808	22.397	19.600	17.292	15.373	13.765	12.409	11.258	10.274	9.427	8.055	7.003	6.177	5.517	4.979	4.160	3.569	3.124	2.778
40	32.835	27.355	23.115	19.793	17.159	15.046	13.332	11.925	10.757	9.779	8.244	7.105	6.234	5.549	4.997	4.166	3.571	3.125	2.778
50	39.196	31.424	25.730	21.482	18.256	15.762	13.801	12.233	10.962	9.915	8.305	7.133	6.246	5.554	4.999	4.167	3.571	3.125	2.778

Index